# ENCOUNTERING GOD

## *El Rachum V'chanun—* God Merciful and Gracious

## Other Jewish Lights Books
## by Rabbi Lawrence A. Hoffman

*My People's Prayer Book: Traditional Prayers, Modern Commentaries,*
Vols. 1–10

*My Peoples Passover Haggadah: Traditional Texts, Modern Commentaries,*
Vols. 1 & 2
(coedited with David Arnow, PhD)

*The Art of Public Prayer,* 2nd Ed.: *Not for Clergy Only*
(A book from SkyLight Paths, Jewish Lights' sister imprint)

*Rethinking Synagogues: A New Vocabulary for Congregational Life*

*Israel—A Spiritual Travel Guide: A Companion for the Modern Jewish Pilgrim*

*The Way Into Jewish Prayer*

*What You Will See Inside a Synagogue*
(coauthored with Dr. Ron Wolfson)

## Also in the Prayers of Awe Series

*Who by Fire, Who by Water*—Un'taneh Tokef

*All These Vows*—Kol Nidre

*We Have Sinned: Sin and Confession in Judaism*—Ashamnu *and* Al Chet

*May God Remember: Memory and Memorializing in Judaism*—Yizkor

*All the World: Universalism, Particularism and the High Holy Days*

*Naming God: Our Father, Our King*—Avinu Malkeinu

PRAYERS OF AWE

# ENCOUNTERING GOD

*El Rachum V'chanun*—
God Merciful and Gracious

Edited by
Rabbi Lawrence A. Hoffman, PhD

JEWISH LIGHTS Publishing

*Encountering God:*
El Rachum V'chanun—*God Merciful and Gracious*

For information regarding permission to reprint material from this book, please mail or fax your request in writing to Jewish Lights Publishing, Permissions Department, at the address / fax number listed below, or e-mail your request to permissions@jewishlights.com.

Grateful acknowledgment is given for permission to use: "Never Will I Hear the Sweet Voice of God" and When You Come to Sleep with Me Like God," from *Wild Light: Selected Poems of Yonah Wallach*, translated by Linda Zisquit (New York: Sheep Meadow Press, 1997), © 1997 by Linda Zisquit; "God of the Straw Mothers," by Orit Gidali, translated by Tania Hershman, © 2015 by Tania Hershman.

**Library of Congress Cataloging-in-Publication Data**
Names: Hoffman, Lawrence A., 1942– editor.
Title: Encountering God : God merciful and gracious : El rachum v'chanun / edited by Rabbi Lawrence A. Hoffman, PhD.
Description: Woodstock, Vermont : Jewish Lights Publishing, [2016] | Includes bibliographical references.
Identifiers: LCCN 2016015870| ISBN 9781580238540 (hardcover) | ISBN 9781580238663 (ebook)
Subjects: LCSH: God (Judaism)—Worship and love. | God (Judaism)—Attributes. | Jewish way of life. | Judaism—21st century.
Classification: LCC BM610 .E53 2016 | DDC 296.3/11—dc23 LC record available at https://lccn.loc.gov/2016015870

Manufactured in the United States of America
Front Cover Design: Jeff Miller
Cover Mechanical Design: Amanda Chiu Krohn

Published by Jewish Lights Publishing
An Imprint of Turner Publishing Company
4507 Charlotte Avenue, Suite 100
Nashville, TN 37209
Tel: (615) 255-2665
www.jewishlights.com

I dedicate this book to someone who will never read it all—and others like her: my daughter Shira, who has suffered her whole life, cruelly and unfairly, from epilepsy. Her many brain surgeries have somewhat (but only somewhat) moderated the severity of her seizures, and at a cost, in that her cognitive capacities are now, as they say euphemistically, "compromised." She regularly wonders what her use is, now that she is no longer able to hold a job, read a book, converse with ease, and live the life that people normally and properly aspire to. The answer, I say, with not a single hesitation, is that her tribulations have not robbed her of her extraordinary kindness. Not a day goes by without her taking time and energy to add cheer to the lives of all she meets and to do whatever she can to help even strangers whom she encounters.

As this book makes clear, God's attributes comprise a list of synonyms for love and compassion, grace and kindness. If that be the case, Shira mastered them long before I ever thought of writing about them. She is the epitome of someone made clearly in God's image.

# Contents

*Anthropology—Encountering the Self*

# Acknowledgments

As always, a book such as this owes an enormous debt to all its contributors, for whom the explication of the liturgy is a labor of love. I am grateful to each and every one of them. In particular, my thanks go to Dr. Joel M. Hoffman, who translates the series but also oversees many of the Hebrew-related issues that inevitably arise.

My thanks go continually also to my extraordinary publisher, Stuart M. Matlins, founder of Jewish Lights, and to Emily Wichland, vice president of Editorial and Production there. It was Stuart who first approached me with the idea for the Prayers of Awe series, as suggested to him by Dan Adler in response to a High Holy Day program developed by Rob Eshman, editor in chief of the *Jewish Journal of Greater Los Angeles*, and David Suissa. Their program sprang from an idea first conceived by Rabbi Elazar Muskin of Young Israel of Century City. Emily continues to amaze me with her wisdom, skill, patience, and perseverance. For her copyediting, my thanks go again to Debra Corman. I happily include as well all the others at Jewish Lights, especially Tim Holtz, director of Production, who designed the cover for this book and typeset the English text.

Special gratitude goes always to my wife, Gayle, who encourages my work—some would say, my obsession—to open the liturgy's magnificence to worshipers. Her support is exceptional.

# About This Book

*Rabbi Lawrence A. Hoffman, PhD*

The synagogue experience on the High Holy Days can be profound but problematic. Its profundity arises largely from the cultural baggage that Jews bring to the occasion: memories of memories, mostly— what they felt as children when the High Holy Days rolled around, a feeling for what their parents and grandparents felt, thanks to the recollections that they too had about the feelings that once gripped their own parents and grandparents, centuries back. Year after year, when August comes, the rest of the world enjoys the fading days of summer; not rabbis, cantors, and synagogue administrators, however, who know full well the heightened expectations for the season and return early from vacation to write sermons, assemble music, and organize the massive effort that goes into the annual New Year reunion of the Jewish People with their God.

---

Rabbi Lawrence A. Hoffman, PhD, has served for more than three decades as professor of liturgy at Hebrew Union College–Jewish Institute of Religion in New York. He is a world-renowned liturgist and holder of the Stephen and Barbara Friedman Chair in Liturgy, Worship and Ritual. He has written and edited many books, including the *My People's Prayer Book: Traditional Prayers, Modern Commentaries* series, winner of the National Jewish Book Award; and the Prayers of Awe series; and he is coeditor of *My People's Passover Haggadah: Traditional Texts, Modern Commentaries*, a finalist for the National Jewish Book Award. He cofounded and developed Synagogue 3000, a transdenominational project designed to envision and implement the ideal synagogue of the spirit for the twenty-first century.

The liturgy for the occasion can frequently be up to the task. Familiar melodies like *Kol Nidre* and *Avinu Malkeinu*, cantorial masterpieces too numerous to name, and sermons that speak to the grand themes of human existence in general and the great concerns of the Jewish People in particular can leave their mark. But equally common are complaints that the lengthy services of prayer are baffling to the point of being opaque. Worse yet, many of the most familiar prayers are more troublesome than touching. They were written, after all, centuries ago, in eras marked with certainties that we now question and by authors who could never have predicted a time when communications connect the globe, and even the exploration of outer space is passé.

I mean no disrespect for the High Holy Day sermons that rabbis labor endlessly to write and to deliver when I say that people expect so much of them precisely because they expect so little of the liturgy. They should expect more from what is, after all, the collected spiritual sediment of Jewish history. In part, that is their appeal, for a time when technology bombards our senses daily, if not hourly, with new compositions that falsely claim depth and seriousness. In part also, however, these ancient or medieval prayers have become impediments to the very spiritual insights that they were intended to convey. We need these prayers now more than ever, but the clarity of their message is occluded by the gulf in understanding between our time and ages past. The human condition has not changed, nor has the wisdom that these prayers contain. But as we have evolved into the complicated century that we now occupy, our estrangement from the ritual we call worship has gotten in the way of having these prayers speak to us as they should.

"Prayers of Awe" is a set of volumes intended to overcome this estrangement. It therefore surveys prayers that are at the center of Judaism's High Holy Day liturgy but that prove problematic to modern worshipers.

At times, the problem is *anthropological*—as when prayer makes statements of *human nature* that we find hard to accept. *We Have Sinned: Sin and Confession in Judaism in* Ashamnu *and* Al Chet, for example, looks at the Yom Kippur confessions and the specifically Jewish understanding of moral error and human sin. At times, the problem is *theological*—as when a prayer presents a *picture of God* that we find troublesome. Think of *Un'taneh Tokef* (the subject of *Who by Fire, Who by Water*), which imagines God as devoting each Yom Kippur to deciding who shall live and who shall die. *Naming God*: Avinu Malkeinu—*Our Father, Our King* looks specifically at the difficulty in naming God, as we do in the familiar prayer *Avinu Malkeinu* ("Our Father, Our King"). This volume, a follow-up, handles the even knottier matter of not just naming but actually encountering, and thereby knowing, the divine. Its topic is a small but critical prayer known as the Thirteen Attributes (*Adonai, Adonai, el rachum v'chanun*, "Adonai, Adonai, God merciful and gracious"), a liturgical staple with which Yom Kippur begins and ends.

We begin with two introductory essays to set the tone. The first, "The God of Grace in Judaism," anticipates the rest of the volume by summarizing the history and theology of the thirteen attributes from their biblical origin to their evolution into the liturgy. Most important, it highlights the Jewish insistence that the God of Jewish tradition is a God of love, even grace, a term normally regarded as Christian but equally appropriate, it turns out, for Jews. The second introduction, "Encountering God: Can God Be Known?" tackles the difficult issue of how human beings can know God altogether.

As with other volumes, a new and annotated translation of the liturgy in question—in this case, Thirteen Attributes—follows (as part 1). The rest of the book generally utilizes this translation, although here and there, authors preferred a more traditional translation or substituted their own, so as to illustrate their respective points more clearly. The rest of the book is given over to the many questions that these attributes raise—and the insights they provide.

The first set of contributions (part 2, "The Attributes of God: Their History and Meaning") is historical and straightforward. What exactly are these thirteen attributes? How does the Bible present them, and what did the Rabbis do with them? How did they become so central in Jewish tradition? An overall synopsis of their evolution is provided at the outset by Rabbi Charles H. Middleburgh, PhD; Dr. Marc Zvi Brettler and Rabbi Andrea L. Weiss, PhD, then explore their biblical roots. Their liturgical usage and their medieval relationship to medieval Kabbalah are the topic of the next two essays, by Rabbi Margaret Moers Wenig, DD, and Dr. Sharon Koren. With all that in mind, we introduce the notion of "grace" as a Jewish concept—first, in the Bible itself (Dr. Marc Zvi Brettler again) and, second, through Jewish tradition more generally (Rabbi David Ellenson, PhD).

The attributes, overall, deal with different terms for God's compassion, or (as we saw) grace, but one term appears as an outlier, "truthfulness." Why does a set of attributes so singularly devoted to compassion, mercy, and love insist also on truth—not necessarily a component of compassion, after all? Part 2 of this book concludes with some tantalizing treatments of the way God's truth is interwoven with God's grace to provide a balanced understanding of how God is met and known, in Jewish tradition.

Part 2, then, looks carefully at the thirteen attributes of God in detail. But we have yet to inquire about the actual way we know this God. More precisely, can finite human beings claim *really* to know an infinite God? Then, too, we are said to be made in the divine image, so to some extent, these are idealized human attributes as well. What, then, are the implications of these attributes for the way we view human nature in general, ourselves in particular? And finally, for Jews, the communities in which we gather matter profoundly—it is there, gathered in community, that we become most deeply aware of God and self.

Part 3 thus turns to a second set of questions raised by the interweaving of God, self, and community, all three of which are informed or transformed by the attributes in question. Appropriate to this trifold focus, part 3 is divided into theology (encountering God); anthropology (encountering the self); and what we call "communology" (encountering the community). The term "anthropology" (from the Greek *anthropos*, "human being") is usually associated with the academic (and secular) study of humanity and its many societies and cultures. Here, we mean it in the religious sense of defining human nature, the way we confront our own selves as the human beings we are and want to become. The word "communology" is altogether new, but the concept is not. It is the Jewish equivalent of what Christians call "ecclesiology," the doctrine of the church as a gathering of individuals into a "sacred" and "priestly community."[1] Jewish sources are rich with discussion of the role of Israel, the people, as the locus of knowing God. We simply have no readily recognizable word for it. Part 3 begins with its own overview by Rabbi Asher Lopatin. There then follow several enlightening essays on what we call "The Sacred Triangle: God, Self, and Community."

As an extension of the community, moreover, we have a separate set of essays (part 4) that address the secular Jewish culture of Israel. Even there, it turns out, there is a search to encounter God. Rabbi Dalia Marx,

PhD, and Dr. Wendy Zierler look at Israeli poetry as an alternative search for the divine. The search for the ultimate is obviously part of everyday spirituality now, not only among those who claim Jewish affiliation religiously, but for those who do not. These final two offerings round out the book by expanding the purview of what it means to encounter God ritually—in this case, through the artistry of poetry, in a society where Jewish religious offerings outside of Orthodoxy are still limited.

⌘

# The God of Grace in Judaism

*Rabbi Lawrence A. Hoffman, PhD*

The fear of the number 13 is so commonplace as to be part of everyday wisdom, and not just in English-speaking countries, where hotels have no 13th floor, airports omit their "Gate 13," and offices have been known to close on Friday the 13th. Streets in Florence give the house between 12 and 14 the number 12½, and in France, an actual society called *quatorziens* ("the 14ers") once rented themselves out as guests to parties that otherwise would have only 13 invitees. Around 1911, this common affliction received its own name, "triskaidekophobia," from the Latin *phobia* ("fear") and the Greek *treiskaideka* ("thirteen").

How and why it all began is not entirely clear. Norse mythology describes a banquet of the gods in which an uninvited thirteenth guest, the trickster Loki, killed Balder the Beautiful, the god of joy and happiness. The same idea lies behind the identification of Judas (the betrayer of Jesus) as the thirteenth attendee of the Last Supper. The crucifixion occurred on Friday (and by extension, some Christian lore identifies Cain as killing Abel on that fateful day)—hence the specially dangerous day of Friday the thirteenth, the fear of which goes by the even larger tongue twister "paraskevidekatriaphobia," from the addition of the Greek for Friday, *Paraskevi*.

Whatever the case, neither paraskevidekatriaphobia nor triskaidekophobia is a disease affecting Jews! If anything, Friday is a day eagerly to be anticipated as Erev Shabbat, the day before Shabbat. And as for thirteen itself, a number directly relevant to this volume, it turns out that several positive items in rabbinic lore number thirteen. Already in the second century, a midrash known as *Sifra* offered thirteen principles by which Torah is to be interpreted. In the Middle Ages, Maimonides produced his famous Thirteen Principles of Faith. And in modern times, Menachem Mendel of Satanov (1749–1826), a master of the Jewish Enlightenment called *Haskalah*—an admirer, therefore, of Maimonides and influenced also by the reading of Benjamin Franklin's ideas on moral reform—drew up his own list of thirteen ethical character traits to be pursued. The Passover song "Who Knows One?" (*Echad Mi Yode'a?*) ends with the verse "Who knows thirteen?"

It should not surprise us, therefore, to find the Talmud announcing thirteen attributes of God.

These attributes go back to the Bible, of course, primarily Exodus 34 and the story of the golden calf; and then Numbers 14, where Moses cites them back to God as a means to soften God's anger at the spies who have lost faith in God's ability to lead Israel to victory over the Canaanites. So well known did they become that parts of them are cited by both prophets and psalms, as, apparently, a commonly held understanding of God's attributes well before the Rabbis enshrined them in Jewish consciousness. We even have a liturgical version in Greek, in an extra-biblical account (somewhere between the second century BCE and the first century CE) called the *Prayer of Manasseh*.[1] These attributes of God were very well known early on; the essays in part 2 of this book provide ample detail of the way they run as a sort of mantra throughout the biblical imagination.

The Exodus account from which they are originally drawn is storytelling at its best. While still atop Mount Sinai, Moses learns from God that the Israelites are worshiping a golden calf. He convinces God to renounce the dire punishment that the people deserve (Exodus 32:14), then descends the mountain only to become so angry himself that he smashes the tablets that he has just received (v. 19). God's pardon of the people notwithstanding, Moses dispatches his fellow Levites, who slaughter some three thousand of the rebellious idol worshipers (v. 28). Again, Moses entreats God to show compassion, and even though God sends a plague to kill off the truly wanton sinners (v. 35), the rest of the people are spared.

Emboldened by God's promise of a new beginning, Moses asks to see God's glory, only to learn that no mortal can see God's face and live (Exodus 33:20). God does promise, however, to station Moses in a cleft in the rock whence he will be able to see God's back pass by (vv. 22–23).

So the next day, when Moses again climbs the mountain (34:2), this time to get a second set of tablets, he takes up residence in a crevice from which he observes:

> Adonai, Adonai, merciful and gracious God, endlessly patient, most kind and truthful, extending kindness to thousands, forgiving sins and transgressions and misdeeds, but by no means cleansing. He visits the iniquity of parents upon children and children's children, upon the third and fourth generation. (Exodus 34:6–7)

The entire account is memorable, consequential—and problematic.

Some of the problems are literary. Scholars are likely to point out obvious redundancies, for example. God duly pardons Israel early on (Exodus 32:14), but Moses nonetheless sends the Levites to punish them (vv. 25–29) and then feels the need to entreat God's pardon a second time (v. 30)—as if the first were not enough. Then the Israelites suffer punishment by plague (v. 35), as if the Levitical purge had never occurred. Furthermore, when Moses promises to attain the second pardon from God, he says, "I will now go up to Adonai" to do so (32:30). But according to Exodus 34:2 and 32:4, Moses does not reclimb Mount Sinai until the next day. Did he climb it twice or three times? If three times, when did he come back down from the second ascent?

What we seem to have here is a literary narrative woven together out of several earlier accounts, all of which recollect a general motif that is present in Israel's relationship with God from the very beginning. God graces Israel with the loving gift of Torah, itself but a stage in a larger promise going back to the patriarchs: the guarantee that God has chosen Israel and will redeem it from slavery so that it may travel to the Promised Land and there serve God properly. Israel is only human, however; it sins but is granted pardon anyway, possibly after some form of punishment that is not fatal to the larger mission of continuing its journey as God's chosen people.

Whether Moses climbed the mountain once, twice, or three times is irrelevant to the larger tale of sin and pardon. Whether actual punishment occurred or not, whether such punishment was the Levitical purge or a divinely dispatched plague, is likewise insignificant relative to the larger message of Israel's destiny to be chosen, to fail on occasion, but to be pardoned and then to take up the divine task all over again.

The second set of problems is theological. Say what you will about pardon in the end, God emerges here as woefully short-tempered—no better than Moses, actually, who loses his cool, smashes the tablets to smithereens, and lashes out with deadly force against the people.

As it happens, however, Judaism as we know it is less biblical than it is Rabbinic, and the Rabbis, who may have known nothing about textual or literary analysis, were very much attuned to the theological difficulties of a story that pictures a God of vengeance. The final compilation of books that compose the Bible was itself decided by the Rabbis, and the meaning of the various books, chapters, verses, and even words are not just what the Bible meant originally but also what it came to mean after the Rabbis had reshaped it through their commentaries upon it.

This Rabbinic reshaping of what the Bible might mean occurred throughout several centuries, most particularly during the same era that gave us Christianity as well. The Rabbis trace their origins to a founding genius, Hillel, who lived at the same time as Jesus. Paul wrote his letters defining nascent Christianity during the period that Jews recollect as the time of the debates between the House of Hillel and the House of Shammai. The war against Rome and the Temple's destruction in 70 CE were traumatic for both parties, one of which composed gospels to proclaim the good news of Christ's death and resurrection, while the other wrote narratives of law and lore (halakhah and midrash) that would become basic to Rabbinic Judaism in all its fullness. Both parties, that is, were faced with the need to understand the times in which they lived and such human universals as the proclivity toward sin and the need for divine pardon, care, love, grace, and mercy.

Both Jews and Christians wrote emphatically of the ultimate God of love. Their respective interpretations differed, but they are alike in approaching the problems inherent in adopting the Hebrew Bible as formative. To be sure, the Christian case might have worked out differently. However much Jews may find the teachings of Paul problematic, Paul was at least convinced that the Hebrew Scriptures retained their sacrality even for Christians who dated their origins with the more recent life and death of Jesus. Others—most significantly a theologian known as Marcion of Sinope (85–160)—argued against Paul's stance. Had Marcion won the day, what Jews call the Bible would not have been accepted into the sacred canon of the church, there would be no Western culture with the "Old Testament" stories at its core, and the issues of God's nature raised in the story of the golden calf would be a Jewish problem only. But Marcion's position did not prevail, so Jews and Christians alike had to face the complexity of the kind of God whom the Hebrew Bible portrays. Is God merciful or vengeful? Does God pardon freely, or are our sins visited upon us, our children, and even further generations as well? We will look briefly at the Christian claim, below. For now, however, we can turn to the immediate issue raised by this book: how the Rabbis redefined God as essentially loving and merciful—and how they did so by a creative misreading of the biblical account of God's attributes.

Getting at Rabbinic theology is no easy task, however, because the Rabbis couched even their theological speculation in Talmudic discourse, a combination of law (halakhah) on one hand and an embellishment of the biblical narrative (midrash) on the other. Christian authorities, by contrast, were trained in Hellenistic rhetoric, the basis for philosophical argumentation and a way of thinking that became central to the West. When people ask for demonstrations of what, exactly, Jews think about God, they expect creeds, dogmas, Aristotelian syllogisms, or at least philosophically cogent arguments and their attendant list of simple declarative sentences that provide a summary of Jewish belief. But the Rabbis give us none of that. Instead, they provide legal discussions with understandings of God that are, at best, just implicit; or stories that portray God one way or another and from which we can derive what the Rabbis believed about God, the Jewish People, and the world. It is not as if there is no such thing as Rabbinic theology, but the theology must be intuited from material that does not look very theological on the surface.

Among the stories is this short but trenchant Talmudic account that elaborates fancifully on what really happened when Moses stepped into the cleft of the rock atop Mount Sinai:

> "God passed before him [Moses] and said" (Exodus 34:6): [This means that] the Holy One of Blessing wrapped Himself [in a *tallit*] like a prayer leader and showed Moses the order of prayer. He said to him, "Whenever Israel sins, let them do this before Me, and I will forgive them." (Babylonian Talmud, Rosh Hashanah 17b)

The precise Hebrew leaves room for interpretation. It reads, literally, "Whenever Israel sins, let them do this order before Me," and Jews have universally interpreted "order" to refer to the list of attributes spoken by God to Moses. Upon sinning, therefore, we are to recite the thirteen attributes as our means of attaining divine pardon.

But what attributes does the Talmud have in mind? Not all of them, apparently, because tradition hands down only the merciful ones for us to recite. It is that "mercy-only" version that enters the liturgy:

> God, You instructed us to recite the thirteen attributes. For our sake, remember the covenant of the thirteen attributes today, as you once revealed them to the Humble One [Moses], as it is written, "Adonai descended in a cloud, and he stood with him there, and he said God's name. Then Adonai passed before him and said, 'Adonai, Adonai, merciful and gracious God, endlessly patient, most kind and truthful, extending kindness to thousands, forgiving sins and transgressions and misdeeds, cleansing.'"

The selectivity with which the Rabbis view the biblical text of Exodus 34:6–7 is mind-boggling. First, they simply omit the last half of what God says. We get only the merciful side of God (from v. 6a), while hearing nothing at all of the God's punishing potential (vv. 6b–7): the promise (or threat) that God "visits the iniquity of parents upon children and children's children, upon the third and fourth generation." Second, and more subtly, the Rabbis exercise exceptional editorial license even on the part of the biblical citation that they include. Literally speaking, the word we translated here as "cleansing" (from the Hebrew root *n.k.h*) appears in a grammatical construction that reads *nakeh lo y'nakeh*. The last two words of the Hebrew (*lo y'nakeh*) is a simple third-person imperfect verb (*y'nakeh*) preceded by the negative *lo*, meaning "God will not cleanse [us of our sins]." But biblical Hebrew has a relatively infrequent grammatical part of speech called an infinitive absolute. The infinitive absolute is a simple statement of the root of the verb (in this case, *nakeh*), which can precede a negative instance of the verb in question so as to emphasize that negativity. The actual meaning of *nakeh* (the infinitive absolute = "cleansing") and then *lo y'nakeh* (the negative *lo* and the imperfect *y'nakeh* = "He [God] will not cleanse") is "He [God] will *surely* not cleanse." The Rabbis conveniently cut the grammatical unit in half, lopping off the last two Hebrew words, but including the first one, the infinitive absolute *nakeh*. By itself, punctuated as it is, the word means only "cleansing" but it gives the impression that God intends to cleanse, whereas the original biblical citation said just the reverse. We are left, in the end, with only thirteen good attributes and no bad ones.

It is not, however, clear that we even have thirteen. To begin with, the introductory Hebrew, *vayomer Adonai Adonai* can mean "He [God] said: Adonai Adonai...." This usual understanding gives us the double repetition of God's name (Adonai Adonai) as the first two attributes. But the first *Adonai* can equally well be taken as the subject of the verb *vayomer* ("[He] said"), giving us "God [—that is,] *Adonai*—said: *Adonai*...." In that rendering, we get only one *Adonai* as part of God's speech, and only a single *Adonai* that can be counted as among the attributes. Jewish tradition reads it both ways. The *Tosafot* (Franco-German commentators from the twelfth and thirteenth centuries) follow Rabbenu Tam (Rashi's grandson, 1100–1171) in preferring the first; but the Spanish commentator Rabbenu Nissim Gerondi ("of Gerona") preferred the second.[2] Rabbenu Tam has generally come down to us as the preferred reading— because it accompanies the Babylonian Talmud as one of its main commentaries. But Rabbenu Nissim's alternative is by no means a modest outlier to Rabbinic tradition. Indeed, the Torah text itself is printed with a small vertical line separating the first *Adonai* from the second one, as if the two "Adonais" really are not intended to be read together as the same parts of speech. That reading goes back at least to Saadiah Gaon, a noted grammarian and philosopher (882–942), who is cited as saying, "When the light of God passed by Moses, Adonai called out to him, 'Adonai....'"[3]

A simple way to determine the right reading might be to try it both ways and see which way gives us the proper number of thirteen. But the problem with that solution is that, unfortunately, neither way of reading the phrase produces the proper number thirteen. The only reason we imagine there are thirteen to start with is that the Talmud cites Rav Yehudah (a third-century Babylonian authority) as saying so—"A covenant has been made regarding the thirteen attributes," he insists.

But how, then, shall we count the thirteen? The systems abound, but none of them seems inherently more obvious than the others. Some (like thirteenth-century Joseph ben Abba Mari Ibn Kaspi and the fifteenth-century Isaac Abravanel, both of Spain) include all the biblical attributes of the Exodus passage—even the negative ones—to get at the number thirteen. Others, like Bachya ibn Pakudah of eleventh-century Spain and Isaiah Horowitz, the sixteenth-century kabbalist of Prague, counted only the positive commandments that the liturgy enshrines.[4] No single computation is authoritative, and in fact, even Rav Yehudah of the Talmud may not have had any particular way of counting in mind. It might be that the number thirteen was considered lucky, auspicious, or just indicative of all good things, so he said there were thirteen attributes, but he was using the number symbolically.

All of which takes us back to the way this essay began: the realization that Jews have customarily looked positively on the number thirteen. So convinced were they, in fact, that after deciding there must be thirteen attributes, they then went out of their way to find the same number thirteen in all sorts of liturgical formulas—the blessing over Hanukkah candles, for example—which they then arbitrarily assigned, word for word. Similarly, the fact that in leap years an extra month is added to the usual twelve, thus giving us thirteen, allowed the *Zohar* to assign each separate month to one of the attributes.[5] It may be, then, that there were no thirteen attributes to begin with; rather, the Talmud identified the attributes as a covenantal assurance of God's pardon, then named it with the auspicious number thirteen, after which authorities sought vainly to discover the original numbering system—as if there had actually been one. The number thirteen, then, in the thirteen attributes, as elsewhere, was chosen for its symbolic value rather than its accuracy as the actual number of attributes that God happened to have.

More important than the number is the decision to insist on just the attributes of mercy as the content of the covenant that the liturgy contains. We return here to the issue of God's nature as first- and second-century Jews and Christians alike struggled to know it. It is commonplace by now to identify Christianity as the tradition that most emphasizes God's merciful love. In fact, however, Judaism too emphasizes God's compassion, as its choice of the merciful attributes alone readily demonstrates. It is incorrect to identify Judaism as the religion of the "Old Testament" with its God of justice and vengeance—a charge that Jews have had to abide for centuries, albeit more rarely in recent years.

A more subtle issue has been the exact definition of divine love in the first place. For Christians, that love has been identified as "grace," a common noun in English but with technical connotation in Christian theology. A very important question is the extent to which the Rabbinic idea of God's love is anything like what Christians call grace.

An easy (and not inaccurate) way to understand grace is from the well-known Christian hymn "Amazing Grace," first penned in 1779 but now popularized by singers and situations the world over.[6] For our purposes here, the first two stanzas tell us all we need to know.

> Amazing grace! How sweet the sound
> That saved a wretch like me!
> I once was lost, but now am found;
> Was blind, but now I see.

> 'Twas grace that taught my heart to fear,
> And grace my fears relieved;
> How precious did that grace appear
> The hour I first believed.

The lyrics are Christian through and through; the idea of being "lost" and then "found" comes from the gospel parable of the prodigal son, for example (Luke 15:11–32). More significantly, we see not just the imprint of Christian theology (the doctrine of God) but Christian anthropology (the doctrine of human nature) as well: the idea that human beings are inherently sinful. It was "grace," we are told, "that saved a wretch [!] like me." It did so by instilling "fear" of God so that "I first believed."

All of this goes back, in part, to Paul's view of Christianity, but it was given classical theological shape in the thinking of the great philosopher and theologian Augustine of Hippo (354–430). To be sure, theological doctrines are far more complex than a single statement of them. The thinking of thirteenth-century Thomas Aquinas differed significantly from Augustine's view, for example, but Augustine's classic view influenced Martin Luther and John Calvin, the primary thinkers behind most of the Protestant churches that settled America.

The Christian idea of grace goes back to the assumption that human beings inherit sin as a sort of human DNA, the legacy of Adam's first and primal sin in the garden. Sinful to our core, we are indeed "wretches." But we are also recipients of God's loving gift of Christ, who died for our sins, and in whom we must believe if we are to be saved. Since we live in a state of sinfulness, we are never worthy of such a gift. It is therefore a gift not just of love, but of grace—*grace being divine love offered even when it is entirely unwarranted.*

When viewed through this prism of Christian theology, it would seem that Jews do not believe in grace. Unlike Paul, Augustine, Luther, and Calvin, Jews do not believe in original sin altogether. The classic Jewish model of the divine-human relationship is, overall, covenantal: God meets us through our communities, with whom God makes covenants, and then holds us (as members of those communities) liable for the terms of the covenantal agreements. As individuals, we do indeed have an evil or sinful side (what the Rabbis call the *yetzer hara*), but equally, we have the inclination to goodness (the *yetzer hatov*). At times, we actually do deserve God's beneficence.

But theology is one thing, basic human sentiment another. "I do believe," said William James, in his classic account of religious experience, "that feeling is the deeper source of religion, and that philosophic and theological formulas are secondary products, like translations of a text into another tongue."[7] All this Christian theology, therefore, is to some extent just layer after layer of philosophical justification added on to the basic psychological sense that we are indeed beneficiaries of more than we deserve. Who doesn't awaken (some days at least) to a brilliantly clear and sunlit morning with the sense that we are fortunate indeed just to be alive, that life itself is a gift, and that we have done nothing to deserve it? To the extent that the religious personality intuits the hand of the divine in making a universe with all its blessings available to us, how can we not imagine God's love as a gift we did nothing to merit?

The difference is that by and large, Jewish theology went in a different direction. Instead of focusing on sin as primary, it retained faith in human nature to choose good or evil. With no sense of original sin, Judaism had no widespread need for the doctrine of grace as the only kind of love that we can expect.

Yet at times, Jews too invoke the doctrine of grace. Dr. Marc Zvi Brettler (pp. 21–26) reminds us there are biblical precedents for the doctrine, and it turns up regularly in the liturgy. The daily morning service has a prayer that insists:

> Master of all worlds, we do not offer our supplications before You based on our righteousness, but rather based on your great mercy. What are we?... Are not all mighty ones as though they were nothing before You, men of fame as though they never existed, the educated as though without knowledge, and the wise as though without insight, for most of their acts are without value and the days of their

life worthless before You! Man barely rises above beast, for
everything is worthless.[8]

This may not be a statement of original sin, but it certainly reflects a sense
of the human condition in a state of nature, meriting nothing whatever.
Christian tradition overlays this portrait of humanity with sinfulness and
then identifies Jesus as the gift of grace that saves us. The Rabbis omit the
emphasis on sin and see the covenant with the patriarchs (and then the
Torah at Sinai) as God's grace, for despite the fact that we do not deserve it,

> we are your people, the children of your covenant, the
> children of Abraham your love, to whom You took an
> oath on Mount Moriah; the descendants of Isaac, his only
> son, who was bound on the altar; the community of Jacob,
> your first-born, whom You called Israel and Jeshurun on
> account of your love for him and joy with him.... How
> wonderful is our lot, how great our destiny, and how beau-
> tiful our heritage![9]

Nowhere is this sense of God's merciful love—God's grace, we can
now call it—more evident than in the High Holy Day liturgy, where
the accent on sin is indeed added. The signature prayer for the occasion,
*Avinu Malkeinu*, pleads, "Our father, our king, be gracious to us and
answer us, for we have no merit."[10] This is not the same as claiming original sin all the way from Adam. But it is clearly a claim about the extent
to which God's graciousness is a gift of grace—"graciousness" being just
a fancy word for "grace." "Be gracious to us" is the English equivalent of
the Hebrew *choneinu*, from the root *ch.n.n*, the same thing we get in the
thirteen attributes when we say *Adonai Adonai el rachum v'chanun* (from
*ch.n.n* also). Indeed, the entire context of the attributes is the scene of the
golden calf, a biblical reminder par excellence that Israel deserves nothing, but, somehow, receives God's pardon as a gift of grace anyway. As
Rabbi Margaret Moers Wenig, DD, points out (p. 33), our liturgical
use of the thirteen attributes combines this story of the calf with a second
instance of Israel's disobedience, the scouts dispatched to spy out the land
of Canaan (Numbers 13:1–14:45). There, the sin was their loss of faith
in God's ability to bring victory. Not for nothing do the Rabbis combine
these two accounts to give us the liturgical recitation that bookends Yom
Kippur—as part of the opening *Kol Nidre* service, but also as a staple for

the concluding service of *N'ilah*. In both cases, we get the thirteen attributes from Exodus and from Numbers too, a double reminder of Israel's sinfulness—and by extension, ours as well.

Both Judaism and Christianity, then, preserve the elemental human sense of being unworthy of all the benefits we receive simply by virtue of God's love. But they frame it differently. For classical Christianity (at least in its Augustinian form), sin is not just elemental but original, all-pervasive, and inescapable. For the Rabbis, sin is real but balanced by the possibility of human goodness that God codifies as the divine expectation inherent in the covenant God makes with us.

In the morning prayer, cited above, we saw the covenant made originally with the patriarchs—even though "man barely rises above beast, for everything is worthless." So, too, we have seen how the later covenant at Sinai came about despite the rankest idolatry, enough surely to make us unworthy of the gift of Torah. And with these two covenants in mind, we can return to "the covenant of the thirteen [attributes]," as the Talmud and our liturgy call it. There, too, the context is human sin, for the entire Talmudic account is predicated upon the insistence that "whenever Israel sins, let them do this before me, and I will forgive them."

Is grace, therefore, part and parcel of Judaism, not just Christianity? It certainly is—not with the same theological overlay of original sin and the need for faith in Christ, but with the Rabbinic understanding that sin is indeed at least part of our human makeup and that God makes covenants with us: first, the covenant with Abraham; then, the covenant at Sinai; and, for moments when we sin, the covenant of the thirteen attributes. These are the Jewish gifts of God's grace.

Our treatment of grace has allowed us to make a very important discovery: the difference between human sentiment, on one hand, and the theological conceptualization of that sentiment, on the other. Theology is precisely that: the consciousness of human sentiments and the recasting of them into terms that invoke God. More precisely, religious thought uses not just theology, but (as we saw) anthropology, too—a doctrine of human nature; and even cosmology—not the scientific version, but a religious understanding of the universe into which we have been cast (for simplicity's sake, we usually use "theology" to refer to all three). Religious thought is the process of taking human sentiments seriously—our certainties and fears, our successes and failures, all of the human condition—and locating these in some logical space that uses words like

"God," "sin," "grace," and so on as useful ways to do justice to the depth and breadth of the experiences we know ourselves to have. Liturgy is very largely the public proclamation of those understandings, so as to come to terms with what we know of life—beyond what science is capable of telling us. Theology, then, is not scientific, but not a negation of science either. It is just a different way of describing human experience. The next chapter turns to this theological inquiry: how we say we can "know" God altogether.

ↄ౫౫అ

# Encountering God
## CAN GOD BE KNOWN?

*Rabbi Lawrence A. Hoffman, PhD*

The previous chapter looked at the history of the thirteen attributes through the Bible, the Talmud, medieval thinkers, and the liturgy. We saw that the Bible includes both pardon and punishment as dual aspects of God's goodness. The Rabbis, however, include only the pardon, so it is pardon alone that the liturgy proclaims as well. For all intents and purposes, then—unless they take the time and effort to trace the attributes back to their biblical origin—it is God's mercy, not God's justice, that average Jews encounter.

One old and established way of thinking about the Bible, in fact, is not as the book that sits on your shelf in its entirety but as just the set of selected readings that we encounter experientially, largely through prayer. Most Jews never read the whole Bible; they get only chunks of it, embedded in the liturgy: the *Sh'ma* may be the best example; holy day Torah readings (like the *Akedah,* the binding of Isaac) and the Ten Commandments are similar instances. The thirteen attributes of God, which, as it were, play to live audiences every Yom Kippur, are also part of the Bible "as known" rather than the Bible for what it really is, the entire set of books from Genesis to Chronicles that only experts read from cover to cover. The Bible that Jews know firsthand, then, presents a God whose self-revelation is entirely merciful.

That being the case, our first chapter also attended to what is meant by divine mercy and decided that it is the kind of love that is best captured in the English word "grace"—not precisely as Christians think of grace, but as Jews do. Having concluded that chapter with a Jewish theology of grace, we are ready now to circle back to the title of this volume,

*Encountering God.* How indeed do we encounter this God of grace? And what are the implications of the Torah's insistence that God's face cannot be seen? Don't we know people primarily through their faces? If God has no face, can God be encountered altogether? If so, how?

Of the two questions, what we mean by God's mercy (from the last chapter) and how we encounter this God of mercy (this chapter), it is the second one that proves more difficult to answer. Yet this volume would be incomplete without at least a preliminary attempt to tackle it. Our title, after all, is *Encountering God*—a companion inquiry to the topic of the prior volume, *Naming God*. Naming God differs from encountering God, however, in that naming is a third-person sort of thing—it is not personal—while encountering is a first-person experience of directly knowing a second-person "other."

Indeed, we name all sorts of things that we never encounter personally: Siberian winters (which most of us have only read about), the Napoleonic Wars (which we know only through history), the abominable snowman (who doesn't even exist), and the very atoms that, we are told, underlie the universe of things (though we must take it on faith that they are there). But God, we say, is not just a Being whom we name; God can be also known, encountered, and experienced as real. Especially on the High Holy Days, we say that we encounter God. As the Rabbis put it long ago, Rosh Hashanah is the time when "all who come into the world pass before You," like sheep, or like soldiers lining up in military formation to pass muster.[1]

This volume therefore looks at the abiding issue of how we encounter God directly, not just as a matter of naming some third-person entity that we may only have heard about, but as a first-person experience of a genuine second-person reality. That is what the tale of Moses on the mountain is all about: the way God provides the revelation of Self—to the point where Moses asks to see God's face. God denies that possibility, but Moses sees God's "back" (*achorai*) at least (Exodus 33:23), in the shape of what we call the thirteen attributes.

The easiest entry into this perplexing question is through the familiar theory of Martin Buber (1878–1965), who inherited a long line of German thought over the question of how human beings go about the process of encountering and, thereby, knowing anything.

The most obvious method by which we know goes by the German verb *erklären*, "to elucidate or explain" along the lines of science. *Erklären* applies to data that philosophers call empirical—what we see, hear, taste, touch, and smell—and, by extension, the scientific facts we deduce from that data to tell us about the world. That kind of knowing seems inadequate, however, for some things—for example, our knowledge of history, where all we have are historical documents, not the facts to which the documents purport to testify. Even if the documents are accurate, how do we achieve a deep understanding of the historical actors involved? Why did Brutus stab Julius Caesar? What led Paul to become a Christian? Why did Rabbi Akiva side with the rebels in the Bar Kokhba revolt?

For that sort of knowledge, a second verb was selected: *verstehen*, "to understand." History, said Wilhelm Dilthey (1833–1911), the philosopher most associated with justifying history as something we can know, requires a deep human understanding, the empathy that one human being (the reader) has for the other (the actor in history).[2] To know the atoms that constitute nature, we need no empathy. To know people in history, we do. What goes for history goes for our own time as well. Sociologists like Max Weber, therefore, investigated the role of *verstehen* in comprehending how societies operate round about us. If we wish to know why someone does something, we need to understand that person's motives—a matter we deduce from empirical evidence, on one hand, but also an innate feeling for the way the person thinks and feels, on the other.[3] In characterizing the uniqueness of historical "understanding" (*verstehen*), Dilthey turned specifically to the way that "the self receives nourishment" through its "understanding of other persons" and, in so doing, described a way of knowing that combines the knower and the person known in combination, or, as he put it, "the I and the Thou, together." Buber made that relationship central in his famous dichotomy of "I-Thou" (the way we know a person) versus "I-It" (the way we know a thing). Eugene B. Borowitz, the master interpreter of Buber, gives the example of a scientist bringing a friend to her laboratory to meet her colleagues. As she is about to introduce the friend, she is called out of the room, so she says, "Get to know my friend while I am gone." What do the other scientists do? They could weigh her, take her temperature, test her blood type, and subject her to all manner of laboratory analysis. But they don't. Even though they would thereby compile a lot of knowledge about the person in question, they know full well that no such data could actually let them "know" her. That sort of scientific analysis is for things, not people. It is an I-It, not an I-Thou manner of knowing.

Sometimes, the I-It attitude is appropriate. When doctors send out blood samples for laboratory tests, they get back an I-It collection of data, properly quantified and fully describable. Employers too (at least partially) may approach an applicant's aptitude for a job as an I-It task, as when poet Stephen Burt complains of being "weighed and measured, tested and standardized."[4] Similarly, for the tasks of daily life, we usually choose to know people as an It—when we approach a sales clerk, for instance. These purely utilitarian transactions do not require the deeper "understanding" of *verstehen*. At times, we even treat people we love that way—as when we divide the household chores among family members or charge someone in the family with an errand—a message to deliver to a neighbor, for example.

In any given circumstance, we have a choice of how to know another person. At first, I am likely to approach a sales clerk as an It: our relationship is utilitarian; if the person serving me goes on coffee break, I continue the conversation with someone else; the person is interchangeable. But the very same clerk may well, over time, engage me personally; eventually, I may get to know him, and as I do, I begin treating him as a Thou. I ask specifically for him when I come into the store; we share things about each other's lives. I look askance if he tries to hand me off to someone else for service. At times, I revert to the I-It attitude (business, as they say, is business), but at times, the clerk is a Thou to me: a singular person unto himself, not just a means to an end. People, then, can be an It or a Thou to us.

So, too, can animals, plants, and even inanimate objects. Think of how we relate to a favorite picture of our parents, placed strategically in our line of sight on the dresser; how a gardener lovingly transplants a scrawny dying plant in hope that it will reflower; how we embrace the reality of the massive oak tree that has stood in our backyard from our childhood days on. These things too can be an It one day, a Thou another.

God, however, is different, Buber says, because God, by definition, can *only* be known as a Thou—never as an It. That is why an encounter with God cannot be adequately described to anyone who has never had one; why mystical experiences are mystical in the first place—they can be explained scientifically perhaps, but the explanation never quite gets at what the person reporting it thinks it was all about. The outsider can only provide an "explanation" (*erklären*), not an "understanding" (*verstehen*). By definition, the objective explanations of science deal with any given phenomenon as an It, whereas mysticism (also by definition) entails a sense of a Thou.

People regularly have experiences of God, particularly in what sociologist Emile Durkheim called the effervescent experience of ritual—singing, dancing, chanting, holding hands in a circle, or even listening intently to a master preacher deliver a message to a congregation intently fixed on the experience. These ritual ways of knowing may also invoke something other than God, but akin to God, in that they seem to be windows onto the ultimate. Indeed, theologian Paul Tillich famously defined God as the object of ultimate concern. Importantly, such moments of ritual are not mere entertainment. They have a moral quality to them; whether positively (a civil rights gathering, singing "We Shall Overcome") or perversely (a Ku Klux Klan meeting half a mile away), ritual knowledge moves people to express their deepest held commitments.[5] As a sociologist, Durkheim was endeavoring to explain what makes such moments "work."

Durkheim's explanations ring true, but they are only just that—"explanations" (*erklären*) of the experience, not "understandings" (*verstehen*) of the I-Thou reality that the people themselves claim they have gone through. They cannot be the latter, because even the people having the experience find it impossible to explain just what it was they found so moving. "You had to have been there," they say. Outside observers may treat the "explanation" as sufficient to deny the deeper significance that the people experiencing the event cannot even successfully articulate. "You thought it was God," they may say, "but really you were just carried away by the music and romance of the whole thing." They thus explain away religious experience by positing natural causes for what was "really" going on—an exercise in what has been labeled the "mereological fallacy,"[6] debunking real experiences by claiming they are "merely" something lesser than what they actually are. Explanation is not understanding, however. To be sure, it may be the music that opened people to whatever they experienced. But the question always remains: just what did they experience? Scientific explanation cannot properly deny the reality of what the person involved claims with all certainty to have taken place.

Philosophers call this confusion a "category error." It is akin to explaining away a masterful musical recital by providing the physics of sound. The science is one thing, the aesthetics is another, and both are true.

It does not follow that *every* claim of religious experience should be taken as spiritually inviolate. We regularly make judgment calls on such things—as when we rule out the probability that God is addressing someone through the television set. More likely, the person involved is having schizophrenic delusions. But it does not follow that *all* claims of knowing God are delusional. Freud frequently spoke as if they were, but in his more careful moments, he differentiated delusion from illusion, allowing at least the possibility that the latter had some basis in reality—even though he thought he knew the scientific explanation for it. He could say, that is, what the scientific cause of religious experience was; whether there was any spiritual reality behind the cause remained an open question. Overall, Freud was apt to discount the reality of anything deeper, but Freud's erstwhile follower Jung—who also claimed to know the scientific mechanism of the psyche and the cause, therefore, of spiritual phenomena—was quite certain that the phenomena existed in their own right, regardless of the science that explained them.

When we say that an effervescent spiritual experience has content, we can mean two things. On the one hand, the content can be what Durkheim called moral: the inculcation of certain beliefs and values. Americans who gather to say prayers at Thanksgiving dinner, for example, are likely to believe that they are blessed and that they ought to be grateful. Both the ritual of gathering (implicitly) and the particular prayers that are said (explicitly) contain just that moral content. But equally, an experience can have no other content than itself—the recognition, that is, that one is gathering with family, friends, or loved ones in a moment of solidarity, support, or comfort—or for no particular reason at all. Buber's I-Thou moment has that less tangible kind of "content." We walk away from such moments simply knowing, somehow, that we "connected" in an important way, even though we cannot fully describe what occurred because the experience is over and gone, and all we have left is the I-It recollection of it.

It is important to see that simply arriving somehow at the logical conclusion that my family, friends, or community support me is considerably different from actually experiencing that support ritually and then reporting its existence thereafter. The former is an academic exercise, a theoretical statement of what I believe is the case. The latter is a claim rooted in the immediacy of experience that I know I have had.

That is why ritual matters so much. It is its own way of knowing, separate from pure rational cognition and far more compelling. To be sure, the knowledge we gain from it is then processed, after the fact, by our rational and moral faculties. We may decide that the effervescence of the group experience led us to an ethical or logical position that, in retrospect, we do not like. In the first case (ethics), the group experience moves us by its values; in the second (logic), we are moved by its claims to truth. They go together, of course, because truth has ethical implications, and behavior has logical underpinnings. Think, for example, of a Ku Klux Klan rally, where the group solidarity convinces a chance visitor that the Klan's cause is proper and just—that the "black and white races really are not equally endowed by God" (a so-called truth) and that discrimination based on color is, therefore, justified (a "value"). The next morning, in the sober light of day, he is likely to feel shame at even thinking that. Equally, albeit less toxically, there are reported cases where people attending nineteenth-century revival meetings found the sermons so convincing that they opted for immediate conversion—only to wonder about their decision when they got home. Any group at all may temporarily convince a visitor that the truths and values for which it stands are believable. After the fact, when they are weighed against logic and reason, they may be rejected as reflecting the emotional impact of the moment.

But equally, the morning-after review might be insufficient to wipe away the certainty of the night before, especially when the ethics or truths that the ritualizing impressed upon us is not shameful, but instead the sort of thing that makes us proud of who we are. An effervescent moment might emphasize the truth of human dignity, the values of love and compassion, and the obligation to stand up for what is right and just. These are things we have likely always suspected to be true and worthy of our championing; we may know also that we often fall short of such lofty goals. When the truths and values of the ritual are what we have always admired, we are likely to remember the ritual moment as affirming what we hoped was true and likely also to believe it and to act upon it. Ritualizing thus becomes a powerful means of becoming the better person we always wanted to be—far more powerful than simply arguing our way to a truth that we then fall short of internalizing as part of our daily lives.

We thus return to the thirteen attributes, which are rooted not in logic but in ritual. The Bible might well have stated them simply as a matter of objective truth. That is, they might have been reported the way the Bible begins: just "God has the following attributes," like "In the beginning God created the heavens and the earth." They are couched instead, however, as part of an encounter, the immediate content of an experience that Moses has directly with God. The Talmud reiterates the context of meeting, this time in a tale of a Rabbi who encounters God directly and receives instructions for all of Israel to recite the attributes in similar encounters whenever its members sin. Insofar as God is known directly through encounter, the actual I-Thou experience cannot be fully weighed and measured by an after-the-fact I-It recollection of what transpired. But the content of that encounter can be, and has been, passed along as the experience of what we have labeled divine grace.

Philosopher Roger Scruton makes the remarkable discovery that the Bible describes both God and Israel as homeless. Much of Torah is the process by which Israel finds a home in the land that God once promised Abraham. But equally, it is a record of Israel making a home for God, the desert Tabernacle (the *mishkan*) and then, later, the Temple itself. God, too, apparently, is constantly in search of a place to land—to settle down, to be present, to be known, to be encountered. Both God and we, says Scruton, are like butterflies, looking for a perch where we can be appreciated—the way a butterfly lands gently but deftly on a flower, briefly to be sure, but enough to be encountered. Encountering God, then, is a two-way street, where both parties deliberately situate themselves relative to one another for the encounter to happen. The encounter can hardly be experienced as a case of meeting just another human being, however, because God is, by definition, other than human. Were we to believe anthropomorphically in a God of human proportions, the matter would be different, but when God is understood in the philosophical way that most moderns find appealing, "a direct personal encounter with God ... is no more possible than a direct personal encounter with the number 2."[7] How can you have an I-Thou relationship with the equivalent of a number?

Actually, our experience with numbers, which is to say, with mathematics, can be profoundly moving. It is precisely the mathematical order of the universe that entailed the spiritual experience to which both Newton and Einstein attested. That the universe has such things as numbers in it, or, at least, that mathematics somehow maps the universe, Newton said, is the mind of God. When scientists, mathematicians, and philosophers encounter the universe as a Thou, they walk away with the content of that experience, not as an actual replication that does the experience justice, but with numbers and equations as the building blocks of what the universe actually is. So too with Moses, the Talmud, and our ritualized experience of Yom Kippur when we recite the thirteen attributes: precisely the ritual nature of the experience provides us with a sense of meeting God, not the way we meet any other object or person, but the way mathematicians meet the number 2. We then walk away from that experience with the sense that the building blocks of the universe include the attributes that we call the divine: the practice of love, mercy, grace. We are answerable to both measures: the scientific set of numbers, weights, and measures, but, equally, the spiritual practice of empathic acceptance and pardon rooted in love.

The divine-human encounter is possible in the first place because of the uniqueness of both sides of the equation. God, we say, is utterly unique, knowable as we know another person, but still, not a person; always a Thou, never an It. Doubt as to God's existence follows inevitably when we try to reduce God to It-like status, at which time we find ourselves unable to frame a sense or definition of God that does not somehow seem laughable. God does not, after all, have a face. Draw one, so to speak, and it will surely fail.

But the specific form of uniqueness that typifies human beings is equally important. It can be summed up in the realization that only humans have rational self-consciousness, in the sense that only we have a sense of a self with a life and a story line that is our own. The degree of consciousness typical of other life-forms is constantly being studied, but there does seem to be a quantum difference between them on one hand and humans on the other. Only humans have the richness of language that goes into constituting a story of who we are and why we are here. Only humans have a sense of self. Selves are not like other entities in the state of nature. "I refer to myself," Scruton says, "but this does not mean that there is a self that I refer to. I act for the sake of my friend, but there is no such thing as a sake for which I am acting. Sakes are not objects in the world of objects. Neither are selves."[8] Selves are not actual things, then; they are first-person perspectives that no one can doubt; we simply know we have them. Indeed, their validity has been doubted all the way back to the great eighteenth-century skeptic David Hume (1711–76), who could see no cogent reason to believe in the continuity that we naturally assume about our lives—no reason to say for sure that the person we remember as a youth, or even from yesterday, is really the same person we know ourselves to be today. But reasonableness aside, even Hume had to contend with his subjective sense of having such a self, just as René Descartes, the father of modern philosophy, a little over a century before (1596–1650) concluded that the single most certain thing anyone can say is that "I think; therefore I am"—that however little we know about what or who we are, we at least know that we are.

The human project is largely the attempt to find reasons for our being, a narrative plot for how we got to where we are and where we think we still might go, a rationale for the odd circumstance that we find ourselves here on earth without ever planning it and that we will die with equally little plan in mind. Religion is the search for such reasons. Not causes, mind you. We confuse reasons and causes at our peril, an easy mistake to make because both cause and reason answer the question "Why?" But the question "Why?" has more than a single kind of answer. Science explains the *cause* of our being here, the way in which forces of nature produced our species in general, our own selves in particular. It does not provide *reasons* for that existence, however. For reasons we look to religion—and to God. The encounter with God comes about in the search for life's reasons. What is the point of it all? Why are we alive? Toward what end?

And there, the thirteen attributes have something to say. It is worth thinking for a moment what they are *not*. They say nothing about, say, accomplishment; we all know that human beings naturally strive for achievements, but God's essential qualities say nothing about achieving. We also strive for enjoyment, but unlike the gods of Olympus, the God of Sinai is not an enjoying deity. We similarly strive to learn—we are curious by nature, after all (witness Adam and Eve in the Garden of Eden, insisting on eating the fruit of the tree of knowledge). And indeed, "truthfulness" (unlike accomplishment and enjoyment) is among the attributes, but even it is hardly central. What we get, almost exclusively, is the accent on love, mercy, grace, and kindness. The only other "self" in the universe, the one in whose image we say we are made, is God, and God's very essence, we are told, is love.

Unlike God, we have faces and know each other best from them. Think here, primarily, of Jacob and Esau. Jacob our forebear steals his brother's birthright and robs him of his blessing. He has good and cogent reasons to believe that Esau would love nothing better than to kill him. But years later, a rich man now, en route to reclaim his patrimony in the Land of Israel, Jacob reconnects with Esau and wonders, the night before, what the dreaded experience will be like. He takes steps to send his family and possessions ahead of him across the river to safety, just in case Esau really does wreak vengeance on him—and given what Jacob stole from him, who would blame him? But the next day, when they actually do meet, Esau surprises him. Both brothers have prospered. Esau holds no grudge. Like God, Esau too has no interest in revenge, even revenge that we might consider to have been his due. He displays, instead, what is surely an instance of grace—love freely offered to a brother whose past behavior makes it certain that he has no claim to merit it. Recognizing Esau's very personification of grace, Jacob says, "Seeing your face is like seeing the face of God" (Genesis 33:10).

God has no face; God surpasses all description; God cannot be described with any accuracy; God cannot be known as an It. God can only be encountered as a Thou, after which we may even doubt whether the encounter occurred at all, so extraordinary is it. But we know what that encounter is like: it has a content that we carry away with us and recognize again when we look into the face of another human being, especially the face of a long-lost brother whom we have wronged but who now pardons us, showing us the grace that is God's—and ours as well.

Here is the reason for our being: we are here to show love, to be kind, to forgive, and to exemplify the grace that is God's and, therefore, ours. This reason for being is at the core of the thirteen attributes. We say them to encounter God in the ritual moment of worship and to carry them with us into our dealings with others, as we build a story of who we are—as made in the image of God.

⚬⟶⟶⟶⟵⟵⟵⚬

# PART I
# The Liturgy

# The Thirteen Attributes

## Translation and Commentary

*Dr. Joel M. Hoffman*

[1] God is a king seated on a throne of mercy, governing graciously, pardoning the sins of his people, removing the first, first, extending pardon to sinners and forgiveness

אֵל מֶלֶךְ יוֹשֵׁב עַל כִּסֵּא רַחֲמִים, [1]
מִתְנַהֵג בַּחֲסִידוּת, מוֹחֵל עֲוֹנוֹת
עַמּוֹ, מַעֲבִיר רִאשׁוֹן רִאשׁוֹן,
מַרְבֶּה מְחִילָה לַחַטָּאִים, וּסְלִיחָה

*(prayer text continues on page 6)*

[1] *God is a king seated*: Others, "God, king, sitting ..." The line is based on Proverbs 20:8, according to which "a king sitting on a throne of justice" can do away with evil with just his eyes (perhaps, "by a glance").

---

Dr. Joel M. Hoffman lectures around the globe on popular and scholarly topics spanning history, Hebrew, prayer, and Jewish continuity. He has served on the faculties of Brandeis University in Waltham, Massachusetts, and Hebrew Union College–Jewish Institute of Religion in New York City. He is author of four books about Hebrew and the Bible, including *And God Said: How Translations Conceal the Bible's Original Meaning*, and has written for the international *Jerusalem Post*. He contributed to all ten volumes of the *My People's Prayer Book: Traditional Prayers, Modern Commentaries* series, winner of the National Jewish Book Award; to *My People's Passover Haggadah: Traditional Texts, Modern Commentaries*; and to *Who by Fire, Who by Water—Un'taneh Tokef, We Have Sinned: Sin and Confession in Judaism—Ashamnu and Al Chet, May God Remember: Memory and Memorializing in Judaism—Yizkor, All the World: Universalism, Particularism and the High Holy Days*, and *Naming God: Our Father, Our King—Avinu Malkeinu* (all Jewish Lights).

By contrast, God here is not on a throne of justice, but instead on a throne of mercy, the shift from justice to mercy being a major theme of Yom Kippur. According to the Midrash (*Leviticus Rabbah* 23:24), God normally sits on a throne of justice, but upon hearing the shofar blasts of the people Israel, God stands up and moves to a throne of mercy. This occurs, says the Midrash, "in the seventh month," that is, during the High Holy Days.

[1] *Throne*: Literally, "chair."

[1] *Governing*: Literally, "acting."

[1] *Graciously*: Literally, "with grace." Others, "with righteousness," based on other ways the root of this word (*ch.s.d*) is used.

[1] *First, first*: Our English reflects the enigmatic phrasing of the Hebrew. The reference is to a Talmudic debate (Rosh Hashanah 17a) on the nature of God's mercy, as prompted by the Hebrew phrase "most kind." Referring to the scale God uses to weigh the balance of merit and sin, the House of Hillel says God tips the scales that weigh merit against sin. The Rabbis wonder how that works. Some say that God presses down on the side of merit; others counter that God lifts up the side of sin. A third opinion is that God "removes the first, first," which is to say (according to some) that God first removes the first sin—the first one in the record, presumably—and then weighs only the sins that remain against all the merit, so that even a person with equal sin and merit (prior to one sin being removed) will still end up being judged as meritorious.

A pithy paraphrase might be "the first sin doesn't count," except that the Rabbis thought of this, too. They note that the first sin doesn't count for the weighing, but neither is it erased. If, after the first sin is removed, the sins still outweigh the merits, the sin is returned to the scales and counted among a person's overall sins for which atonement must be made or punishment meted out.

[1] *Extending*: Literally, "increasing." The Hebrew word here, *marbeh*, lies at the foundation of a set of common Hebrew idioms—for example, *marbeh tz'dakah marbeh shalom* (Mishnah Avot 2:8), which means, literally, that one who gives a lot of charity increases peace; that is, charity leads to peace. Our English "extending" here misses one nuance

of the Hebrew, namely, the notion that God doesn't just extend pardon but does so in some superlative manner beyond the ordinary. But other English options—like "increasingly" or "often"—don't help.

[1]*Pardon to sinners ... forgiveness to transgressors*: As is often the case when translating Hebrew for the High Holy Days, we are limited by the fact that, compared to English, Hebrew has many words for "sin" (and "sinner"). When the Hebrew word varies, we would prefer varying the English as well. Here, for example, we have the common word *chataim* ("sinners," related to *chet*, "sin"); also, just above, we have *avonot* (plural of *avon*, also "sin"). Whereas Hebrew uses *chet* and *avon* to indicate a fine difference of meaning between the two, our English misses the distinction. We might have recourse to a rarely used English word, such as "miscreant," for one, but both *chet* and *avon* are relatively common in Hebrew, and we generally prefer retaining the same register as the Hebrew in our English equivalents. So we have chosen to use "sin"/"sinner" here for both *chet/chataim* and *avon/avonot*. We immediately encounter yet a third term after these two, *poshim*, for which we use the English "transgressors."

We confront a similar dilemma regarding the verbs "pardon" and "forgive," which in English have to suffice for three common Hebrew near synonyms, from the roots *m.ch.l*, *s.l.ch*, and *k.p.r*.

[1]*Dealing generously*: Literally, "does generous things," with the common Hebrew word *tz'dakah* used here not in the widespread contemporary sense of "charity" but the related idea of something generous.

[1]*Living beings*: Literally, "flesh and breath." "Flesh and blood" would have been another translation option. Given the context—sin and God's response to it—we would imagine that the sense here is not actually all life, but human life alone, although from the Hebrew itself we cannot tell if God's generosity is being predicated toward animals as well.

to transgressors, dealing generously with all living beings. [2]You do not treat them according to their evil. [3]God, You instructed us to recite the thirteen attributes. [4]For our sake, remember the covenant of the thirteen attributes today, as You once revealed them to the Humble One, as is written, "Adonai descended in a cloud, and he stood with him there, and he said God's name. Then Adonai passed before him and said,

לְפוֹשְׁעִים, עוֹשֶׂה צְדָקוֹת עִם כָּל בָּשָׂר וָרוּחַ. [2] לֹא כְרָעָתָם תִּגְמוֹל. [3] אֵל, הוֹרֵיתָ לָנוּ לוֹמַר שְׁלֹשׁ עֶשְׂרֵה, [4] זְכוֹר לָנוּ הַיּוֹם בְּרִית שְׁלֹשׁ עֶשְׂרֵה, כְּמוֹ שֶׁהוֹדַעְתָּ לֶעָנָו מִקֶּדֶם, כְּמוֹ שֶׁכָּתוּב: וַיֵּרֶד יְיָ בֶּעָנָן, וַיִּתְיַצֵּב עִמּוֹ שָׁם, וַיִּקְרָא בְשֵׁם יְיָ. וַיַּעֲבֹר יְיָ עַל פָּנָיו וַיִּקְרָא:

[2] *Treat them*: Or, "reward them." The Hebrew word here means "treat in kind," as in "to reward goodness with goodness and evil with evil." Unfortunately, the English word "reward" by itself generally refers specifically to good things, so we use the more general "treat" here. The point is that goodness is deserving of goodness and evil deserving of evil, but in this case, God disregards the evil.

[3] *Thirteen attributes*: In Hebrew, just "the thirteen."

[4] *For our sake*: Literally, "to us," an example of what linguists call the "benefactive dative"—that is, using the preposition "to" to indicate who benefits. We don't have such a construction in mainstream English, but we see something related (although without the preposition) in the dialectal "I'm going to get me a burger." There, the "me" emphasizes that the burger is for my enjoyment. English does have something similar—a *malefactive* dative, which indicates who suffers, as expressed with the preposition "on." In the English "Someone ate the last bagel on me," the phrase "on me" adds the information that I was negatively affected by the bagel eating. In our Hebrew here, we ask God to remember the covenant to our benefit.

[4] *Revealed*: Or "instructed."

[4] *Humble One*: A frequently found poetic term for Moses, whom the Rabbis call "the humble one."

⁵'Adonai, Adonai, merciful and gracious God, endlessly patient, most kind and truthful, extending kindness to thousands, forgiving sins and transgressions and misdeeds, cleansing.'"

⁵ יְיָ יְיָ, אֵל רַחוּם וְחַנּוּן, אֶרֶךְ אַפַּיִם, וְרַב חֶסֶד וֶאֱמֶת. נֹצֵר חֶסֶד לָאֲלָפִים, נֹשֵׂא עָוֹן וָפֶשַׁע וְחַטָּאָה, וְנַקֵּה.

⁴*As is written*: Commonly the ungrammatical, "as it is written." But that is not how standard English works. For instance, we don't say, "as it is written in the Declaration of Independence ..." but rather, "as is written ..."
⁴*He stood with him*: Our translation, like the Hebrew text, uses "he" for both God and Moses, so we don't know from the text if God stood with Moses or Moses with God.
⁵*Adonai*: Or "the Lord."
⁵*Merciful and gracious*: These are two reasonable options for the Hebrew *rachum* and *chanun*. We no longer know the exact nuances of the ancient words. Even if we did, it would be difficult to find exact English matches for them. For instance, instead of "merciful" we might prefer "compassionate."
⁵*Endlessly patient*: Or "slow to anger."
⁵*Most*: In the sense of "very." The Hebrew literally reads "abundant in ..."
⁵*Kind*: Others, "loving-kindness" or "steadfast love."
⁵*Kindness*: The Hebrew here, *chesed*, is the same word we just translated as "kind." (We used "kind" to match "most kind," as opposed to the literal but less idiomatic "great in kindness" in English.)
⁵*Thousands*: Presumably, thousands of generations, which is to say, "lots" of generations.
⁵*Forgiving*: Literally, "carrying." The Hebrew word, *nosei*, is what connects the attributes to the overall theme of the High Holy Days. We nowadays think of the theme as "forgiveness," so that *nosei* implies, for us, "forgiving" sin. In its original context, however, the word *nosei* meant just what it normally does to us, "carrying."

What we see here is an evolving metaphoric understanding of sin. According to our modern view, sins have to be punished or forgiven, but that simple understanding does not convey the whole gamut of thought behind the idea of sin and how God deals with it.

By the first century CE or so, just as the Rabbinic era was dawning, sin was understood as constituting a debt, which, as we still say today, could be "forgiven," but also repaid. This is why sins are placed on one side of a balance scale and merits on the other (see above, "First, first"). Merits offset sins, just as credits offset debts. A similar financial metaphor describes good deeds as principal upon which interest is earned (see *My People's Prayer Book*, vol. 5, Birkhot Hashachar [*Morning Blessings*], p. 130).

In the Bible, by contrast—prior to the Rabbis, that is—a prominent metaphor was sin as a weight to be borne, or, as we have it here, "carried." In Leviticus 24:15, for example, the punishment for people who sin is that they must "carry" the burden of what they have done.

The thirteen attributes are biblical in origin, so in understanding what they meant originally, we should interpret them according to the biblical metaphor, not the Rabbinic one. What seems to be promised here, then, is that God carries the burden for us. This may be different from forgiving, in that "forgiving" implies that there will be no consequences anymore, while "carrying" may imply that the consequences remain but that God is—perhaps only temporarily—assuming them for us.

The issue is particularly important in light of the follow-up in the very next words in the Bible—the part of the thirteen attributes that the Rabbis chose not to include in the liturgy. Lacking from the liturgy is the promise that God will certainly not "cleanse" the sins; rather, God will visit the sins of the parents upon their children and their children's children and the third and the fourth generations. If so, what the Bible may be saying in its original context is that God will temporarily assume the burden of the sins, but the sins will remain a burden to future generations. This is almost the opposite of forgiveness!

Another possibility—commonly reflected in translations—is that God carries some but not all of our sins. This leads to the JPS (Jewish Publication Society) translation "yet He does not remit all punishment" (Exodus 34:7). But this seems less likely as the intended biblical meaning, because the Hebrew doesn't contain anything to the effect of "yet" or "but" or "however."

⁶Pardon our sins and transgressions, and take possession of us. ⁷Forgive us, our father, for we have sinned; pardon us, our king, for we have transgressed. ⁸For You, Adonai, are good and forgiving and most kind to all who call on You.

⁶ וְסָלַחְתָּ לַעֲוֹנֵנוּ וּלְחַטָּאתֵנוּ
וּנְחַלְתָּנוּ.
⁷ סְלַח לָנוּ אָבִינוּ כִּי חָטָאנוּ, מְחַל
לָנוּ מַלְכֵּנוּ כִּי פָשָׁעְנוּ.
⁸ כִּי אַתָּה, אֲדֹנָי, טוֹב וְסַלָּח וְרַב
חֶסֶד לְכָל קוֹרְאֶיךָ.

So it seems that the original biblical intent was that God carries but does not erase sin—which is why sin remains for future generations.

The Rabbis, however, lopped off the follow-up in order to include only the part about God's kindness, as an exemplary indication of God's forgiving nature. We therefore use "forgive" here, in accord with what the Rabbis intended.

⁵*Cleansing*: The Hebrew word *nakeh* is the first part of a larger phrase (*nakeh lo y'nakeh*) that means "certainly not cleansing." A quirk of Hebrew grammar lets the Rabbis lop off the end of the phrase and recast it positively rather than negatively—just the opposite of the biblical intent. Still, the Hebrew is not quite grammatical, which is why our English, too, lacks the word "and." (Technically, the lack of "and" isn't ungrammatical. Rather, it's a rare grammatical construction called "asyndeton," perhaps most famous from Julius Caesar's "I came, I saw, I conquered.")

⁶*Sins and transgressions*: Once again we have to compromise as we find English words for various Hebrew near synonyms. In this case, we use "sin" and "transgression" for two different Hebrew words, even though we used "sin" for the same two words in verse 1, above.

⁶*Take possession of us*: Or "take us as an inheritance" or even "adopt us." The line forms the second part of Exodus 34:9, following the thirteen attributes (from 34:6–7). The attributes speak of generations, and the Hebrew root here is often connected to inheritance. (The biblical text omitted in our prayer—Exodus 34:8 and the first words of 34:9—reads: "Moses quickly bowed low to the ground. And he said ...")

☙

PART II

# The Attributes of God

## Their History and Meaning

# Overview

# Will the Real God Please Stand Up?

## BALANCING CLASSIC ACCOUNTS

*Rabbi Charles H. Middleburgh, PhD*

The thundering echo of the thirteen attributes of God, revealed by the Almighty to Moses, reverberates down the millennia. They occur as Moses reaches the Sinai summit with the second set of stone tablets in readiness for the re-inscription of the Ten Commandments—to replace those he had shattered in his anger at the Israelites' worship of the golden calf. The first time around, the conversation was almost entirely about the people and what they needed to do to live goodly and godly lives; this time, the words appear to be about the nature of God.

Whatever we may think about the meaning of these attributes, and their implications for our lives, it is undoubtedly the case that they became something of a mantra in ancient Israel, beginning in Exodus 34—according to some scholars, the earliest strand of the Torah—whence the

Rabbi Charles H. Middleburgh, PhD, is the dean of Leo Baeck College in London, where he has taught since 1984. He is coeditor with Rabbi Andrew Goldstein, PhD, of the Liberal Judaism *Machzor Ruach Chadashah* and the anthologies *High and Holy Days: A Book of Jewish Wisdom* and *A Jewish Book of Comfort*. He contributed to *Who by Fire, Who by Water*—Un'taneh Tokef; *All These Vows*—Kol Nidre; *We Have Sinned: Sin and Confession in Judaism*—Ashamnu *and* Al Chet; *May God Remember: Memory and Memorializing in Judaism*—Yizkor; *All the World: Universalism, Particularism and the High Holy Days*; and *Naming God: Our Father, Our King*—Avinu Malkeinu (all Jewish Lights).

attributes had plenty of opportunity to become widely known. They are quoted in six different biblical books, the latest being Nehemiah (9:17), datable to the late fifth century BCE. Their occurrence in two specific books, however, most intrigues me: the relatively little-known prophecy of Nahum and the very well-known tale of Jonah.

The book of Nahum, one of the so-called Twelve Minor Prophets, is a pre-exilic diatribe against the capital of Assyria, Nineveh. In the year 612 BCE an army of Medes captured and destroyed the city; Nahum's book (likely written thereafter) is without question one of the most chilling prophecies in prophetic literature.

In the third and final chapter Nahum spits out the following diatribe:

> Ah, city of crime, utterly treacherous, full of violence, where killing never stops! Crack of whip and rattle of steel, galloping steed and bounding chariot! Charging horse-men, flashing swords, and glittering spears! Hosts of slain and heaps of corpses, dead bodies without number—they stumble over bodies. (Nahum 3:1–3)

Yet he exults:

> Desolation, devastation, and destruction! Spirits sink, knees buckle, all loins tremble, all faces turn ashen. (2:11)

This is terrifying language, made even worse by the way Nahum takes the Exodus text and twists it to fit his context. This is not a benign God, comforting wayward human beings with attributes that give hope and encouragement. To the contrary, in Nahum's view:

> Adonai is a passionate, avenging God; Adonai is vengeful and fierce in wrath. Adonai takes vengeance on his ene-mies, He rages against his foes. Adonai is slow to anger but great in power, and Adonai does not exonerate the guilty. (1:2–3)

There can be little doubt that this travesty of the Exodus 34 attributes of God has a direct and devastating purpose: to frighten and to dash all hope. God is vengeful, not forgiving. God is *erekh apayim*, translated in this book as "endlessly patient," with the connotation of being "slow to anger," but Nahum takes it to mean "endlessly staying angry / extending anger"; and instead of being *rav chesed*, "most kind" (in the sense of being filled with covenant love), Nahum's God is *ug'dol ko'ach*, "great in power," the power to destroy.

The final quotation, *v'nakeh lo y'nakeh*, is directly from Exodus 34 and is particularly terrifying, so much so that the Rabbis, who use it liturgically, drop the last two words to make it say just the opposite of what it actually means. Our liturgy simply says *v'nakeh*, literally, "cleansing" (in our translation) but implying, more precisely, "exonerating the guilty." Nahum cites the original unflinchingly: *v'nakeh lo y'nakeh*, God will "not cleanse"—"God will not exonerate the guilty" (Nahum 1:3). The citizens of Nineveh, the archetypal wicked city, are doomed.

The book of Jonah, which we read every Yom Kippur afternoon, provides its own dramatic allusion to the thirteen attributes—quite the opposite of Nahum!

Jonah, the most petulant of prophets and the prophetic "everyman," is each and every one of us—a normal human being. But in the end he successfully fulfills his mission and becomes the most effective prophet of all. And where is the reluctant Jonah sent? To Nineveh! Yet again this stereotypical evil city is the focus of a prophetic book, but this time not that it may be destroyed, but that its people may abandon their evil ways and be forgiven by Israel's God. They are not part of Israel's Sinai covenant, but they may still merit divine forgiveness.

Jonah, as we all know, is disinclined to do what God orders. He has an intimate relationship with God, like a child to a parent, and indeed, he even tries to run away, as a frightened child might. He takes passage on a ship and hides below deck as if God will not find him there. He thinks he knows what God will do anyway and doesn't want to be a bit-part player on a great stage where the final scene has already been written.

But God calls the wayward child Jonah to his responsibility. God first dispatches a storm that threatens to capsize the ship and then a conveniently located large fish to swallow him and dump him back on land. Jonah must prophesy!

When the Ninevites hear Jonah's proclamation, "Repent or else," everyone from the beast of burden to the king himself responds positively—exactly as Jonah had feared all along! Jonah is peeved, extremely so, and because he has the easy relationship he does with his God, he lets all his frustration out. "I knew this is what would happen," he says, in effect. "You are, after all [quoting Exodus 34], a merciful and gracious God, endlessly patient, most kind" (Jonah 4:2). But he does not complete the quotation! We expect the continuation of the attributes all the way to *v'nakeh lo y'nakeh*, "not exonerate the guilty." Instead, we get *v'nicham al hara'ah*, "renouncing evil," a phrase that harks back to the Israelite rebellion of the golden calf, when Moses persuades God not to destroy the idolatrous Israelites and says to God, "Renounce the evil plan to punish your people" (Exodus 32:12).

And when did *this* exchange occur? Just before Moses smashed the first covenant tablets—and when he returned to Sinai with the second set, the thirteen attributes were first expressed!

As I mentioned before, the Rabbis altered the thirteen attributes liturgically to make it beyond question that God exempts the guilty from punishment—that there is nothing for which a contrite heart cannot be forgiven. We generally assume that they took the scissors to Exodus 34:7 just to fit the context of the Days of Awe, but there may have been a greater motivation at work.

Look again at the thirteen attributes as given in Exodus, Jonah, and Nahum. The Exodus prototype comes in the aftermath of idolatry; God is merciful but also punitive and very angry. Moses will have to curtail God's anger. Jonah's version is in the context of a cliché-wicked city whose evil citizens, nonetheless, deserve God's love if they repent. Nahum knows nothing of repentance; he portrays a petrifying and remorseless God, whose positive attributes have been changed into negatives.

Who is Israel's God, then? Exodus 34 leaves us in doubt. God is both pardoning and punishing. Nahum's God is all-punitive. Jonah's God is eager to forgive. Recognizing this overall biblical inconsistency, the Rabbis opt to disallow the God of the Jewish People being vengeful, endlessly angry with sinners, and almost delighting in punishment. So they edited the biblical message, changing its totality from a mixed but ultimately negative message to one of positivity and hope, a message bringing comfort and the promise of divine love to repentant sinners—especially on the holiest day of our year.

# Biblical Beginnings

# God, Merciful and Compassionate?

*Dr. Marc Zvi Brettler*

The High Holy Day prayer we call the Thirteen Attributes misrepresents the Bible, even though it comes directly from it. It quotes selectively, using only those verses that depict God as benevolent and merciful. Such selectivity typifies the liturgy's use of the Bible. Prayers are not interested in—and have no obligation to be representative of—the Bible in all its diversity; rather, they utilize only those biblical texts that further their composer's agenda—in this case, the message that prayers are heeded by a forgiving deity.

The attributes are introduced with the biblical image of a human king from Proverbs 20:8, "The king seated on the throne of judgment can winnow out all evil by his glance," but an important word in this verse is switched (liturgy, line 1a): *din*, "judgment," becomes *rachamim*, "mercy," "compassion," or "graciousness" (like the word "grace")— a change that emblemizes what will happen throughout this prayer, as

Dr. Marc Zvi Brettler is the Bernice and Morton Professor of Judaic Studies at Duke University. He contributed to all volumes of the *My People's Prayer Book: Traditional Prayers, Modern Commentaries* series, winner of the National Jewish Book Award; and to *My People's Passover Haggadah: Traditional Texts, Modern Commentaries*; *Who by Fire, Who by Water*—Un'taneh Tokef; *All These Vows*—Kol Nidre; *We Have Sinned: Sin and Confession in Judaism*—Ashamnu *and* Al Chet; and *Naming God: Our Father, Our King*—Avinu Malkeinu (all Jewish Lights). He is coeditor of *The Jewish Annotated New Testament* and *The Jewish Study Bible*, which won the National Jewish Book Award; coauthor of *The Bible and the Believer*; and author of *How to Read the Jewish Bible*, among other books and articles. He has also been interviewed on National Public Radio's *Fresh Air* by Terry Gross.

verses about judgment are either omitted or altered to highlight mercy instead. The Thirteen Attributes thus becomes a synopsis of a very one-sided God, a God of mercy.

Much of this introductory paragraph would have been foreign to ancient Israelites, who would never have heard of "thirteen attributes"—far less, that they constituted their own "covenant"—even though the word *b'rit* ("covenant") does occur earlier on in the same biblical chapter (Exodus 34:10), a fact that may have contributed to the Rabbinic idea later on. Nor would they have thought that the attributes were given to Moses so that he might equip future generations to recite them as a means of invoking God's mercy through prayer.

At the same time, these ancient Israelites would have appreciated the balanced, parallelistic cadences of the introductory lines that follow God as supreme king of mercy (liturgy, lines 1b–4), for these are typical of biblical poetic style:

a. "extending pardon to sinners" (*marbeh m'chilah l'chata'im*)
a1. "and forgiveness to transgressors" (*us'lichah l'fosh'im*)
b. "dealing generously with all living beings" (*oseh tz'dakot im kol basar varu'ach*)
b1. "You do not treat them according to their evil" (*lo kh'ra'atam tigmol*)
c. "You instructed us to recite the thirteen attributes" (*horeta lanu lomar sh'losh esreh*)
c1. "For our sake remember the covenant of the thirteen attributes today" (*z'khor lanu hayom brit sh'losh esreh*)

They would have also known that *anav* ("Humble One," liturgy, line 4) was a biblical epithet of Moses (see Numbers 12:3, "Moses was a very humble man, more so than any other man on earth"). Also, even though the word *chasidut* ("righteousness"—"graciously," in our translation, line 1) is not biblical, its form (an abstract noun ending in *ut*) is, and attributing *chasidut* to God is based on biblical precedent (see esp. 2 Samuel 22:26 = Psalm 18:26, "With the righteous, You deal righteously," *im chasid titchasad*). Thus, the liturgical introduction (lines 1–4) shows clear affinities with the Bible, even while introducing words and ideas that appear biblical but are not. Religions typically innovate this way—cloaking the new in the guise of the old.

At times, religions even say expressly that they are quoting the old as part of the new; so we get (in line 4) "as it is written" (*k'mo shekatuv*), a post-biblical formula, but similar to the Bible's own *kakatuv* (e.g., 2 Kings 14:6), the way the Bible cites itself—in this case the author of 2 Kings is citing Deuteronomy 24:16.

But our hypothetical biblical readers would have been aghast at the liberties taken in the liturgical citation of Exodus 34:7, the second verse of the divine attributes. The biblical original ends with the guarantee that God "visits the iniquity of parents upon children and children's children, upon the third and fourth generation." That second half of the verse is altogether omitted. In addition, the three words prior (*v'nakeh lo y'nakeh*) are broken apart in such a way as to altogether alter the original meaning. These three words form a single grammatical unit, like the English "I can't bow out of that obligation," a sentence in which "bow," "out," and "of" are inseparable. The biblical three-word expression *v'nakeh lo y'nakeh* must also be read as a whole. It means "yet He does not utterly cleanse [us from the sins for which we deserve punishment]." As the Rabbis dismember it, we are left with *v'nakeh* alone (liturgy, line 5), implying just the reverse, that God indeed "cleanses" us from such sin. After their initial shock at all of this "whitewashing" of God, my ancestors might heave a sigh of relief with the ending (line 6): "Pardon our sins and our transgressions, and take possession of us!"—the second half of just a few verses later, Exodus 34:9, quoted accurately.

I can even imagine these biblical forebears appreciating line 7 (*s'lach lanu avinu ki chatanu; m'chal lanu malkeinu ki fashanu*), easily divisible into synonymous parallelism:

    1. "Forgive us, our father, for we have sinned;"
    1a. "pardon us, our king, for we have transgressed."

It is not biblical; it even contains a post-biblical word, *m'chal* ("pardon," from a post-biblical root *m.ch.l*), but its style follows typical biblical synonymous parallelism, where

- each line can be divided into two,
- each part says more or less the same thing,
- the second part is grammatically similar to the first,
- and the second part uses synonyms to words found in the first part, to form word pairs.

In this case, two words even repeat identically (*lanu, ki*), while other words are synonymous: "forgive" and "pardon"; "our father" and "our king"; "we have sinned" and "we have transgressed." These lead seamlessly into a concluding quotation from Psalm 86:5: "For You, Adonai, are good and forgiving and most kind to all who call on You." Psalm 86 is particularly appropriate here, because verse 15 actually cites some version of the thirteen attributes themselves: "But You, O Adonai, are a merciful and gracious God, endlessly patient, most kind and truthful."

We saw before how our liturgy engages in grammatical violence in citing God's mercy (of Exodus 34:6–7a) but omitting the promise of intergenerational punishment (of Exodus 34:7b). But the version in Psalm 86 also cites a "kinder, gentler" God, with no mention of punishment. The Rabbis were not the first, therefore, to see God as altogether merciful. They had this precedent in Psalms (and several other biblical passages) to guide them.

Exodus 34:5–7 follows the story of the golden calf and Moses climbing the mountain a second time to receive the tablets of laws. Exactly why these attributes should be revealed to Moses then is not clear, however. On the face of it, they are a response to Moses's request of 33:13, "Now, if I have truly gained your favor, pray let me know your ways, that I may know You and continue in your favor." But most scholars believe this verse is from a different document or source and thus originally unconnected to the attributes.

In any event, Exodus 34 is not the first time that some form of these attributes is found in the Torah. They are also in the Decalogue (the so-called Ten Commandments) of Exodus 20:5–6 (see also Deuteronomy 5:9–10), as part of the ban on following false gods:

> You shall not bow down to them or serve them. For I, Adonai your God, am an impassioned God, visiting the guilt of the parents upon the children, upon the third and upon the fourth generations of those who reject Me, but showing kindness to the thousandth generation of those who love Me and keep my commandments.

Here, the context is the prohibition of idolatry specifically (see Exodus 20:3), not general attributes of the deity. And the two descriptions of God's nature, although similar, are not identical; in Exodus 20, God's threat of intergenerational punishment precedes the description of divine graciousness, while Exodus 34 has the reverse order. Nor is the wording identical. Yet both know of intergenerational punishment and insist that God is at least 250 times more beneficent than punishing—intergenerational punishment covers four generations, while the picture of the compassionate God assigns mercy to thousands (of generations).

Earlier biblical scholarship tried to figure out which of the two lists (Exodus 20 or 34) was earlier or if, alternatively, they were both indebted to a common third source. Such attempts are somewhat out of fashion now, as we have come to believe that a variety of parallel lists once coexisted side by side—there probably was no single original for us to find. Nor is it possible to know when and how such lists were used, though it is easy to imagine that they were intended, as in the High Holy Day prayers, to invoke divine mercy.

Even while recalling intergenerational punishment for four generations, both Exodus 20 and 34 insist that God is much more gracious than reproving! Furthermore, they function to deflect the punishment from the worshiper to others down the line. Still, they believe that sins must be punished, not totally forgiven. And for some in ancient Israel, such guaranteed punishment, especially across generations, was inherently problematic. Deuteronomy 7:9–10 quotes the divine attributes but polemicizes against the inclusion of intergenerational punishment among them: "God ... keeps his covenant faithfully to the thousandth generation of those who love Him and keep his commandments, but ... instantly requites with destruction those who reject Him." Ezekiel 18:4b categorically declaims, "The person who sins, only he shall die." And Isaiah 43:25 promises simply that Adonai "blots out ... transgressions" altogether.

This inherently difficult issue of intergenerational punishment—either for following other gods (Exodus 20) or more broadly (Exodus 34)—helps explain why the divine attributes circulated in an alternative form (as in Psalm 86:15) where such punishment is missing. This truncated formulation is best known from Jonah 4:2, where Jonah says he fled "for I know that You are a compassionate and gracious God, slow to anger, abounding in kindness, renouncing punishment." Here, too, we see no reference to intergenerational punishment. In fact, had Jonah believed in it, Jonah would have expected God to punish the Ninevites even if they repented, on account of the sins of their parents, grandparents, and great-grandparents, and the whole point of the book of Jonah would be moot.

Yet, other biblical texts do cite intergenerational punishment. In its discussion of the fate due an enemy, Psalm 109:14, for example, requests, "May God be ever mindful of his father's iniquity, and may the sin of his mother not be blotted out." Nahum 1:2–3a also reads:

> Adonai is a passionate, avenging God; Adonai is vengeful and fierce in wrath. Adonai takes vengeance on his enemies, He rages against his foes. Adonai is slow to anger and of great forbearance, but Adonai does not wholly cleanse [*v'nakeh lo y'nakeh*].

Here is the very phrase from Exodus 34:7b, which our prayer excises.

These verses are not alone in depicting God as angry, unpredictable, or vengeful—just the opposite of the merciful deity depicted in the positive thirteen attributes. Psalm 94, for example, opens, "God of retribution, Adonai; God of retribution, appear!" In truth, the Bible does not usually depict God as predominantly compassionate or fair-minded.

In sum, our liturgical use of Exodus 34:5–7 does indeed misrepresent the Bible, taken as a whole. But it follows the precedent already found in Psalm 86:15 and Jonah 4:2, where, as we saw, the divine attributes connected to intergenerational punishment are lacking.

The reworking of Exodus 34:5–7 is really part of a larger issue: Is selective memory good? Sometimes it is our very ability to forget—to see and remember selectively—that allows us to move on with life, especially, perhaps, at times of introspection, such as the High Holy Days. We know all too well that we are affected by previous generations' wrongs—none of us was really born with a clean slate. But can we imagine a High Holy Day prayer that paraphrases Lamentations 5:7, "Our fathers sinned and are no more; and we must bear their guilt"? The High Holy Days are imaginatively designed to evoke great hope, hence its themes of a book of life, the sweetness of honey, unburdening ourselves of sin, and starting life afresh. The daring choice to emphasize only the merciful attributes of Exodus 34:5–7 is a constructive part of that process.

# Seeing God through the Metaphoric Imagination

*Rabbi Andrea L. Weiss, PhD*

After the burning bush, after the Exodus from Egypt through a wall of water, after the words delivered through thunder and lightning atop a mountain, after the golden calf and the tablets smashed to pieces, Moses finally asks to see the invisible, allusive divine presence: "Please, show me your glory" (Exodus 33:18). God responds, "You cannot see my face, for no human can see Me and live" (Exodus 33:20). So God hides Moses in the cleft of a rock and calls out while passing before him, "Adonai, Adonai, merciful and gracious God, endlessly patient, most kind and truthful, extending kindness to thousands, forgiving sins and transgressions and misdeeds, cleansing" (Exodus 34:6–7).[1] Moses discovers that when it comes to God, verbal description takes the place of a visible apparition.

Still, the inability to see God's physical manifestation did not prevent our biblical ancestors from metaphorically imagining what God was like. The thirteen attributes of Exodus 34:6–7 pile up a list of abstract terms to describe God's qualities and character. Their very abstractness, however, makes it difficult to picture what they actually imply, so we must turn elsewhere in the Bible to find metaphors that visualize how these characteristics might manifest themselves. How, for example, might

Rabbi Andrea L. Weiss, PhD, was ordained in 1993 from the Hebrew Union College–Jewish Institute of Religion in New York and received her PhD from the University of Pennsylvania in 2004. She serves as associate professor of Bible at the Hebrew Union College–Jewish Institute of Religion in New York. She is associate editor of *The Torah: A Women's Commentary*.

we conceive of a "merciful and gracious" God? To what might we compare a God "most kind and truthful"? The Bible answers these questions with metaphors that bring the thirteen attributes to life.

The first adjective in Exodus 34:6 depicts God as *rachum*, "merciful" or "compassionate." This root (*r.ch.m*) repeats in Psalm 103:13: "As a father has compassion [*rachem*] for his children, Adonai has compassion [*richam*] for those who revere Him." This verse suggests that God looks like a parent when displaying the type of love and caring conveyed by the adjective *rachum*. The same root links God with the image of a merciful parent in two additional passages. Jeremiah 31:20 begins with a rhetorical question about the people Israel, here referred to as "Ephraim": "Is Ephraim my dear son?" God responds affirmatively by asserting that in spite of the pronouncements against them, God recalls Israel with affection, just like a parent with a beloved child: "My heart yearns for him; I will assuredly have compassion on him [*rachem arachamenu*]." In Isaiah 63:15–16, the prophet turns Jeremiah's words into a plea to God to act on Israel's behalf: "Look down from heaven and see from your holy and glorious height! Where is your zeal, your power, your yearning, and your compassion [*v'rachamecha*]?... Surely You are our father ... You, O Adonai, are our father." Together, these three passages establish that *el rachum v'chanun*, a "merciful and gracious God," resembles a parent, likely a father in the biblical context: an authority figure who treats the metaphoric child with affection and benevolence if the child remains loyal and obedient, but with rebuke if the child fails to meet the parent's expectations. Proverbs 3:11–12, for instance, warns, "Do not reject the discipline of Adonai, my son; do not abhor his rebuke. For whom Adonai loves, He rebukes, as a father the son whom he favors."

When Israel disobeys and rebels against God, the prophets also portray God as a husband betrayed by his unfaithful wife. Jeremiah 3:19 begins with the parent-child metaphor: "I had resolved to adopt you as my child ... and I thought you would surely call Me 'Father.'" But in the subsequent verse, the metaphor quickly shifts to the husband-wife analogy: "Instead, you have broken faith with Me, as a woman breaks faith with her lover" (Jeremiah 3:20). This picks up on a theme found earlier in the chapter: "If a man divorces his wife, and she leaves him and marries another man, can he ever go back to her?" (Jeremiah 3:1).

Jeremiah lived and wrote prior to the Babylonian exile; but later, after the Israelites endure exile, the prophet whom we call Deutero-Isaiah returns to Jeremiah's theme and attempts to convince his audience that God is ready to reconcile with Israel, "a wife forsaken and forlorn" (Isaiah 54:6). In Isaiah 54:7, the metaphoric husband admits, "In a fit of rage I deserted you," yet he then declares, "But with great compassion [*uv'rachamim g'dolim*], I will gather you back." In the following verse, God reiterates this sentiment: "In an outpouring of anger, for a moment, I hid my face from you. But with everlasting kindness [*chesed olam*], I will show you compassion [*richamtich*]" (54:8). In this passage, the notion of God as merciful (*rachum*), kind (*rav chesed*), and forgiving takes the shape of an estranged husband who pledges to turn from anger to love with renewed tenderness and devotion.

The adjective *rachum* relates to the noun *rechem*, meaning "womb," and to the unusual word *m'rachem*, which refers to a young mother who has recently given birth. This word introduces another way to imagine a "merciful and gracious God": as a mother. Banished to Babylon and far away from the Promised Land, the Israelites fear that God has forsaken and forgotten them (Isaiah 49:14). Attempting to counter this perception and reassure the people of God's unending love, the prophet asks, "Can a mother forget her baby or a young woman [*merachem*] the child of her belly?" Although we anticipate a negative response to this rhetorical question, the verse surprises us: "Though they might forget," God contends, "yet I never could forget you" (Isaiah 49:15). This verse reminds us of the limits of metaphor: God may indeed be compared to a devoted mother, but ultimately, Adonai "is God, not human" (Hosea 11:9). God alone can promise never to sever the bond with Israel and to remain "endlessly patient, most kind and truthful, extending kindness to thousands" (Exodus 34:6–7).

In Isaiah 66:13, the prophet draws upon the same maternal metaphor to console the exiles: "As a person whose mother comforts him [*t'nachamenu*], so I will comfort you [*anachemchem*]; and you will find comfort [*t'nuchamu*] in Jerusalem." Repeated three times, the root *n.ch.m* ("to comfort") reminds us that we witness God's mercy and grace (*el rachum v'chanun*) when we sense God's loving, comforting presence.

These divine qualities manifest themselves in a metaphor found in perhaps the most familiar passage in the Bible. Following the declaration, "Adonai is my shepherd," Psalm 23 describes the shepherd conscientiously guiding the sheep to food and water and protecting the sheep from harm. In spite of the potentially precarious conditions, the sheep experiences no fear, "for You are with me; your rod and your staff—they comfort me [*y'nachamuni*]" (Psalm 23:4). Not surprisingly, the same metaphor recurs in words of the prophet whose very mission is to "comfort, comfort My people [*nachamu nachamu ami*]" (Isaiah 40:1). Isaiah 40:11 shows how the divine shepherd diligently tends to each and every animal: "Like a shepherd He pastures his flock. He gathers the lambs in his arms and carries them in his bosom; gently He leads the ewes." These depictions of an attentive and loving shepherd concretize what it means to be *el rachum v'chanun*, a "merciful and gracious God."

As part of the thirteen attributes, Exodus 34:7 describes God extending kindness to thousands: *notzer chesed la'alafim*. The verb translated here as "extend" (*n.tz.r*) means "to keep" or "to preserve" (others translate the phrase as "keeping kindness"), and elsewhere, this verb means "to watch" or "to guard." In Isaiah 27:2–6, the song of a "delightful vineyard," this verb appears twice as the metaphoric farmer promises to protect his vineyard (*notzrah ... etzorenah*) and water it "every moment," lest any harm befall it. The farmer in this tale acts with *chesed*, kindness and dedication. As a result of his vigilance and care, the vineyard thrives: "Jacob will strike root, Israel will blossom and sprout; and the whole world will be filled with fruit" (v. 6). This passage provides another way to imagine what it means for God to be "merciful and gracious ... endlessly patient, most kind and truthful, extending kindness to thousands." Psalm 121 employs the synonymous verb *sh.m.r.* ("to guard") to depict God as a guard who watches over us night and day, never sleeping, ever attentive, so that we do not stumble: "Adonai will guard you from all harm.... Adonai will guard your coming and your going now and forever" (Psalm 121:7–8).

Guard, farmer, shepherd, mother, husband, father—these metaphors transform the abstract terms in the thirteen attributes into concrete images that explain who God is and how God works in the world, especially in relationship with the people Israel. The metaphoric creativity of the Bible thus allows us to see God in our imaginations, if not with our own eyes.

☙❧

# Post-biblical
# Reinterpretation

# How the Bible Became the Prayer Book

## NOT THREATS OF PUNISHMENT BUT RABBINIC PROMISES OF FORGIVENESS

*Rabbi Margaret Moers Wenig, DD*

The Torah is full of punishment: Adam and Eve expelled from the garden; the generation of Noah drowned in the Flood; the builders of the Tower of Babel scattered; Deuteronomy's many threats (27:11–26), chanted only in a whisper; Lamentations' gory chastisements (2:1–3:20); and more. Yet, during the season of repentance, our liturgy features promises of forgiveness, not threats of punishment. Verses of the Torah are truncated to highlight forgiveness and hide punishment. Brazenly the liturgy quotes only the first half of Exodus 34:6–7—*Adonai, Adonai, el rachum v'chanun* ..., "Adonai, Adonai, merciful and gracious God, endlessly patient, most kind and truthful, extending kindness to thousands, forgiving sins and transgressions and misdeeds, and cleansing"—while deliberately omitting the second half—"but by no means cleansing from

Rabbi Margaret Moers Wenig, DD, teaches liturgy and homiletics at Hebrew Union College–Jewish Institute of Religion in New York and is rabbi emerita of Beth Am, The People's Temple. She contributed to *Who by Fire, Who by Water—Un'taneh Tokef*; *All These Vows—Kol Nidre*; *We Have Sinned: Sin and Confession in Judaism—Ashamnu and Al Chet*; *May God Remember: Memory and Memorializing in Judaism—Yizkor*; *All the World: Universalism, Particularism and the High Holy Days*; and *Naming God: Our Father, Our King—Avinu Malkeinu* (all Jewish Lights).

33

sin but visiting the iniquity of the parents upon children and children's children upon the third and the fourth generation."

This citation, "Adonai, Adonai, merciful and gracious God, end-lessly patient ..." (or, "the Thirteen Attributes of God's Mercy"), is litur-gically more important to Yom Kippur than *Kol Nidre*, more often recited than *Avinu Malkeinu*, and more central than *Un'taneh Tokef*.[1]

Placed in a larger liturgical unit called *s'lichot* (prayers for God's pardon), the thirteen attributes are repeated again and again each night or early morning, from shortly before Rosh Hashanah to the close of Yom Kippur or, as is the custom of some Jews, beginning a whole month before Rosh Hashanah and continuing until the end of Sukkot.

The recitation of the thirteen attributes is not a purely intellectual exercise. The mere proclamation of a doctrine would require only a sin-gle recitation, not the constant repetition we have here. Repetition does more than express ideas; it engenders feelings. Some leaders of prayer understand the feeling of *s'lichot* to be that of desperate pleading. The liturgical context in which the thirteen attributes are recited, however, belies that assumption. The context, in the inherited Ashkenazi version of *s'lichot*, alludes to a midrash in which God is imagined fashioning a new covenant with forgiveness at its core:

> God, king seated [*El melekh yoshev*] on a throne of mercy, governing graciously, pardoning the sins of his people, removing the first, first, extending pardon to sinners and forgiveness to transgressors, dealing generously with all liv-ing beings. You do not treat them according to their evil. God, You instructed us to recite the Thirteen Attributes. For our sake, remember the covenant of the Thirteen Attributes today, as You once revealed them to the Humble One [Moses], as it is written, "Adonai descended in a cloud and he stood with him [Moses] there, and he recited God's Name [Exodus 34:5]. Then Adonai passed before him [*vaya'avor Adonai al panav*] and said: Adonai, Adonai, merciful and gracious God [*el rachum, v'chanun*] ... [Exodus 34:6–7a]."[2]

Despite the claim of the prayer above, in the book of Exodus God never "instructs us" to recite the thirteen attributes. In a midrash, however, God does.

In Exodus the story goes like this: In furious reaction to his people's construction of a golden calf, Moses smashes the set of tablets God has just bestowed upon him. God, who is equally enraged, punishes the people with a devastating plague and vows to abandon them forever. Moses convinces God to annul the decree and asks to see God's face. For Moses's own safety ("Human beings cannot see Me and live" [Exodus 33:20]), God denies Moses's request, but places Moses in a cleft in the rock and then, "Adonai passed before him [*vaya'avor Adonai al panav*] and said [*vayikra*], "Adonai, Adonai, merciful and gracious God ..." (34:6). Moses entreats God, "Pardon our iniquity and sin" (34:9). God relents and says, "I hereby make a covenant" (34:10), and Moses delivers a second set of tablets to the Israelites (34:32).

The midrash extends the biblical account. It imagines that God relents not only *in this case* but *in all future cases as well* as long as Israel properly repents, and it portrays God imparting to Moses not only a second set of commandments but also a liturgical formula to be recited when Israel violates them. God's *onetime* act of pardon is thus midrashically transformed into a *perpetual promise* of pardon. S'lichot, and thus much of the Yom Kippur liturgy, was fashioned with this promise in mind.

On what does the midrash base its imagined scenario in which God teaches Moses how to pray for forgiveness? Through a clever rereading of the Hebrew phrase *al panav*. In Exodus 34:6, *vaya'avor Adonai al panav* means "God passed over [or by] his [Moses's] face," that is, "God passed before Moses." The midrash reinterprets *panav* to suggest that "God passed [something] over his *own* face," namely, a *tallit*.

> The Holy One wrapped Himself like a leader of prayer, *passing [a tallit] over his [God's] own face*. God showed Moses an order of prayer [i.e., *Adonai, Adonai ...*] and said to him, "Every time Israel sins, enact before me this order [of prayer], and I will forgive them" (Talmud, Rosh Hashanah 17b).[3]

The thirteen attributes become the terms not only of a promise, but of a new covenant, referred to laconically in Exodus (34:10) and named officially by the Rabbis as the *b'rit sh'losh esrehi*, "the covenant of the thirteen [attributes]."

The biblical story of the golden calf, told in mythological terms like the plot of a Wagnerian opera, minces no words. Betrayal exacts a terrible price, suffering inevitably ensues, but the story does not end there. A similar drama is played out in the book of Numbers (13:1–14:45) when twelve spies are sent to survey the Land and ten of them bring back a pessimistic report. In response, rather than trust God, the Israelites despair and clamor to return to Egypt. Once again God vows to abandon the people (14:12), only this time *Moses* recites the very words that God had pronounced on Sinai, "*Adonai, Adonai ...*" (14:18); and sure enough, God responds, "I have pardoned, as you have asked" (14:20)—but more literally, in the Hebrew, "I have pardoned, *according to your words* [*kidvarekha*]," namely, the words of the thirteen attributes.

These two stories of (1) Israel's idolatry (the golden calf) and (2) lack of faith (the spies) become the two iconic Jewish tales of breaking, but then reestablishing, the covenant. To drive that idea home, the famed eleventh-century rabbinic commentator Rashi works out an elaborate connection between the two. The initial set of tablets, he says, is broken on the seventeenth of Tammuz (a minor fast day). Then, after two forty-day sojourns on the mountain, Moses is given the second set of tablets—on none other than the tenth of Tishrei, Yom Kippur itself, making Yom Kippur the day par excellence of pardon and covenant renewal. And then, as if the two stories were one and the same, Rashi portrays God proclaiming to Moses on Sinai (story 1), "I have pardoned [*salachti*]," even though, in the biblical text, that proclamation appears not in that story at all (the Exodus story of the golden calf) but, as we saw above, in story 2, the Numbers story of the spies (Numbers 14:20). As Rashi conflates these two stories, so too does the *s'lichot* liturgy, mixing verses from both stories (Exodus 34:5–9 and Numbers 14:19–20) as if they were one.

Yom Kippur is about forgiveness, not punishment.[4] Were punishment the point, the Rabbis might have prescribed, as Yom Kippur Torah readings, the punishments meted out following the sin of the golden calf or the sin of the scouts. Were punishment the point, our liturgy would not have omitted the second part of the divine attributes revealed on the mountain—the part that promises punishment, not just mercy.

The Israelites' sins of building the golden calf and of losing faith in God are fictional, but also, oh so true. Many relationships suffer breaches that prove irreparable. Not forgiveness but destruction lies in their wake. In these iconic biblical stories, however, what stands out as remarkable is not the fact that the relationships were breached but that they were restored!

It is the promise of forgiveness that makes restoration possible. It is the promise of forgiveness that makes confession and repentance (*t'shuvah*) possible. Imagine you are a child who has hit a softball through a neighbor's window. What would more likely inspire you to confess your error and repair the damage: anticipating a beating or knowing that you will be forgiven? Confession and reparation, two of the crucial steps in the process of *t'shuvah*, depend upon an expectation of forgiveness. Appropriately, then, during *s'lichot*, the thirteen attributes are recited *before* the confessions. In fact, during the *S'lichot* service prior to Rosh Hashanah, the thirteen attributes are recited *four times* before the confessions, and again four times during the *s'lichot* of Yom Kippur evening.[5] And, when the long, long day of Yom Kippur is nearing its end (in the concluding service of *N'ilah*), the thirteen attributes are recited again—not just four times now, but no fewer than eight![6]

The season of repentance begins with a promise of forgiveness, and Yom Kippur concludes by immersing us in that promise. Imagine: all around us, in front of us, behind us, to our left and to our right, young and old, sweet-sounding and gravelly, in and out of tune, everyone reciting these words in his and her own voice.[7] In this closing service, imagine hearing, and singing, again and again:[8]

> Adonai, Adonai, merciful and gracious God, endlessly patient, most kind and truthful, extending kindness to thousands, forgiving sins and transgressions and misdeeds, and cleansing.

On the very day we are not permitted to bathe or to drink, these words become our *mayim chayim*, "living waters," the promise of forgiveness in which we bathe and are purified. This is the purification, the *taharah*, promised on Yom Kippur evening: *Ki vayom hazeh y'khaper aleikhem, l'taher etkhem mikol chatoteikhem. Lifnei Adonai tit'haru*, "For on this day shall atonement be made for you to purify you from all your sins. Before God, you shall be pure" (Leviticus 16:30).[9]

⚬⚬⚬

# Thirteen Attributes or Ten *Sefirot?*

## THE GOD OF MEDIEVAL MYSTICS

*Dr. Sharon Koren*

The quest to know God personally runs deep in Jewish mysticism—but it begins with the Bible and is nowhere more evident than in Moses's personal request following the sin of the golden calf. Emboldened, perhaps, by his success at assuaging God's anger, he adds, "If I have truly gained your favor, pray let me know your way so that I may know You.... Let me see your glory" (Exodus 33:13, 33:18). Moses desires to know God's way—God's method of interacting with the world; but also, God's glory—the visual representation of what God "really" is. Moses has had many interactions with God since his first revelation, at the burning bush, but only now does he seek to know God's very nature. God actually grants Moses's wish! True, no mortal can survive seeing the divine "face," God says, but God allows Moses to see the divine back, and then the divine character as well:

---

Sharon Koren, PhD, is associate professor of medieval Jewish culture and the Dr. Norman Cohen Chair for an Emerging Jewish Scholar at Hebrew Union College–Jewish Institute of Religion in New York City. She completed her doctorate in medieval studies at Yale University. She is a contributor to *My People's Prayer Book Volume 8: Kabbalat Shabbat (Welcoming Shabbat in the Synagogue)* and the author of *Forsaken: The Menstruant in Medieval Jewish Mysticism.* She is currently working on a book on the matriarchs in medieval Kabbalah.

> Adonai, Adonai, merciful and gracious God, endlessly patient, most kind and truthful, extending kindness to thousands, forgiving sins and transgressions and misdeeds, cleansing. (Exodus 34:6–7)

This revelation has been the entry point to understanding God ever since. In the golden calf account, it is God who reveals them. Later on, when the spies dispatched to scout out the Land lose faith in God's ability to produce victory, Moses hurls them back in God's face, nearly verbatim, to soften God's ire (Numbers 14:18); the same certainty of divine mercy becomes the summary conclusion to the prophecy of Micah (7:18–20) and a feature of the Psalms as well (86:15, 103:8). By the Rabbinic period, these qualities were deemed the "thirteen attributes of mercy" and became central to Rabbinic conceptions of prayer and forgiveness.[1] They were incorporated into our earliest known prayer book (*Seder Rav Amram*, c. 860 CE) and still serve as the foundation of the Yom Kippur liturgy.

Like Moses in the Bible, medieval mystics too sought knowledge of God and a glimpse of God's glory. They, however, did not have Moses's ease of divine access. A mystical circle in the twelfth- and early thirteenth-century Rhineland (the *Chasidei Ashkenaz*, or "German Pietists") used innovative forms of exegesis, like numerology and letter manipulation, to uncover the secrets of the divine encoded in Scripture. Thoroughly familiar with the primacy and importance of the thirteen attributes in prior Jewish thought and liturgy, they interpreted allusions to the number thirteen elsewhere as references to God's thirteen attributes—the thirteen letters that make up the Hebrew names of the three patriarchs and the four matriarchs, for example. Eleazar of Worms (c. 1176–1238), one of the most prolific German Pietists, connected the thirteen Hebrew words in Psalm 81:4–5 ("Blow the horn on the new moon, on the full moon for the feast day. For it is a law for Israel, a ruling of the God of Jacob") to "the thirteen attributes of mercy, for the Holy One blessed be He, is filled with mercy through the blowing of the shofar on account of the thirteen letters in the names of the patriarchs of the world."[2] He notes too that the first verse of Song of Songs, which he interpreted as a love poem between God and Israel, had thirteen syllables to call attention to God's thirteen attributes of mercy. Such aggressive interpretation may seem forced to us, but medieval exegetes believed that every detail of the biblical text was rife with esoteric meaning.

These German Pietists were just one school of medieval Jewish mysticism, however. Other mystics known as kabbalists preferred a system of speculation based on ten attributes known as *sefirot*. Given the primacy of the thirteen attributes in Jewish tradition, why would kabbalists—whose very name derives from the Hebrew term for "tradition"—choose a different approach?

These thirteenth-century kabbalists did in fact draw on tradition, but a different one—the Bible's fondness for the number ten (ten plagues and the Ten Commandments, for example). The Hebrew verb *vayomer*, "and God said," occurs nine times in the first creation account, but creative exegetes managed to bring the tally to ten, thereby beginning a tradition that God created the world through ten utterances (in Hebrew, *asarah ma'amarot*; Talmud, Rosh Hashanah 32a; *Pirkei Avot* 5:1). The Talmud further posits (Chagigah 12a) that God created the world not just by ten utterances, but also by ten qualities: wisdom, understanding, reason, strength, rebuke, might, righteousness, judgment, loving-kindness, and compassion.[3] One of the earliest works of Jewish cosmology, the *Sefer Y'tzirah* (*The Book of Formation*), says God created the world by means of the twenty-two letters in the Hebrew alphabet and ten *sefirot*.

The meaning of the term *sefirot* is unexplained there, but it likely derives from the Hebrew root *s.f.r*, whence we get the verbs "to speak," "to write," and "to count." *Sefer Y'tzirah* thus enlarges upon the power of language, making creation the result not just of speech alone (*ma'amarot*, the Rabbinic "utterances") but of all modes of communication.[4] It takes great pains to underscore the total of ten *sefirot*—"they are 10 and not 9; 10 and not 11"—along with the fact that these ten are the basis of creation.[5] The *sefirot* include the dimensions of beginning and end, good and evil, above and below, east, west, north, and south. "The unique Lord, a trustworthy divine king, rules over them from his holy abode forever and ever."[6] The wise are encouraged "to test" and "to investigate them" and, in so doing, "restore the creator to his place."[7]

Though *Sefer Y'tzirah* is almost impossible to date—it may be as early as the first or second century or as late as the tenth—by the end of the twelfth and beginning of the thirteenth centuries the text was central to the Jewish esoteric tradition and elicited commentaries from scholars as varied as Saadiah Gaon in tenth-century Baghdad and Isaac the Blind, one of the earliest kabbalists in thirteenth-century Provence.

Mystics in southern France were developing a theology to draw closer to God. Some of them—those known as the *Iyyun* circle—based their understanding on the thirteen attributes of God.[8] Ultimately, however, the dominant schools of Kabbalah chose the *sefirot*. Where the thirteen attributes focus on God as merciful judge, the sefirotic system—first articulated in the earliest kabbalistic treatise, called *Sefer Habahir* (c. 1180), and later independently crystallized in the works of Isaac the Blind (early thirteenth century)—ultimately provided more possibilities for understanding an infinite God.

These Provençal kabbalists were faced with the challenge of Maimonidean philosophy. In his *Guide for the Perplexed*, first translated into Hebrew in Provence in 1204, Maimonides argues that God is completely unknowable, unchangeable, and unmovable. One can make no positive assertions about God because any such act would limit God's infinite essence. Such an infinite power is completely beyond the realm of human cognition and completely removed from our lives. But if so, to whom should we pray? Why should we perform the commandments? Why should we even remain Jewish? These early kabbalists harmonized Maimonides with the needs of the devout by developing a unique form of Jewish philosophy that provides a God with two facets or sides: one that is completely hidden and another that is manifest in the world. They saw it as their task to uncover the manifest and, therefore, approachable aspects of God, the only ones we can hope to know. To do so, they drew upon Neoplatonism, the philosophy of the fourth-century scholar Plotinus, whose thought was philosophically respectable and hospitable to a religious worldview.

Simply put, Plotinus believed that there were three aspects to what we understand to be God: the unknowable side, reason, and the world soul. The unknowable side was the source of all being and reality. Both reason itself and the world soul flowed from this ineffable source. This triadic system influenced early Christian understandings of the trinity and, eventually, medieval Kabbalah as well. Paralleling the "unknowable side of God," they posited a divine aspect beyond the realm of human knowledge, known as the *Ein Sof* (literally "without end"); as their equivalent of the world soul, they imagined ten knowable emanations of God that inhere in the world and can be known by reason. By the middle of the thirteenth century, these attributes were outfitted with language from the system of *sefirot* and known as Crown (*Keter*), Wisdom (*Chokhmah*),

Understanding (*Binah*), Loving-kindness (*Chesed*), Fear/Judgment (*Pachad/Din*), Beauty (*Tiferet*), Victory (*Netzach*), Splendor (*Hod*), Foundation (*Y'sod*), and Presence/Kingship (*Shekhinah/Malkhut*).

But even while choosing the sefirotic system, medieval kabbalists did not completely abandon the thirteen attributes of mercy. Some sources embed the thirteen attributes within the *sefirot*—locating three of the thirteen attributes within the *Ein Sof* and/or *Keter*.[9] One section of the *Zohar* (*Idra Zuta*), the most popular work of medieval Kabbalah (1280–1305), imagines this merciful triad of *Ein Sof* and/or *Keter* as a patient long countenance, a "holy old man," and the "Ancient of Days" (*Arikh Anpin* or *Atika Kadisha*), who exists in contrast to an impatient and judgmental short-faced countenance (the *Ze'ir Anpin*, a name given to all the other seven *sefirot* combined).[10] Another section of the *Zohar* (*Idra Rabba*) imagines that God has twenty-two attributes of mercy—the thirteen mentioned in Exodus 34:6–7 and the nine listed in Numbers 14:18. These attributes are so integral to the sefirotic structure that they are symbolically described as curls on God's beard. Thirteen curls on the beard of the merciful long countenance, or Ancient of Days, and nine on the judgmental short countenance. Hence the *Zohar* teaches:

> When this forehead (the forehead of the Short Countenance) is revealed, all Masters of Judgment are aroused, and the whole world is delivered to Judgment—except when the prayers of Israel ascend before the Ancient of Days, and he wishes to have compassion on his children: He reveals the forehead of the Will of Wills and illumines that of the Short Countenance, and Judgment is soothed.[11]

Rather than ignore the thirteen attributes of mercy, then, many medieval kabbalists make God's mercy an essential and even "physical" aspect of the divine. Indeed, the *Arikh Anpin*, the patient long countenance, is an Aramaic translation of *erekh apayim*, usually translated as "slow to anger" ("endlessly patient" in this book's translation) but, literally, meaning "long countenance." The Zoharic authors of the *Idra Rabba* and *Idra Zuta* develop a belief whereby mercy inheres in God's most elemental aspects. They, too, would have hoped to stir the compassion of the creator on Yom Kippur. The other sefirotic attributes, such as wisdom, understanding, and righteousness, however, ultimately allow for other forms of contemplation and engagement with an infinite God.

These other ways of approaching God are quite another matter, of course, well beyond the topic of this book. Here, we need only note how medieval mystical masters chose ultimately to focus on the tradition of ten, rather than thirteen, but to do so in an expansive way that allowed for endless creativity. Even in so doing, however, the thirteen attributes were not lost and the ultimate concern for God's merciful ways remained primary.

ᏰᎳᏍ

# *Mercy or Grace?*

# "By the Grace of God"—A Biblical Idea?

*Dr. Marc Zvi Brettler*

Many of my Jewish friends shudder at the word "grace," which they feel is Christian. Indeed, in the entire Jewish Publication Society *Tanakh*—the official Jewish translation of the Bible for North America—a concordance search for the English word "grace" turns up only nineteen uses of the word, in only seventeen verses—and some of these do not even refer to God! Far from being a distinctive trait of the divine alone, "grace" is a more general English rendering of a variety of words, including the nouns *chen* (and the related root *ch.n.n.*), *chesed*, *tzedek*, and *emunah*. Both the paucity and the generality of usage might suggest that the God of the Hebrew Bible is indeed short on "grace."

Only at first glance, however! A closer look at biblical texts suggests that it is the translators, not the Bible, that make God graceless. The Jewish aversion to the word probably derives from the widespread impression that the "God of grace" is so central to Christianity that all

Dr. Marc Zvi Brettler is the Bernice and Morton Professor of Judaic Studies at Duke University. He contributed to all volumes of the *My People's Prayer Book: Traditional Prayers, Modern Commentaries* series, winner of the National Jewish Book Award; and to *My People's Passover Haggadah: Traditional Texts, Modern Commentaries*; *Who by Fire, Who by Water*—Un'taneh Tokef; *All These Vows*—Kol Nidre; *We Have Sinned: Sin and Confession in Judaism*—Ashamnu *and* Al Chet; and *Naming God: Our Father, Our King*—Avinu Malkeinu (all Jewish Lights). He is coeditor of *The Jewish Annotated New Testament* and *The Jewish Study Bible*, which won the National Jewish Book Award; coauthor of *The Bible and the Believer*; and author of *How to Read the Jewish Bible*, among other books and articles. He has also been interviewed on National Public Radio's *Fresh Air* by Terry Gross.

Jews, not just Jewish translators, must avoid it. This is a grave mistake! It simply runs contrary to the facts, and it fuels the mistaken image of the Old Testament God as a "God of wrath and justice," and the New Testament God as a "God of love and mercy."

To be sure, the Hebrew of the Bible does not support the full-blown Christian theological notion of "grace" as "the free and unmerited favor of God, as manifested in the salvation of sinners and the bestowal of blessing."[1] But it certainly knows of a God who dispenses "divinely given talent(s) or blessing(s)."[2] More to the point, the God of the Hebrew Bible does so even when these blessings are not fully deserved, making them, therefore, the result of "grace."

This Jewish conception of grace is embedded in the beginning of the thirteen attributes, where God is described as *chanun*, "showing favor, grace, mercy, or compassion." Almost twenty times, a psalmist implores Adonai in the imperative, *choneini*—"Be *chanun* to me," that is, "Show me favor!"—and in many of these cases the psalmist offers no reason why God should do so; if "grace" is the dispensation of God's loving favor even without warrant, the psalmist is, by definition, requesting "grace."

That Adonai is sometimes a God of grace is evident in the biblical "historical books" as well. Referring to Israel's subjugation by the Arameans, 2 Kings 13:23, says, for example, "[But] Adonai was gracious and merciful to them, and He turned back to them for the sake of his covenant with Abraham, Isaac, and Jacob." The people are forgiven even though they do not repent in this instance; God's grace and mercy are bestowed upon them simply because God recalls the ancestral covenant, not because the people themselves deserve it.

Such texts have influenced the High Holy Day liturgy as well—for example, *Ki Hinei Kachomer* ("For behold, like clay ..."), a poem examined in a previous volume of this series, which pleads, "Look at the covenant" (*labrit habet*), a call for God to invoke his attributes of grace and memory not because we deserve it but because of a covenant that promises God's love anyway (see Prayers of Awe, *Naming God: Our Father, Our King*—Avinu Malkeinu, 64).

Even more striking is Judges 2:11–19, which presents the settlement in Canaan as a cyclical set of events in which (a) Israel forsakes God; (b) God turns Israel over to its enemies; (c) Israel complains to God; (d) God raises up a judge who saves them; (e) a period of peace ensues—and then the cycle starts anew. Nowhere does this paradigm mention contritely praying to God for forgiveness. Some texts—such as Judges 4:3 (in the Deborah episode)—speak of Israel "cry[ing] out to Adonai," but in context this seems little more than "God help us," not a full-blown prayer for assistance, complete with contrition and repentance. In fact, Judges mentions repentance only in one section (10:10, 10:15), and many scholars believe (with good reason) that this is a later addition to the book! Thus, Judges presents the period of settlement as replete with divine grace—time and time again, Israel is forgiven and saved from its enemies, even though it is not deserving.

Grace did indeed become a central notion in Christianity, but only because it is one of many cases where early believers in Jesus took a theological idea in the Jewish Scriptures and made it much more central. This appropriation fit the developing belief system of early Christianity—but it does not imply that it was not already Jewish in its origin or that Judaism must therefore abandon it as no longer Jewish. The belief in a God of grace began in the Hebrew Bible, after all; it can be as authentically Jewish as it is Christian.

ᏮᏟᎷᎶ

# By the Grace
# (Yes, Grace!) of God

*Rabbi David Ellenson, PhD*

A s a boy, I always loved the recitation of the Thirteen Attributes in the liturgy of the synagogue—both on the High Holy Days and on the three Pilgrimage Festivals of Passover, Shavuot, and Sukkot. I loved the chant, and I loved the words. Our teacher drummed home the fact that the entire congregation must recite all the attributes aloud and in unison. He said that congregations where the *sh'liach tzibbur* (prayer leader) would first chant the attributes and only then have the *kahal* (congregation) repeat them were guilty of a *minhag ta'ut*, a serious infraction of Jewish law and custom.

Our teacher traced the need to say it all together to a famous Talmudic exposition of Exodus 33:18–22 and 34:6–7. The Israelites had

Rabbi David Ellenson, PhD, is currently director of the Schusterman Center for Israel Studies at Brandeis University as well as chancellor emeritus at Hebrew Union College–Jewish Institute of Religion (HUC-JIR). From 2001–2013, he served as president of HUC-JIR. Ellenson has been a fellow of the Shalom Hartman Institute of Jerusalem and a fellow and lecturer at the Institute for Advanced Studies as a well as a Lady Davis Visiting Professor of the Humanities in the Department of Jewish Thought at Hebrew University in Jerusalem. He has also served as a professor at the University of Southern California and as a visiting professor at both UCLA and The Jewish Theological Seminary of America. New York University recently appointed him as Distinguished Visiting Professor. His book, *After Emancipation: Jewish Religious Responses to Modernity*, won the National Jewish Book Council's award as outstanding book in Jewish Thought, and he contributed to all volumes of the *My People's Prayer Book: Traditional Prayers, Modern Commentaries* series, winner of the National Jewish Book Award. His newest book, *Jewish Meaning in a World of Choice*, was included in the Jewish Publication Society's Scholar of Distinction Series.

just sinned against God by creating a golden calf. After interceding with God on their behalf, Moses asks God, "Show me your glory" (*Hareini et k'vodekha*), and God wraps Himself in a *tallit*, just like a *sh'liach tzibbur*, and says, "I will make all my goodness pass before you" (33:18–19). Just a couple of verses later God promises to shelter Moses lovingly and protectively in the cleft of a rock (33:21–23), and sure enough, when Moses climbs the mountain and finds the crevice in question (34:5), God explains the meaning of "his goodness" by stating these attributes "Adonai, Adonai, merciful and gracious God, endlessly patient, most kind and truthful, extending kindness to thousands, forgiving sins and transgressions and misdeeds, cleansing [*v'nakeh*]" (34:6–7).

God then explains (Talmud, Rosh Hashanah 17b) that these words should forever be fixed as a part of Jewish prayer and promises that if the people utter these words together before God, they will be guaranteed God's mercy in return. In offering this prayer as one community in shul on each of the holidays, we follow the command of God, just as *Chazal* (our Rabbinic Sages) taught us, and as a result, our community and all of Israel will merit forgiveness for the sins we have committed.

I must confess that as a young boy I found this ritual practice and the teaching that explained it overwhelmingly comforting. I was a child, after all, who thought "sin" was, literally, rebellion against the will of God and subject to some unspecified, but surely severe, punishment. The anxiety this caused me was alleviated by the words of this prayer and by its soothing communal recitation. As I chanted them along with everyone else, I felt the comfort of being part of a community that was bound together in an age-old affirmation of God's essence as the very epitome of kindness and understanding. I understood that despite human weakness that leads to error and wrongdoing, we are loved by a God who will always absolve us (and me) of our (my) transgressions. The *chesed* of God (the "divine grace") was so immense that God would forgive us even if we (I) were (was) unworthy and even when we (I) could not always forgive ourselves (myself). How wonderful the thought of a God so benevolent!

Even as my understanding of sin is today less grave and less fundamentalist than it was when I was a child, guilt about my imperfections still haunts me, and for this reason the recitation of these attributes in our prayers continues to comfort me, as much as—if not more than—it did when I was a child.

I feel that way despite my advanced Jewish knowledge of the way the story got put together. I know, for example, that the prayer-book text of the Thirteen Attributes deliberately lops off two important words of Exodus 34:7. It concludes with *v'nakeh*—"cleansing" in the sense of "granting pardon"—even though the original biblical verse continues, *lo y'nakeh*, meaning just the reverse: that [God] will "*by no means* cleanse" (grant pardon to) the guilty. I know also that the Rabbis chose to exclude the last half of the very same verse, which modified any hope for God's compassion by saying that God will visit the sins of the parents upon their children and their children's children to the third and fourth generations. These deliberate Rabbinic misreadings of the biblical text simply reinforce and extend the feeling of comfort that the prayer once provided me as a boy; they only strengthen my intuition that God must be a being of infinite kindness.

The Thirteen Attributes constitutes a prayer of *rachamim* ("mercy"), an extension of God's love for us; all commentators agree on this. However, these same commentators often miss the particular quality of the love being promised. They translate or interpret the Thirteen Attributes of the prayer book as if God's love were contingent upon the prior human act of repentance. They thereby give us a "legalistic" approach whereby we become prisoners standing in the docket who must successfully plead "guilty but repentant" in order to be acquitted.

But that is not love—it is justice. And that is not at all what is being promised here. What the Thirteen Attributes of the liturgy actually guarantees is God's love as unlimited *grace*, the kind of love that is granted unconditionally, no strings attached.

The mistaken legalistic approach is illustrated, for example, by the *ArtScroll Machzor* commentary on this passage, which draws on the Talmud (Yoma 86a) to explain, "God wipes away the sins of those who repent sincerely, as if they had never existed.... *He cleanses* the sins of those who truly repent; but *He does not cleanse* the sins of those who do not repent." Virtually every modern liturgical rendition of the Thirteen Attributes follows suit, even the current Reform and Conservative liturgies, which translate *y'nakeh* as "granting pardon" (the assumption being that we must deserve it by exercising penitence first). The older Conservative *Silverman Machzor* says explicitly "acquitting the penitent," while the Orthodox *Birnbaum Machzor* has "clearing those who repent."

All these translations display (or presuppose) the notion that on Rosh Hashanah, the Day of Judgment (*yom hadin*), *we* stand before God in judgment, with absolution depending upon repentance. God is forgiving, but forgiveness requires contrition as a precondition. Divine forbearance is not unrestrained. The compassion of God is not unlimited.

I want instead to take very seriously the deliberate omission of *lo y'nakeh*, "God will not cleanse," from the official liturgical version of God's attributes. The framers of the liturgy clearly wanted to affirm that the love God has for us and the grace with which God embraces us actually are unbounded. The repetition, at the beginning, of God's name as *Adonai, Adonai* actually highlights this gracious nature of God's forgiveness, because Jewish tradition associates that particular name (*Adonai*) with *midat harachamim*, "the attribute of mercy." The name *elohim*, by contrast, is associated with *midat hadin*, "the attribute of strict judgment." Thus, from the fact that Genesis reads, "In the beginning, *elohim* created the world," *Chazal* (our Rabbinic Sages) determined that initially, God (as *elohim*) intended that persons be judged only in response to their deeds—legalistically, that is. Yet, as *Adonai*, God then realized that the world could not bear such a strict standard of justice. Rav Huna (in Talmud, Yoma 86a) therefore cited Psalm 145:17, "God is just [*tzadik*] in all God's ways, and magnanimous [*chasid*] in all God's deeds," to conclude that God ultimately reestablished the world in accord with *chesed*. As *Adonai*, God endowed us with grace—love that we receive even if not fully deserved—and asked that we emulate such compassion in our dealings with others.

My realization that our Rabbis codified the liturgical recitation of the Thirteen Attributes with *v'nakeh* (= God pardons) but not the next two words (*v'lo y'nakeh* = God actually doesn't) simply strengthens the feelings I had as a boy when I recited this prayer, but in a profoundly theological way. The Thirteen Attributes provides the astounding guarantee that God possesses infinite and uncontingent compassion and kindness. I find this comforting.

⟨ΠΠΠꝘ

# Mercy and Truth

# The Single, Solitary Self That Isn't

*Rabbi Jonathan Blake*

In the thirteen attributes, the paired qualities *chesed ve'emet* (literally, "kind and truthful"—in the translation of this book) are properly to be read as a hendiadys, a word pair that expresses a single concept.[1] Rather than expressing separate qualities, the two words combine to mean something like "covenant faithfulness," "true kindness," or "steadfast compassion."

And yet taken individually, *chesed* and *emet* convey dissimilar constructs, *chesed* occupying the intimate space of human feeling, and *emet* residing in the metaphysical space where the human mind can fathom vast spans of time.

I have long meditated on this paradox of a God who is both immanent and transcendent. As our siddur puts it, "You are as near to us as breathing, yet farther than the farthermost star."[2] The phrase *chesed ve'emet* encapsulates this paradox, of a God who is objectively "eternal," "unwavering," "true" (in the sense of a "*true* friend," i.e., loyal or lasting) but whose presence to us is detected in the intimate sense of "love," "kindness," and "compassion."

Both qualities become evident in meditating on the mystery and miracle of human existence within nature, in contemplating how the

Jonathan E. Blake is senior rabbi of Westchester Reform Temple in Scarsdale, New York, having served formerly as associate rabbi with Rabbi Rick Jacobs, current president of the Union for Reform Judaism. A graduate of Amherst College and ordainee of Hebrew Union College, Rabbi Blake is a regular commentator on Jewish text and Jewish life who has been a featured author for the URJ's *Ten Minutes of Torah*. He is also a contributor to *Text Messages: A Torah Commentary for Teens*, *GQ* Magazine, and the acclaimed documentary films *51 Birch Street* and *112 Weddings*.

blessings that we experience immanently as *chesed* point also to a God who is the unity of all time and space—that is to say, *emet*, truth writ large.

The great and sometimes tragic delusion of human life is how thoroughly we have convinced ourselves of our separateness. From the moment they cut the umbilical cord, we are trained to stand on our own: to survive, thrive, and provide; to become self-aware and self-sufficient.

But the notion of the "self" is much overrated, based, as it is, on illusion. Daniel Matt, a leading authority on Jewish mysticism, puts it this way: "Just because we have words for all the parts of a tree ... does not mean that a tree really has all those parts. All our names are, likewise, only arbitrarily superimposed on what is, in truth, one great seamless reality."[3]

Who are we to say where the branch ends and the bud begins; where the trunk ends and the roots begin; where the roots end and the soil begins? Who are we to say where you end and the universe begins?

At the cellular level, after all, you are little more than a respiring, perspiring, semipermeable bag of mostly water. If you doubt me, then just hold your breath for more than a few seconds and experience the most profound distress a person can feel: to be disconnected from the source of life.

At the atomic level, you are little more than a cloud of electrons buzzing around the nuclei of about seven billion billion billion atoms (a seven followed by twenty-seven zeroes), dancing in sacred chemistry with the atoms of the air you breathe, the matter you touch, the water you drink, the food you eat.

Some of the carbon atoms in the elaborate protein chains of that food began their journey when the nuclear furnaces of newborn stars alchemized that key element for life. These atoms have hurtled through time and space, eventually taking up residency in the seashells that would fossilize into limestone for hundreds of millions of years, break up in an earthquake into rubble and airborne bits, and through the miracle of photosynthesis, find their way back into organic life, into what would become your lunch.[4]

Everything is connected, as these High Holy Days are acutely aware. They are all about sensing God immanently as *chesed* but then realizing how our human experience of warmth, joy, love, tenderness, and connection points simultaneously to the seemingly opposite dimension of *emet*—that which is eternal, lasting, and true.

Picture the Day of Atonement at dawn. You open your eyes, and they flood with light. Your eyes have incrementally improved throughout your time on earth, that is, your billions of years all told—from photosensitive bacteria to the light-detecting blobs on the bellies of primordial flatworms, the primitive peepers of fish and lizards, the keener eyes that let birds navigate and mammals hunt and flee the hunter, to your marvelous, human eyes. Your brain constructs a model of the world, a two-dimensional rendering of a three-dimensional reality, using the light projected onto the back of your retina.[5]

You look in the bathroom mirror. You sometimes see other faces in your own. Your dad's nose. Your mom's eyes. Your brother's ears that, you realize now, are not the only ones in the family to stick out a bit too much. You remember coming to temple on Yom Kippur as a kid. You remember your father's hands, how they would enclose your own. You miss him.

You go downstairs and recognize your child's face. She came up from the city for the holiday, with her husband and their kids who will come here this afternoon for the family service.

Your brain has stored images of your daughter at every age, from the moment you first held her, wrapped in a striped blanket in the hospital, to the moment she stood on the bimah for her bat mitzvah, wearing your pop's striped *tallit.* You see that same *tallit,* now the *chuppah* at her wedding. Even though every cell in her body has replaced itself millions of times over since last you saw her, and even though that face has changed since first you held her—taken on the lines of time and love, strife and success—you know that face; you love that face; you see *your* face in that face.

Outside, you notice the tips of the maple leaves. It's the glucose trapped inside, slowly turning red when daylight diminishes and photosynthesis stops. Soon the leaves will stop breathing altogether and fall. But today, they look resplendent.

You find your seat, next to a family you know. You used to see them all the time when your kids were in school together. Now it takes a Yom Kippur to bring you together, and this year, you notice, they are one fewer. You do the only thing you know how to do in that moment. You put your arms around them. In the instant of that embrace, your love commingling with their sorrow, all the years and all the space and all the divergent paths that carried you each from the other disappear, and you are one.

The music gets to you. You know it's just quivers in the air, the vibrations of human voices, air passing from the lungs over the larynx, fingers striking keys and electronic signals amplifying themselves in patterns that register in your brain as harmony and melody; but, for a few precious moments, there are no measure lines, no notes, only music.

For a little while your eyes stray off the page and you daydream. How can it be that since last you sat here, the earth, the whole planet—every place you've ever visited, every grain of sand you've ever pressed underfoot, and every pillow on which you've placed your head—has taken a journey of 584 million miles around the sun at around 66,000 miles per hour? This sun circles the center of the Milky Way at about 515,000 miles per hour, completing its journey once every 230 million years. And all the while the Milky Way races away from every other galaxy, toward the outer reaches of the universe.

And then you realize: there is no such thing as a self, a self totally self-contained, a self totally separate from its environment.

You are not just *you*. You are blood cells flowing through a river inside you, sixty thousand miles long. You are skin cells shedding themselves into dust in the air. You are the sunlight you absorb into all your tissues. You are the teachings of your mother and father, their parents and grandparents. You are the wisdom of your schoolteachers, the caring of your friends, every song lyric you've ever committed to memory, the prayers of your congregation, a single silken thread in an unknowably vast web of creation. You are the unknowable alterations you've made to the world with words and deeds.

You, yourself, are more than a self. You are the universe unto yourself, a singular expression of the infinite God, the paradox of *chesed ve'emet* reconciled in your very being.

⊙⟊⟊⟊⊙

# The Son of Truth Meets the God of Compassion

*Rabbi Shoshana Boyd Gelfand*

The majesty of a sunset, the sublimeness of a Beethoven symphony, the wonder of a child's birth—certain experiences defy the reach of language to express them. And if this is true with the world at large, how much more must we struggle when it comes to describing God, who is truly beyond human experience. Language simply cannot capture the divine. So whenever we speak of God, we are reduced to inadequate metaphors, whether nouns ("our rock," "our redeemer," "our king") or adjectives ("holy," "awesome," "great"), in a vain attempt to articulate God's essence. Interestingly enough, even God doesn't seem capable of creating a robust self-description. When asked directly, the best the divine being can do is share self-referential truisms ("I am that I am"—Exodus 3:14) or references to historical events ("who brought you out of the Ur Chaldees"—Genesis 15:7).

This gap between human language and the divine essence seems impossible to overcome. Paradoxically, even Moses, the prophet who, on

---

Rabbi Shoshana Boyd Gelfand received her rabbinic ordination in 1993 at The Jewish Theological Seminary in New York. She has served as chief executive of the United Kingdom Movement for Reform Judaism and prior to that was vice president of the Wexner Heritage Foundation in New York. Currently she is director of JHub, an operating program of the London-based Pears Foundation. She contributed to *All These Vows*—Kol Nidre; *We Have Sinned: Sin and Confession in Judaism*—Ashamnu *and* Al Chet; *May God Remember: Memory and Memorializing in Judaism*—Yizkor; *All the World: Universalism, Particularism and the High Holy Days*; and *Naming God: Our Father, Our King*—Avinu Malkeinu (all Jewish Lights).

the one hand, saw God "face to face" (Exodus 33:11), can only, on the other hand, see God's "back" pass before him, while hearing a list of the thirteen attributes: "Adonai, Adonai, merciful and gracious God, endlessly patient, most kind and truthful, extending kindness to thousands, forgiving sins and transgressions and misdeeds, but by no means cleansing. He visits the iniquity of parents upon children and children's children, upon the third and fourth generation" (Exodus 34:6–7).

These self-proclaimed attributes combined with his own direct experience of God placate Moses, but not all biblical characters are as easy to satisfy. One can read the book of Jonah as a critique of Moses's naïve failure to demand more. Jonah—whose full name is Jonah ben Amittai, Jonah "Son of Truth"—will accept nothing short of the truth, the whole truth, and nothing but the truth. Jonah, Son of Truth, challenges God to be a God of truth, the kind of truth that Sir Isaac Newton imagined for a universe that is mechanistically predictable—established by God, but then spun off on its own with no hope of further divine intervention.

The entire story of Jonah questions this Newtonian view of the world, because in the four short chapters that comprise it, just about everyone and everything undergoes unpredictable change. The sailors, the fish, the people (and cattle!) of Nineveh, and even God—all of them "repent" of their initial action and alter their behavior in some profound way: the sailors shift from pagans to "God-fearers," the fish coughs up Jonah onto dry land, the Ninevites perform the complete and utter "turnaround" of repentance (t'shuvah), and even God changes, allowing divine compassion to overcome divine justice.

But what about Jonah himself? Is Jonah capable of similar change? Can a character whose very name is Truth embrace the unpredictability of change that is the essence of t'shuvah? Can Jonah (the stand-in for us all) repent of his own behavior?

The first three chapters don't bode well for our reluctant hero. In defiance of God's order to go and tell the Ninevites to repent, Jonah boards a boat headed in the exact opposite direction. Whereas God's order was to "arise and go" (Jonah 1:2), Jonah "goes down" and "flees" in the opposite direction from Ninevah (v. 3). And just in case we, the readers, have missed the point, the Hebrew verb "to go down" (yarad, vayered) is repeated three times (vv. 3, 5) and then followed by the similar-sounding verb vayeradam, "he fell asleep." Not only has Jonah descended physically as far from his mission as possible; he has also descended from consciousness, "falling asleep at the switch" rather than facing his mission. It's as far away from God's charge to "arise and go" as one could possibly get. Jonah has not only disobeyed the command and rejected his mission, but also he has done so with gusto.

God will not allow his prophet to escape, however. Jonah is thrown overboard by pious sailors and unceremoniously regurgitated onshore in a pile of fish vomit. Left with no choice but to obey, he carries out his assigned task reluctantly and with minimal effort, in the hope that the Ninevites will ignore him. To his surprise, they repent wholeheartedly and change their ways immediately. While most prophets would be delighted at such unmitigated success, Jonah despairs. In the final chapter of the book, we hear why.

Jonah frames his objection by quoting God's own words, the very thirteen attributes that Moses heard. "I knew," Jonah says, "that You are gracious and merciful, endlessly patient, and most kind [*chanun v'rachum erekh apayim v'rav chesed*] so that You would repent of the evil" (Jonah 4:2). This phrase is indeed part of the thirteen attributes revealed to Moses, but with a difference! In the Exodus version, God is "merciful and gracious, endlessly patient, most kind *and truthful*" (*rachum v'chanun erekh apayim v'rav chesed ve'emet*). As Jonah "Son of Truth" recalls it, however, God is merely "merciful and gracious, endlessly patient, and most kind" (*chanun v'rachum erekh apayim v'rav chesed*). Jonah's omission of the word "truthful" virtually screams out at us. It explains why he is so offended by the idea of divine pardon; Jonah's commitment was not to compassion but to the predictability of truth, a quality that he believes God lacks.

It is as if Jonah were saying, "Yes, God, I grant that You are gracious, compassionate, long-suffering, and merciful. All of those attributes are clearly evident in your constant wishy-washy changing of your divine mind. And because of those liberal forgiving qualities, I knew You would change your mind yet again and not hold the Ninevites accountable for their actions. I may not be able to argue with You about that, or You'll send me to time-out in the belly of a fish again. But what I can do is refuse to grant You the attribute of truth, which You claim describes You. For if You were indeed the God of truth, then You would hold people accountable for their actions and there would be consequences to sin. But You don't hold us accountable and therefore the world is unpredictable, and I would rather die than live in that kind of a world where I'm sent to make a prophecy against evil and then You refuse to follow through with the very punishment You've asked me to declare."

Jonah doesn't actually give that speech, but he might as well have. It explains why he is angry enough to want to die. Jonah is the realist among us, the pure scientist for whom the world must have unmitigated causality and utter predictability. If you sin, you are punished. That's just the "truth" of the matter. He cannot abide the idea that God can capriciously "repent" (Jonah 3:10) from actions that the normal working of the world should have determined.

We can appreciate Jonah's desire for predictability. The Hebrew verb for God's "repenting" of the decision to destroy Nineveh is *n.ch.m.* (Jonah 3:10), the same verb found earlier in the Bible when God "repented of" creating the world and sent the Flood to destroy all living things (Genesis 6:6). In both cases, God's "repentance" is triggered by human violence. In Noah's time, God repents childishly, lashing out to destroy the quintessential divine act—creation. By the time of Jonah, God has realized that the covenant requires that justice be tempered with mercy. So this time, God's reaction to human violence is expressed in a more mature manner. Rather than destroy the Ninevites, God shows compassion. God allows an opportunity for the Ninevites to repent so that God can restore life rather than punish it with death. In that sense, it is a more mature rewriting of the Flood story.[1] Jonah, however, is stuck in the draconian paradigm of the Flood story. He has not yet learned to appreciate the power of compassion. At the end of the story, God will have to instruct him that unyielding truth must be tempered with divine compassion if humanity is to survive.

Perhaps the most telling verse in the entire book of Jonah is Jonah's rhetorical question "Who knows whether God will turn and repent, and turn away from fierce anger that we not perish?" (3:9). Indeed, who knows? We don't know. Jonah doesn't know. Perhaps even God doesn't know! From Jonah's perspective, God is not so much compassionate as just downright capricious, and therein lies the rub: God's world is neither knowable nor predicable because, unlike truth, compassion cannot be quantified in scientific notation.

Are we like Jonah, so attached to a notion of truth as complete and utter predictability that we want God to maintain strict justice at the expense of allowing humankind to drown in the consequences of our actions? Or are we like the sailors, prepared to sacrifice our sense of certainty to allow for the possibility of some divine intervention beyond truth to keep us afloat in this unpredictable world?

In the course of Elul and the High Holy Days, we recite the thirteen attributes repeatedly—as part of the daily *s'lichot* (prayers for forgiveness) and when we remove the Torah from the ark on Rosh Hashanah and Yom Kippur. Slowly but surely, as if reenacting the experience of Moses himself, we internalize these attributes as the closest we will come to knowing God. But then on Yom Kippur afternoon, just hours away from the closing of the gates of repentance, our prophetic friend Jonah forces this most fundamental question upon us: As we ask for mercy from God, are we prepared to accept the consequences? Will we insist on remaining Jonah, Son of Truth, where our future follows with mechanical predictability from our actions of yesterday? Or will we choose a world with "God, full of compassion" (*el malei rachamim*), where we cannot know for sure what tomorrow will bring?

It is clear what God wants. That's why God spends the entire last chapter trying to convince Jonah to temper truth with compassion. But the book of Jonah ends with a question mark, as does the *Minchah* (evening) service in which we read it. What will we choose—truth and its consequences, or compassion and its unpredictability? Will we allow God to be described by all thirteen attributes, or will we limit God to just twelve?

⚬═══⚬

# Truth

## CAST DOWN AND RESURRECTED

*Rabbi Elie Kaunfer, DHL*

People are ambivalent about truth. On the one hand, it is the basis of any real relationship; on the other hand, we "can't handle the truth." Of all the attributes ascribed to God, perhaps the most difficult is *emet*—truth. How do we relate to truth on the High Holy Days? What might we learn from its presence—and absence—in our liturgy?

Truth has long been viewed as the enemy of human existence. Indeed, according to a midrash, were it up to truth, people would never have been created:

> When the Holy One was about to create Adam, the ministering angels split into factions, some of them saying: "Create him," and others urging: "Don't create him." ... Love said: "Create him: he will perform acts of love." Truth said: "Don't create him: all of him will be falsehood." ... What did the Holy One do? He cast truth to the ground, as it says: "You cast truth to the ground" (Daniel 8:12).[1]

---

Rabbi Elie Kaunfer, DHL, is cofounder and executive director of Mechon Hadar (www.mechonhadar.org). He holds a doctorate in liturgy and is the author of *Empowered Judaism: What Independent Minyanim Can Teach Us about Building Vibrant Jewish Communities.* He is a contributor to *Who by Fire, Who by Water*—Un'taneh Tokef; *All These Vows*—Kol Nidre; *We Have Sinned: Sin and Confession in Judaism*—Ashamnu *and* Al Chet; *All the World: Universalism, Particularism and the High Holy Days*; and *Naming God: Our Father, Our King*—Avinu Malkeinu (all Jewish Lights). *Newsweek* named him one of fifty top rabbis in America.

In this conception, people can't live with truth. But "truth is God's seal" (Talmud, Shabbat 55a), and in the thirteen attributes of Exodus 34, Moses describes God as "merciful and gracious God, endlessly patient, most kind [*chesed*] and *truthful* [*emet*]." How can God, whose very seal is truth, sustain a relationship with humans, who can't coexist with truth?

But a funny thing happened to God's attributes over time: the aspect of truth disappeared—thrown to the ground, so to speak, as the midrash had predicted. In the eight other appearances of the list of attributes in the Bible,[2] only one (Psalm 86:15) retains *emet*. Moses himself doesn't mention it when defending the people in the sin of the spies (Numbers 14:18). Perhaps most daringly, the review of the sin of the golden calf, recorded in Nehemiah 9:17, simply removes it, even though the original account (in Exodus 34, the one we have here) has it.[3] Perhaps we prefer a God who is not known for truth. After all, if God were truthful about our sinful behavior, who could survive? (See Psalm 130:3, "If you keep account of sin, Adonai, who will survive?")

Yet, truth never fully disappears. Even in the midrash that describes truth as flung to the earth in order for people to be created, truth is resurrected:

> The ministering angels dared say to the Holy One: "Master of the universe, why do You humiliate your seal?[4] Let truth arise from the earth." Hence it is written: "Let truth spring up from the earth" (Psalm 85:12).[5]

I want to examine three places where truth springs up in our High Holy Day liturgy, as a way of understanding better how we might relate to this most difficult attribute.

## Jonah and Truth—A Cautionary Tale

Jonah 4:2 repeats the divine attributes but, strikingly, removes truth from the list: "You are a God, gracious and merciful, endlessly patient, most kind, repenting of evil."[6]

As noted by Devora Steinmetz, Jonah stands in contrast to Moses here. Moses recites the attributes lovingly to protect the people; Jonah does so deploringly because they will prevent his prophecy of Nineveh's destruction from coming true.[7] Jonah wants a God of truth, not a God of kindness. The Ninevites' *t'shuvah* (their "repentance"), he knows, is doomed in the harsh light of truth's reality.

Appropriate to the story, truth appears earlier in it, in Jonah's very name: Jonah ben Amittai, "Jonah, Son of Truth" (Jonah 1:1).[8] God may epitomize mercy, but Jonah embodies truth, and ultimately God's mercy defeats Jonah's truth: the Ninevites are not destroyed; they repent and are saved (3:4–10). Other than Jonah's name in the very first verse of the book, truth disappears from the story altogether. Love conquers truth, which stands for destruction and must be defeated.[9]

## Truth as Precursor to Confession

Although the thirteen attributes are a centerpiece of the Yom Kippur *s'lichot* (the poetry seeking pardon), they appear also that day as an introduction to the *Vidui* (the confession): "We are brazen, but You are *merciful* and *gracious*; we are stubborn but You are *endlessly patient*."

Here, too, truth is nowhere to be found, but as with Jonah, it reemerges—in this case, as the introduction to the confession: *Aval anachnu chatanu*, usually translated "But we have sinned." The Hebrew word *aval* appears only twice in the Torah, however, and both times the *Targum* (the Aramaic translation of late antiquity) translates it not as "but/however," but as *b'kushta*, "in truth."[10] *Aval anachnu chatanu* really means "In truth, we have sinned."

Truth is the necessary precursor to confession, for we can hardly admit our sins if we ignore the sobering truths of who we are and what we have done. In Jonah, truth was the enemy of human existence; here it is our starting point to an honest evaluation of ourselves and our actions. Truth is the first step to taking stock of our life, which, in turn, is the first step to living a different life.

## Calling on God in Truth

Another reformulated list of attributes appears in Psalm 145:8, known liturgically as *Ashrei*: "Gracious and merciful is Adonai; endlessly patient and very kind."

Again, truth is missing, as it is in Psalm 103:8, as well: "Adonai is merciful and gracious, endlessly patient, most kind." Psalm 145 begins, "I will extol You, my God and king," and Psalm 103 starts out with

"Praise Adonai, O my soul." Who wouldn't want to extol or praise a God who is all love unmitigated by truth?

But truth reemerges in Psalm 145:18: "Adonai is close to all who call on Him; to all who call on Him in truth."

It is as if truth has been "cast to the ground" in Psalm 145:8, only to "spring up" in verse 18 as the mode for best calling out to God. In fact, these two verses are linked through a literary clue, noted by medieval authorities.[11] While every other stanza of the psalm is broken into two sections with the conjunction "and" (the Hebrew letter *vav*), these two verses are not.[12] The literary parallelism seems intentional: truth has migrated from verse 8 to verse 18.

What is the significance of calling on God in truth? The phrase is actually quite rare—elsewhere in the Bible, people speak (*daber*) "in truth," but they never call (*karah*) on God "in truth." The psalm implies, however, that truth is a preferred human stance toward God: prayer follows from being *honest* about oneself, *true* to one's emotions, *real* in one's self-representation. This stance of truth is critical: God listens to those who speak in this language of truth.[13]

A final transformation that happens to truth is imagined by one of the poets of the High Holy Day liturgy. Although Psalm 145:18 is quoted faithfully in one of the famous poems, *Le'el Orekh Din* ("To God, who prepares the legal case"), where we read, "God is close to those who call on him in truth,"[14] another *piyyut* for Rosh Hashanah, *Melekh Elyon* ("King on high"), subtly changes the message to "God is close to those who call on him in *love*."[15]

Could "truth" be synonymous with "love"? By accessing truth might we also access a deeper capacity to love? Perhaps truth, as cast down to the earth, is actually the tool that can help us return—to ourselves, to our God, and to our loved ones. We cannot bear a world where God acts entirely in truth, yet we also cannot bear a world with no truth at all—no honesty about ourselves and what we feel, do, and are. A world where the truth of our deepest selves is revealed might become the world of love, for which we so deeply hope and pray.

ommo

# A Cosmos with "Give"—and Moments of Truth

*Rabbi Nicole Roberts*

"What's our 'Come to Jesus' moment?" I once asked a rabbinic mentor, while we stood waiting for a wedding to begin. "Do we have anything like that in our tradition?"

Thankfully, he always met even my most startling, heretical questions with curiosity and thoughtful consideration. "Perhaps at Yom Kippur," he eventually replied. "At *N'ilah*, maybe. I think the moment is *Avinu Malkeinu*. Standing before the open ark. For me, it's *Avinu Malkeinu*."

His "Perhaps at Yom Kippur" caught me off guard. I had thought that my question might prompt a brainstorming of instances when our biblical or Rabbinic ancestors suddenly changed their life course, found faith, or turned to God in rock-bottom helplessness and were met with mercy. That is to say, I had expected a mining of our narrative tradition. I was not thinking liturgically or prayerfully. I was not thinking about when *we* experience such moments in our *own* lives.

His "For me, it's ..." raised the stakes even further, making the conversation personal. He experiences that sort of moment during the chanting of *Avinu Malkeinu*. When do *I*?

---

Rabbi Nicole Roberts was ordained by the Hebrew Union College–Jewish Institute of Religion, Cincinnati, in 2012 and now serves the North Shore Temple Emanuel (Progressive) in Chatswood, New South Wales, a suburb of Sydney, Australia. In addition to her congregational responsibilities, she serves as treasurer of the Moetzah, the Council of Progressive Rabbis of Australia, New Zealand, and Asia. She lives with her husband, David, on Sydney's North Shore.

Before I answer, let me explain what I meant by the original question. Based on how I hear the term used in popular culture, I understand a "Come to Jesus moment" to be a "moment of truth" of great magnitude and transformative potential—the sort of moment that immediately follows an experience that has left us sobered and breathless, face-to-face with a reality no longer dressed up in the adjectives, rationalizations, and denials that typically cushion and enable our race through life. I understand it as that moment a person encounters only rarely, after witnessing the miracle of life—a birth, perhaps—or awakening to the reality of human frailty and mortality, including one's own tenuous hold on life. This is a moment when we recognize, more than we are willing to admit on all the other, ordinary days of our lives, that we depend on either good fortune or divine *leniency*—some sort of *give* in the universe—in order to endure in this world and take part in its blessings. The atheist, in that moment, praises good luck. Our Christian brothers and sisters "come to Jesus." What do Jews do?

We make *t'shuvah*. We turn, we transform, we reevaluate how we live. We stand in awe and humble acknowledgment that the universe has been *forgiving* with us, and for reasons that we do not fully understand. This may sound backwards; the way we usually think of it, we are to make *t'shuvah first* and only *then* experience forgiveness. But, for me, it is the experience of that ration of fore-give-ness—of a cosmos that has *give* in it—that leads to *t'shuvah*, the moment of truth when we begin to transform, reassess our priorities, and change how we live.

That moment of truth confronts me liturgically not when I call upon *avinu malkeinu* to hear my pleas and grant pardon, but when I stand in awe of the leniency that has been granted *without* my having to plead. When the congregation recalls the moment of God's self-revelation to Moses as *Adonai, Adonai, el rachum v'chanun, erekh apayim v'rav chesed ve'emet*, a "merciful and gracious God, endlessly patient, most kind *and truthful*," I am moved to recall those moments of truth in my life. These are the words that remind me each year what is really real and what truly matters.

The poetry and majesty of the High Holy Day liturgy give lofty stature to such moments and embed them indelibly in our spiritual consciousness. But the moments themselves occur elsewhere, often in the trenches of daily life, when we are less primed for them. My husband and I experienced one such moment, which I often describe as "a moment of pure truth," on the road to synagogue one Erev Shabbat. Earlier that day, a major storm had torn through our hometown of Nashville, Tennessee. It was dark outside, but up ahead we saw three teenagers on bicycles. I swerved into the empty left lane to give them what I thought was plenty of space, but upon swerving back, we felt a dreadful, sickening, clunking "thud" on the passenger side of the car.

"What was it?" I panicked, seeing nothing but darkness in the rear-view mirror. My heart was racing. I pulled over instantly. "What did I hit?" It was so dark that I couldn't tell, but my mind imagined the worst: *Was it a person?* Had I not cleared *all* the cyclists in swerving to avoid them?

Paralyzing horror and dread quickly turned to disbelief upon hearing my husband's breathless reply. "It was a cow. A huge black cow." The cow's dark color had obscured it in the night; my husband saw it only as I'd hit it. "You just grazed his head—he walked away. But another instant and we all ..." We stepped out of the car. The passenger side mirror was shattered. Miraculously, the only other damage was a small dent in the back door. Inexplicable. The timing was ... chilling. We were dumbfounded.

Why are "pure truth" the only words I can find to describe what we felt, staring at the splintered mirror? Perhaps because we had come face-to-face with the now undeniable, unadorned, unglamorous truth of just how quickly our fortunes can turn—how life can be transformed in a heartbeat, literally. There was no cloaking that truth in the usual disguises that enable us to power onward, overlooking life's fragility: the rationalizations ("I'm a safe driver"), misguided priorities ("We've got to get there on time"), and distractions ("Turn on the radio; let's get our mind off this"). Life as we knew it could have come to a swift end; that bald reality was plainly visible in the dangling wires where once there was a mirror.

"Let's not fix it," I insisted.

"But it's not safe to drive without a mirror," my husband reasoned.

"Okay ... we'll fix it. But not right away." It seemed important to live for at least a little while in that mirrorless space—face-to-face with the *unfiltered* reality of human perishability—and important, too, to honor and marvel at the give in the universe. We could have taken a life. We could have lost ours. Yet there we stood. How could we just move on? Shouldn't something *change* about how we live? Patching up the mirror would somehow put us at one remove from the realities—and priorities—that, for the moment, seemed so very clear.

He was right, though; "it's not safe." Human beings do not have the luxury of dwelling indefinitely in the flood of emotions that fill our moments of truth: the gratitude, relief, horror, fear, love, awe, humility, shock, and disbelief. God tells Moses, "You cannot see my face and live" (Exodus 33:20)—we cannot experience so much of life's raw Mystery passing before us and still *live* our lives at the same time. God's hand, writes Abraham ibn Ezra (on Exodus 33:22), "served as a shield, the way the [divine] hand covers the sun [as with a cloud], so that one's soul does not separate from the body [causing death]." Moments of truth are too powerful for us to face for any longer than an instant. Ultimately they become moments of *turning*.

A moment of truth changes us. It transforms the assumptions, priorities, and principles by which we live. It creates a distinct "before-and-after" that remains with us for the rest of our days. But we need not dwell in the moment itself. We can replace the broken car mirror without seeing our act as a slap in the divine face. God knows we cannot drive without the mirror, and our world requires us to drive.

Occasionally we do recall the tangle of wires, the shattered glass, the dreadful, sickening thud that shook us. Each year, in fact, Yom Kippur demands this of us: an acknowledgment that life can be taken from us at any time and for any reason, or for none at all. When we stand and chant *Adonai, Adonai ... rav chesed ve'emet*, we recall this sobering truth. Yet in that same moment, we acknowledge the give in the universe—the uncanny fact that we subsist by ways and means beyond our understanding. This moment in our liturgy invites us to relive our moments of truth, yet only for an instant, for if they do not inspire us to turn and live differently, *that* would be a slap in the divine face.

The atheist bows to good luck.

The Christian comes to Jesus.

We make *t'shuvah*, propelled in each moment of truth by the foregiving, revealing, shielding, transforming touch of the divine.

☙❧

# PART III
# The Sacred Triangle
## God, Self, and Community

# Overview

# "God ... God!"
## BEFORE, AFTER, AND FOREVER

*Rabbi Asher Lopatin*

The scene is familiar: A packed shivah house (house of mourning), where the mourner is leading the *Shacharit* (morning) service. Sadly, this is a particularly tragic shivah: parents have lost their thirty-one-year-old son in a horrific car crash—and he had just gotten engaged. The father leads the usual prayers, with an added element, however, because the death occurred right before Rosh Hashanah: *s'lichot* (prayers for forgiveness) and their accompanying thirteen attributes of God's mercy, beginning with the haunting words "God ... God!" (*Adonai ... Adonai*). Over and over they are said, out loud, in unison, and by everyone: mourners, comforters, friends and family of those who are no longer with us.

To everyone gathered in the room that morning, the irony of the situation was poignant. Here was a father who just lost his young son through tragedy—an act of God, as it were—facing east, where the Temple once stood, and proclaiming God's mercy. The same God who blessed the family with children just took one of them away.

This irony reflects so much of Jewish history as well: countless blessings, but tragedies, too. Through it all, the good and the bad, Jews

---

Rabbi Asher Lopatin is the president of Yeshivat Chovevei Torah Rabbinical School, an Orthodox rabbinical school that teaches an inclusive, open, and inquisitive Torah. He is the former rabbi of Anshe Sholom B'nai Israel Congregation, a modern Orthodox synagogue in Chicago, and is a founding rabbi of the multidenominational Chicago Jewish Day School. He contributed to *Who by Fire, Who by Water—Un'taneh Tokef; All the World: Universalism, Particularism and the High Holy Days*; and *Naming God: Our Father, Our King—Avinu Malkeinu* (all Jewish Lights).

show continuing loyalty to God; and despite it all, God shows continuing loyalty to us. Our Rabbis allude to this unfailing bond through life's ups and downs in their explication of these very same thirteen attributes.

The Talmud (Rosh Hashanah 17b) explains: "'God ... God': [That means] I [God] am the one who is with you before you sin; and the one who is with you after you sin and as you repent." The great sixteenth- and seventeenth-century Talmudic commentator the Maharsha (Samuel Edels) explains this phrase thus: We need God's mercy before sinning, for the world was created only with God's mercy as a partner, and we need God's mercy after sinning, to make repentance possible. The Maharsha sees us constantly enveloped in God's mercy: both before and after we do anything wrong—even the most horrific wrongs we might imagine doing. God and God's mercy are a constant; they are simply "there," as a reality of the world we inhabit.

The idea of God being there to support us in good times and in bad is the core that gives strength to every fallible human being. We need God's help in making decisions, in navigating among competing values, and in deciphering the motivations that move us in directions both good and bad. It is the certainty of God's love that allows us to risk making these decisions in the first place; we need to know that God will still be there even if our decision turns out to have been a terrible mistake with harmful consequences. I once had a friend who committed a crime; it occurred to me that he was indeed heading to jail but that God would visit him there! So too with us all: we need to live with the consequences of our disastrous mistakes, but God can be counted on to help us work through our misguided decisions, to learn repentance, and to regain the high ground again. This is God's assurance as we negotiate this difficult world: God's mercy is always with us.

Our Rabbis, however, were not discussing God alone. Through the verse "And you shall go in God's ways" (Deuteronomy 28:9), they derived the need for us to act toward God as God acts toward us. The message of "God ... God" achieves its strongest valence precisely when we realize that we must be like God—we must be "there" for God as God is "there" for us, in mercy and love both before and after.

It is easy to love God when the world works in a loving and awesome way—as so often it does! When we are blessed with success and fulfillment, with love and health and happiness, then the world fairly oozes mercy and joy. But then we hit those moments, where, as it were, the world that God created sins against us—as Jews, as part of humanity, or as individuals—like the parents in the shivah house I describe. It is harder then to say, "God ... God"—"God, we loved You in the good times, and God, we won't abandon You when tragedy befalls us. We know that in these moments of pain, You are still with us; so, too, we will continue to be with You."

So in some ways, the most appropriate place to affirm the thirteen attributes of *s'lichot* is precisely in a shivah home. The mourner, whether leading services, saying *Kaddish*, or just standing, is affirming through the thirteen attributes the commitment not to reject God, despite the pain of the moment.

Moreover, just as we have the metaphor of God visiting us in jail, so we have the metaphor that sometimes we must visit God—that is, in tragic times, we must imagine God to be in an uncomfortable place requiring our steadfast loyalty. Jewish tradition (Talmud, Chulin 60b) pictures God, at the time of creation, forcing the moon to shrink in size relative to the sun. On every new moon, God is said to ask us to offer a sin offering for God (!), so that God may atone for treating the moon so disrespectfully. Especially is that so on the new moon of Rosh Hashanah! As we head toward Rosh Hashanah, the anniversary of creation, with all its inbuilt flaws and tragedies, God needs us to say, "God ... God"—"You are here for us, and we are there for You."

Our faithfulness to God is to be matched by equal faithfulness to fellow human beings. When friends and colleagues are respectful and supportive, when even our enemies are not being difficult, those are easy times to look kindly and lovingly upon them. When people do terrible things to us, however, that is when the challenge of "God ... God" really hits home.

Is it really possible to carry out this commandment to be "there" for people even when they do horrific things? Yes, I believe it is. We are not told that we have to forgive them or absolve them of their crimes, but they must know that even in our anger, we will not utterly abandon them. The Maharsha's vision insists that God's love even for sinners is what makes *t'shuvah* (repentance) possible. I return to the metaphor of visiting sinners in jail: someone has to connect with them; someone has to be there to love them. As our Rabbis see it, the thirteen attributes are God's guarantee to be there for them. We have to follow God and let everyone know, righteous and not-so-righteous, that we will not abandon them in their moment of failing.

Faithful love even in moments of darkness is not easy. Even God needs to be reminded of it, as it were—which is why we recite, pray, shout the thirteen attributes. All the more so do we need to remind ourselves that the attributes apply to us as well. In the house of a tragic shivah, we see how strong human beings can be, how they really can stick with God in a superhuman way. It is irrational and a mystery, but such shivah houses are a manifestation of the merciful world that God created: God is merciful to stay with us, as we are merciful to stay with God.

Perhaps an even greater challenge is to be with people where every fiber in our body tells us to stay away. Again, we are not absolving people of crimes; we are not saying that since it is a friend who did something wrong, it is not so bad. In fact, when someone close to us has done something bad, we may be obligated to be the first to speak out. However, our world's only hope for repair, for that sin offering for God on Rosh Chodesh and Rosh Hashanah, is our readiness to reach out lovingly to those who have failed us, in order to help them reconnect with their inherent goodness.

The hardest place to start may be ourselves. We have to believe that God is there for us when we are hurting and when we have hurt others. God gives us no carte blanche to do whatever we want, but even if we sin, God never leaves us.

We have to believe that—how else can we hope to turn our own lives around? I know God is there for us all, even in difficult moments. I pray that we find people also who are there for us in such times. In a shivah house, despite its tragic and unbearable pain, mourners can discover the miracle of people being there for them—and through those people, they may feel the love of God.

We need community for the thirteen attributes to mean anything, and indeed, according to Jewish law, they are meant to be said in a community. They obligate us (like God) to be present for others in their highs and in their lows. Then, with God's help, others will be there for us. Together, the God of "before and after"—and we, God's beloved creatures "of before and after"—can affirm the comfort, strength, and goodness inherent in "God ... God!"

# Theology—
# Encountering God

# Inviting God Back to the Garden

*Rabbi Angela Warnick Buchdahl*

Just last month, my family and I went on a trip to the Grand Canyon. We hiked to the rim, and as the forest thinned out, the ground fell away, and the canyon's full grandeur came into view. I turned to my teenage son and exclaimed, "Can you believe the beauty of God's handiwork?" His response? "I think that's called erosion, Mom."

I shouldn't take it personally. He's certainly not the only teenager who doesn't readily see God in the world. But as someone in the "God business," it hit hard. How do I talk about God to my determinedly rational, science-oriented son? Or, for that matter, to anyone?

My understanding of God's existence is rather uncomplicated: I know God exists in the same way that I know love exists. But fitting God into definable parameters (like the thirteen attributes)—that's more complicated.

As a child, I had an unself-conscious relationship with God. We were in regular conversation. And singing to God—well that was one of my favorite things to do. I became a rabbi primarily because I wanted to help others recognize God in their lives. But it's difficult to express this intensely personal and ineffable experience to anyone else.

I think God is hard for Jews because, unlike religious traditions that assume faith as a natural condition of belonging, Judaism requires no specific belief, rejects theological dogma, and has no ready image of God in the first place. "God" is not a natural part of our Jewish vocabulary.

Rabbi Angela Warnick Buchdahl was ordained as cantor and rabbi from Hebrew Union College–Jewish Institute of Religion in New York (1999 and 2001, respectively) and is the first ordained Asian American in North America. After serving Westchester Reform Temple in Scarsdale, New York, she joined Central Synagogue in New York City in 2006 as its senior cantor and was selected as its senior rabbi in 2014.

This summer, when a kindly Midwestern woman helped my husband find the cell phone he had dropped on the top of a mountain, the first words she uttered were "Praise the Lord!" How many Jews would have said that, as she did, literally and without a trace of irony?

But our inability to fully explain or understand God did not stop our ancestors from trying. Hence, the thirteen attributes shown to Moses on the mountain.

The problem with such imagery is that it reduces the *experience* of God—a divine *presence*—to a conception of a divine *being*. And that does God a great disservice.

When I ask a classroom of Jewish adults, "How many of you believe in God?" I get just a few tentative hands. When I ask for a time they have felt a divine *presence* of some kind, nearly every hand goes up. Nearly everyone can name or describe a moment when a transcendent presence feels undeniable: the birth of a first grandchild and watching a son become a father; reaching the top of a mountain; being part of a community that comforts a mourner after the death of her husband.

It's not just the big moments that I have in mind. Think of stepping outside after the first winter snowstorm. All the things that were dirty yesterday lie covered with a soft, clean blanket of white. Here in New York, the "city that never sleeps," the eternal din of the streets is momentarily (and miraculously) muted.

Or consider the moment when you finally tune in to your son who has discovered a colony of ants, marching industriously forward with enormous burdens on their backs. For a brief second, you see them through a child's eyes as if you too were young again.

It's not that God endows us with these experiences.

God *is* these experiences.

I have a vivid memory of being five years old and only recently arrived in this country from Korea. Everything smelled and tasted different here. Our apartment was across the street from the synagogue in Tacoma where my father and his father had both been raised. My father took me with him to services, but I didn't speak any English yet, let alone Hebrew, so the only prayer I could recognize was the *Sh'ma*, because we sang it at my bedtime. *Adonai echad*. "God is One."

One night my father took me outside to look for shooting stars. He lay down on the grassy courtyard and laid me across his chest looking up at the night sky.

I kept impatiently asking, "Is that a shooting star?"

"No."

"Is that one?"

"No."

"Just be still," he said.

So I calmed down, breathing alongside his heartbeat, and suddenly I really saw the night sky. It was all I could see, thick with stars. I felt so small and insignificant under this wide horizon, but I knew I was part of it all—my father's breath, the grass below, the stars above. It hit me that this very same sky stretched across the world to my old home. Everything was connected: sky, home, breath, family. *Adonai echad.* "God is One." It was a moment when (as the Hasidim say) heaven touched earth, and I knew that I was not alone, that anywhere could be home, that I was part of something beyond myself, that there is just One.

This is what I call God.

All we need to do is bring to mind such moments of wonder, compassion, presence, transcendence, healing, and connection that we *already know*—and become open to calling them "God." We then naturally experience God in more places, more relationships, some of them helped along by Jewish ritual—a baby naming, a bar mitzvah, Shabbat, for example—but also the faces on the subway, or the kindness of a stranger who finds our lost cell phone on a mountaintop.

You may resist calling these moments "God." I understand. It's not the way you learned about God in Hebrew school, nor how God is presented in our prayers. But we should resist the urge to boil God down to anything tangible—even the thirteen attributes. And this is challenging for us, because the Torah itself can be a stumbling block.

Take the well-known story of Adam and Eve, whom God has placed in the Garden of Eden, a perfect paradise, with the warning not to eat from the tree of knowledge. We all know how the story plays out: a snake tempts Eve, Eve persuades Adam, they eat the forbidden fruit of knowledge and are banished from the garden.

The God depicted in this story—a watchful, all-knowing, and vengeful God—is hard to accept. This God you don't believe in I don't believe in either.

But this biblical view is only one of many in our tradition. The kabbalists offer a very different one, beginning with the Hebrew word *et*, normally an untranslatable grammatical particle that merely introduces the direct object in a Hebrew sentence. The *Zohar*, however, observes that *et* is made up of the first and last letters of the alphabet—the alpha and the omega of the Hebrew language, as it were, and hence the all-encompassing nature of divine speech. It redefines *et*, therefore, as one of God's many names. So when the Torah reads, *Vay'garesh et ha'adam* (Genesis 3:24) literally, "He [God] expelled [*vay'garesh*] Adam [*et adam*]," the *Zohar* translates it as "He [*adam*, that is, Adam] expelled [*vay'garesh*] God [*et*]."

What a radical and powerful notion: God didn't expel humankind from the Garden of Eden; *it was humankind who exiled God.*

Consider the implications of this reading: Having tasted the fruit from the tree, we fell in love with knowledge; we elevated science, technology, and rationality above the simple beauty and intimacy of the garden. Armed with this new truth, we no longer needed God (we thought), became unable even to recognize God, and pushed God out.

But no matter how much we know about the world, we realize eventually how alone we are within it. The fruit from the tree of knowledge can explain how cancer cells reproduce in the body and even help us find our way to a cure. But it cannot assuage the terror of the diagnosis or the anguish of the suffering, nor can it help us die with dignity and peace. Knowledge can explain how the frequency of a sound wave determines its pitch. But it cannot explain why hearing a great symphony makes us weep.

The inadequacy of knowledge is that its truths alone cannot teach us how to stretch the capacities of our hearts, to live courageously in our suffering, or to reach beyond ourselves to find purpose and meaning in our lives.

As I read this kabbalistic text, our error was not in eating the fruit—knowledge is good. It was in imagining we were no longer in the garden and losing appreciation for the beauty and mystery that is still all around us. Abraham Joshua Heschel urged us to cultivate the "awe [that] enables us to perceive in the world intimations of the divine, to sense in small things the beginning of infinite significance, to sense the ultimate in the common and the simple."[1]

More than belief, deeds, or faith, it is awe that constitutes the primary outlook of a religious person, because awe brings "intimations of the divine." Awe paves the way for God's return to the garden.

A famous midrashic parable describes a king's son far from his father's home. His friends advise him, "Return to your father," to which he replies, "I am unable." Whereupon his father sends word, saying, "Go as far as you are able, and I shall come the rest of the way to you."

In the traditional reading of this midrash, it is we who have strayed from God. But perhaps we are the ones still sitting in the garden, and God is far from us because we have sent God away. The thirteen attributes may help us think about God at a distance—who God is, how God works—but they can also get in the way of experiencing God directly, as a presence in the garden, right beside us.

⚭

# Being Honest about God

*Rabbi Andrew Goldstein, PhD*

The thirteen attributes in Exodus 34 might just as well be a single act in a larger drama that begins two chapters earlier:

Prologue (Exodus 32): Moses atop Mount Sinai; having received the Ten Commandments, he is sent back down by God, only to find the Israelites dancing round the golden calf.

Act 1: A wonderfully human (even slightly comical) conversation ensues as God and Moses blame each other for the Israelites' sin. God insists the Israelites are "your people." Moses insists that God, not he, brought Israel out of Egypt—they are *God's* people, then, not *his*!

Act 2: In mutual frustration at Israel's apostasy (and maybe by their mutually recriminatory conversation as well), Moses smashes the tablets of stone, and God threatens to wipe out the people as well.

Act 3: Horrified at the turn of events, Moses pleads with God on Israel's behalf and seeks to reaffirm his mission face-to-face with God, only to be told (Exodus 33:12–23) that the best he will get is an intimation of God's presence passing by.

Act 4: Moses ascends the mountain again, to get a duplicate set of tablets to make up for the ones he broke. Protected in a crevice of rock,

Rabbi Andrew Goldstein, PhD, is the president of Liberal Judaism, UK; the vice president of the European Union for Progressive Judaism; and coeditor of *Machzor Ruach Chadashah*. He contributed to *Who by Fire, Who by Water—Un'taneh Tokef; All These Vows—Kol Nidre; We Have Sinned: Sin and Confession in Judaism—Ashamnu and Al Chet; May God Remember: Memory and Memorializing in Judaism—Yizkor; All the World: Universalism, Particularism and the High Holy Days; and Naming God: Our Father, Our King—Avinu Malkeinu* (all Jewish Lights).

God does indeed pass by—revealing the divine thirteen attributes (Exodus 34:6–7) under consideration here.

Denouement: Moses descends the mountain; the people observe that his face is "radiant" (Exodus 34:35).

The entire drama has probably never actually been portrayed on stage or film, but every Rosh Hashanah and Yom Kippur (and festivals as well) we make a mini-drama out of the thirteen attributes at least. The ark is opened to reveal the Torah scrolls resplendent in their white covers. The music is solemn, a pleading melody, repeated three times to add to the intensity. Worshipers cannot help but be moved by the moment, to the point where only the pedantic academic or theologian bothers analyzing the words or counting the attributes. And such is the cadence and mystical power of the passage that phrases from it get repeated often in the Bible and later liturgy.

Over time, I have had much opportunity to meditate on these attributes. They are introduced by "Adonai passed before him [before Moses] and said, 'Adonai, Adonai ...,'" but in my youth, I had a "Woody Allen" sort of thought that maybe it was not God speaking, but Moses, and Moses had a stutter, no doubt more pronounced when in an excited state. "*Adonai, Adonai ... el rachum....*"

Some time later, when I looked up the passage, as a rabbinic student at Leo Baeck College, I spotted the symbol |—a vertical line between the repeated divine names—and realized that the meaning really could be "Adonai said, 'Adonai, a merciful and gracious God....'" And now, fifty years later, I know (from the definitive *Gesenius' Hebrew Grammar*) that such a vertical line is indeed included "between words which are liable to be wrongly connected."

Perhaps then, I was right: Exodus 34:6–7 should be understood as "Adonai said: Adonai, a merciful and gracious God...." Traditionally, however, each "Adonai" counts as a separate attribute. If the first one is just the subject of the sentence ("Adonai said"), then we would be left with only twelve attributes of God, not thirteen!

Would that really matter, however? Don't we regularly play fast and free with the biblical verses that we use liturgically?

My biblical drama cited above, for instance, omitted Exodus 34:10–17, where God instructs Moses that when the Israelites enter the Promised Land, they should "destroy the altars and images" of the indigenous peoples, whom God has already driven out, "for Adonai, whose name is Jealous, is a jealous God." Quite the opposite of the "merciful and gracious, endlessly patient, most kind" God of the verses that precede this passage!

Even the thirteen attributes of God as we have them in the liturgy is a case of selective citation. I have always used the prayer books of the British Liberal Movement, beginning with the 1923 version edited by Rabbi Dr. Israel Mattuck, who was influenced by the *Union Prayer Book* of North America, which he must have used when he was still a student at the Hebrew Union College. Following its precedent, he lopped off the last word of the Thirteen Attributes found in the traditional liturgies (*v'nakeh* = "and pardoning" [literally, "cleansing"]). This omission was repeated in our British Liberal *Gate of Repentance*, which was edited by Rabbis John Rayner and Chaim Stern and published in 1973. In 2003, however, I coedited with Rabbi Dr. Charles Middleburgh the latest edition of our High Holy Day prayer book, *Machzor Ruach Chadashah*, where we restored the missing word, translating it "and granting pardon."

Were we right in doing so? The word is really part of a complex grammatical form that altogether reads *v'nakeh lo y'nakeh* and implies an emphatic negative. Rather than "granting pardon," the biblical claim is precisely the reverse—that God "*surely* does *not* grant pardon, but, rather, visits the iniquity of parents upon their children and children's children, upon the third and fourth generation." The traditional inclusion of *v'nakeh* alone in the prayer book is the exact opposite of what the biblical text intends, a perversion of God's dramatic declaration! Our Liberal predecessors removed it because they wanted to avoid using a grammatical sleight of hand to misrepresent the biblical text to worshipers.

Sometimes Liberal or Reform Jews have been attacked for shortening or bowdlerizing their liturgy or skipping over passages in the Bible that make them feel uncomfortable, but here we see that selective citation is not at all just the penchant of these progressive movements. From earliest times (at least from the text of our first extant prayer book, *Seder Rav Amram*, in the ninth century), Jews have omitted the uncomfortable guarantee that God visits parental iniquity throughout the generations and kept just the reassuring promise of God's kindness and compassion.

Perhaps we are being too protective of the divine—like parents who will not listen to any criticism of their child, wanting only positive and constructive reports. But surely God can handle it! God is indeed forgiving and compassionate but also fair and strict, unlikely to pass blithely over our errors. Surely on Yom Kippur of all days we should face this truth about God—which reflects the truth about ourselves: yes, there is much that is good and positive in our lives, but we also make mistakes, with a wake of unfortunate consequences. Yes, God pardons us, but yes also, God holds us guilty and responsible for what we do.

If I could, I would reorder the thirteen attributes of God. I would count "Adonai" as one (the first *Adonai* being an introduction). I would end with *v'nakeh lo y'nakeh* and understand it as "yet not remitting all punishment to the guilty." This would surely be a true reflection on the nature and purpose of the Days of Awe.

Yet I recognize that too much talk of sin and punishment may prove dispiriting for a congregation that (just like Moses at Sinai) wants reassurance of God's comforting presence. So I will stick with the traditional liturgical fudge that sings only of God's mercy. And let me interpret Moses's beaming face at the end of Exodus 34 as a sign of the contentment born of experiencing whatever presence of God there is to know. As we leave the synagogue at the end of Yom Kippur, may we too have had an intimation of God's presence; may we too feel forgiven and perhaps even glow from the sense of the peace we feel with ourselves and with God.

# God—Still All-Good and All-Powerful

*Rabbi Walter Homolka, PhD, DHL*

On the High Holy Days especially, I am acutely aware of the way our tradition pictures God. This is the day of judgment, when an all-good and all-powerful God weighs our sins. But if such a God created human beings in God's own image, just how is it that people can do evil? Why does God allow it? Is God really all-good and all-powerful? If so, how can God permit the kind of evil witnessed during the Shoah? What kind of God is this, anyway?

In the wake of Auschwitz, we all should wonder: how can an all-good and all-powerful God allow evil?

I often pass the villa at 56–58 Am Grossen Wannsee in the leafy western suburbs of Berlin. There, on January 20, 1942, SS-Obergruppenführer Reinhard Heydrich called a meeting to unveil the "Final Solution," the plan to round up European Jews from west to east and send them to extermination camps in the General Government (the occupied part of Poland), where they would eventually be killed.

The meeting was held to ensure the cooperation of the administrative leaders of the various departments required to implement the

---

Rabbi Walter Homolka, PhD, DHL, is professor of contemporary Jewish thought and executive director at the School of Jewish Theology of the University of Potsdam and rector of the Abraham Geiger College in Germany. He is author of many books, including *Jesus Reclaimed: Jewish Perspectives on the Nazarene*, and coauthor with Hans Küng of *How to Do Good & Avoid Evil: A Global Ethic from the Sources of Judaism* (SkyLight Paths). He contributed to *We Have Sinned: Sin and Confession in Judaism—Ashamnu and Al Chet*; *May God Remember: Memory and Memorializing in Judaism—Yizkor*; and *All the World: Universalism, Particularism and the High Holy Days* (all Jewish Lights).

plan: secretaries from the Foreign Office; the justice, interior, and state ministries; and representatives from the Schutzstaffel (SS). The surviving minutes of the meeting make for horrifying reading. Mass murder is reduced to matters of bureaucratic efficiency and inter-office collaboration. Reading the minutes you encounter evil beyond comprehension—treated merely as an organizational challenge. The array of public servants who worried over the managerial details raised no personal moral objections and showed no individual hesitation about what they were being asked to do.

How can God's goodness and omnipotence be defended given the existence of evil such as this?

In his 1984 lecture "The Concept of God after Auschwitz," the Jewish philosopher Hans Jonas proposed the notion of a compassionate God who, nevertheless, is not all-powerful.[1] I admit that I am not totally comfortable with this solution. For me, a God who commiserates with humans but cannot or will not engage in alleviating human pain and disaster resembles a grandpa-type figure to whom we can turn for consolation but not for help. Is this King Lear–like god the God we proclaim in our liturgy? No, it is not.

Christians confront suffering with the image of a suffering God. In Trinitarian theory, Jesus is the revealed side of God while God the father is the *deus absconditus*, the hidden, unrevealed aspect of the divine. God the father commiserates with the divine son: "For God so loved the world, that He gave his only begotten son, that whoever believes in him shall not perish, but have eternal life" (John 3:16). Suffering, thus, becomes the route to redemption. God has, as it were, given up the power to eliminate suffering but has sent, instead, his own suffering-servant son to demonstrate suffering as the way to eternal life.

For a purely Jewish approach, however, the idea of God as all-good but not all-powerful is rather more difficult to manage. I would like, therefore, to offer an alternative line of thought that is in keeping with the story of creation and is generally called the "free will defense."

Central to Judaism is the doctrine that God made human beings in the divine image. It follows that we must have freedom of will and may choose to do good rather than evil. Judaism down the centuries has been very clear and consistent on this point: the good in us is a consequence of our being made in the image of God (as in Genesis 1:27 and 5:1). One of the greatest rabbis, Rabbi Akiva, observes, "Human beings are loved because they were made in God's image. That they were created in God's image was made known by a special love, as it is said, 'For God made human beings in the divine image'" (Mishnah Avot 3:14).

What about evil, then? Where does evil come from?

The answer begins with a look at Jewish literature from antiquity. Ben Sirach (second century BCE) was a gentleman farmer whose book of proverbial wisdom never made it into the Jewish Bible but was well known to the Rabbis and treated as authentic Jewish wisdom nevertheless. We have the book extant in several ancient languages, including Hebrew, although the Hebrew is a translation. According to Ben Sirach, God made human beings "according to His own image.... He gave them knowledge of understanding, and showed them good and evil.... Having made man in the beginning, He left him in the hands of his own decision."[2]

So Ben Sirach adjudges human beings responsible for their own actions. But then, the evil counterpart to the "*good* impulse" requires explanation. Rabbinic Judaism succinctly supplied it: just as God created the good impulse (*yetzer hatov*), so too did God create the evil one (*yetzer hara*), so that human beings have the possibility of, and responsibility for, choosing between the two. The noun *yetzer* is derived from the verb *yatzar*, "to form," and therefore means something like "a fundamental aspect of human nature" or "a fundamental human disposition." Of course, this raises the question how a good God can create an evil impulse,[3] and the surprising answer is that at least to a large degree, and despite its name, the evil impulse is not fundamentally evil.

We quoted Ben Sirach as saying that God "left man in the hands of his decision." In the Greek version of Ben Sirach the word for "decision" is *diabole*, which becomes *diabolus* in Latin, a word that gives us the English "diabolical" and carries the meaning "devil." Hence the Christian explanation of evil as devil-sent. But Ben Sirach need not have meant that. The Hebrew translation renders "decision" as *yetzer*, just what we find in the Rabbis.

But, again, if all the works of God are good, even the *yetzer hara* cannot be evil in and of itself. The Midrash makes this very clear when discussing the creation of human beings. The biblical text judges that creative act "very good" (Genesis 1:31). The Rabbis understand the pleonastic (i.e., logically superfluous) word "and" with reference to the two human impulses (good *and* evil) so that the verdict "very good" refers to them both. The Midrash explains, "Can, then, the evil impulse be very good? That would be extraordinary! Were it not for the evil impulse, however, no man would build a house, take a wife, and beget children; and thus said Solomon: I have also noted that all labor and skillful enterprise come from men's envy of each other (Ecclesiastes 4:4)."[4]

This illuminating text makes it clear that *yetzer hara* is a blanket term for acts of self-preservation or of pleasure and power, but also for desiring possessions, securing a good reputation, seeking popularity, and so on. These impulses are not in themselves evil. On the contrary, they are good in the sense that they are biologically useful. But they are extremely powerful, and if they are not controlled by a lively conscience, they can quickly lead us to disregard justice and the needs of others or even to do them harm. In this sense, and because it so often drives us to do wrong, the *yetzer hara* can be viewed as evil. But it does not need to be: the psychic energy for which it stands can also be directed to good ends; as Ben Sirach concludes, God "commanded no man to be ungodly, gave no one permission to sin."[5]

It is possible for human beings to control the *yetzer hara*. "Who is mighty?" asks Ben Soma in the Mishnah. "One who controls his *yetzer* [evil impulse]" (Mishnah Avot 4:1). The problem, of course, to put it simply, is how to cultivate and activate the good impulse so that it can exercise the necessary control.

Hans Jonas (mentioned above) explained the possibility of such human activity with the kabbalistic concept of *tzimtzum*, the act of self-limitation by which God withdrew God's presence to allow space in which to create a world. "By forgoing its own inviolateness," God "allowed the world to be. Having given Himself whole to the becoming world, God has no more to give: it is man's now to give to him."[6]

Another Jewish philosopher, Emmanuel Levinas, himself a former prisoner of war in Nazi Germany, declared theodicy itself to be "blasphemous," because any theory that explains or justifies evil must also be the "source of all immorality." Rather than justify God in the face of evil, he maintained, we are to live godly lives ourselves; rather than speculating fruitlessly on whether God was present during the Holocaust, we must build a world where goodness will prevail.[7]

In September 2008, the Nobel Laureate Elie Wiesel startled his audience at a Holocaust Educational Trust appeal dinner in London when he declared, "I was there when God was put on trial at a concentration camp." In response to Rabbi Jonathan Romain and Rabbi Dan

Cohn-Sherbock, who cast doubt on the account, Wiesel replied, "Why should they know what happened? I was the only one there. It happened in Auschwitz at night; there were just three people. At the end of the trial, they used the word *chayav*, rather than 'guilty.' It means 'He owes us something.' Then we went to pray."[8]

We Jews are known to argue with God at times—after all, as part of the covenant God owes us something. But we too owe God. This is why—after arguing with the divine majesty—we dutifully pray as the sacrifice of our hearts and from there go on to build a better world.

⚭

# God Forgives Because He Has No Choice

*Rabbi Delphine Horvilleur*

D o you suffer from triskaidekophobia? Few people know the scientific name for this very unscientific phenomenon: the irrepressible fear of a simple number whose very existence brings bad luck. The superstition is deeply rooted in Christian theology, thirteen being the number of guests at Jesus's table during the Last Supper. The fear of bad omens frequently goes as far as skipping over the thirteenth row in planes and the thirteenth floor of buildings. There is no "13" in elevators! In Jewish theology, thirteen is not associated with bad luck, but neither is it "neutral"; it is attached instead to the notion that stands at the core of High Holy Day theology: forgiveness.

An entire season of the Jewish calendar, known as the season of repentance, focuses on this idea. And Yom Kippur constitutes its apotheosis. We repeat constantly then this adage from the Mishnah (Yoma 8:9): "For the wrongs we commit against God, Yom Kippur atones; but for the wrongs we commit toward one another, Yom Kippur does not atone until we are forgiven by the person wronged."

Supposing, to begin with, that each of us has indeed sincerely asked forgiveness from our family and friends, our neighbors and colleagues, and even our enemies; and that, in keeping with tradition, we have been

Rabbi Delphine Horvilleur is the rabbi of congregation MJLF (Mouvement Juif Libéral de France) in Paris. She was ordained at Hebrew Union College–Jewish Institute of Religion in New York in 2008 and became the third woman rabbi in France. She is the creative director of Le Café Biblique, a pluralistic group of Jewish study, and chief editor of *Tenou'a*, a French magazine of Jewish thought. She contributed to *Who by Fire, Who by Water—Un'taneh Tokef; All These Vows—Kol Nidre; We Have Sinned: Sin and Confession in Judaism—Ashamnu and Al Chet;* and *May God Remember: Memory and Memorializing in Judaism—Yizkor* (all Jewish Lights).

freed from our blunders and our mistakes. We have still to understand how the greatest of miracles could occur: that on this day, by a sort of "abracadabra," God resets the counters to zero.

Why on this particular day are past errors suddenly erased—like a preview of the now famous front page of the magazine *Charlie Hebdo* "All is forgiven" (a highly controversial front page of the satirical magazine published shortly after the attacks of January 2015, where a sad-faced prophet Muhammad makes that declaration)?

The answer is to be sought within the liturgy and more specifically the number thirteen.

From the month of Elul, in my community, we recite an early morning *S'lichot* service commencing at dawn, before the day has even begun. This strange hour removes routine from our prayers and the spiritual torpor in which our habits have settled us. These *S'lichot* services consist of what, to me, resemble a packaged gift: beautiful wrapping around a core idea.

The packaging consists of liturgical poems and supplications that vary according to place and tradition. Again and again, we ask God to answer us, to reign, to be present, to hear our prayers, to inscribe us in the book of life. How strange for us to ask forgiveness, to beg or even demand that God grant us things—as if we can control what God does.

But that is just the packaging. The heart of the *S'lichot*—the actual gift, so to speak—is a three-line biblical quotation from Exodus 34:6–7 and 34:9.

1 (v. 6a). Adonai passed before him and said,
2 (vv. 6b, 7a). "Adonai, Adonai, merciful and gracious God, endlessly patient, most kind and truthful, extending kindness to thousands, forgiving sins and transgressions and misdeeds, cleansing."
3 (v. 9b). You will pardon [*v'salachta*] our sins and transgressions and take possession of us.[1]

Three sentences: The first is in the *past* as a reminder of a particular situation in our history. The second lists God's attributes in the *present*—what the Rabbis call the thirteen attributes of the divine. The third promises God's forgiveness in the *future*.

Why are past, present, and future tenses juxtaposed here without any obvious coherence?

The solution to the mystery lies in the biblical context from which this text is drawn (Exodus 32–34). Moses has been atop Mount Sinai for forty days, receiving Torah—a very long time for a people just out of Egypt and accustomed to the reassuring presence of a leader, especially in a world where idols are always conveniently available. So the people, impatient and anxious, build a golden calf.

For the Rabbis, this episode becomes the mother of all misdeeds, the most terrible sin in the Jewish People's history. When Moses comes back down Mount Sinai with the tablets in hand, he is furious at what he discovers, and he smashes the tablets of stone. God then considers destroying this stiff-necked people, thereby putting an end to God's project. The situation is catastrophic. The scene is set: Will the Hebrew people be forgiven? And if so, how?

In Exodus 34, Moses ascends the mountain again to obtain forgiveness for Israel. Needing himself to regain strength to guide the people, he has already (Exodus 33) made a special request of God, "Show me your presence" (v. 18)—to which God has replied, "No one can see my face and live" (v. 20). Yet God has agreed "to make all my goodness pass before you" (v. 19), and when Moses climbs the mountain (Exodus 34:4), God descends in a cloud (v. 5), and only then, precisely then, do we get the first two lines of our formula (the third will come later):

1 (v. 6a). Adonai passed before him and said,
2 (vv. 6b, 7a). "Adonai, Adonai, merciful and gracious God, endlessly patient, most kind and truthful, extending kindness to thousands, forgiving sins and transgressions and misdeeds, cleansing."

From that moment, the people of Israel receive miraculous forgiveness; now Moses can go back down the mountain.

To understand what is at stake on Yom Kippur, we need the dates on which all of this occurred. The Hebrews built the golden calf on the ninth of Av. Moses went back up Mount Sinai on the first of Elul and stayed there forty days, making his return to the people on the tenth of Tishrei, the exact date of Yom Kippur, year after year! It is on that date, and no other, that Moses came back down the mountain with an improbable pardon that will save us.

Yom Kippur is thus the anniversary of the greatest pardon ever accorded to the Jewish People, the annual moment in time, therefore, when we say to God, "If the tenth of Tishrei was the day You pardoned our ancestors for such an enormous thing as the golden calf, You must be able to do as much for us today. Because today we replay the scene. We reiterate the choreography, repeating the exact same words that You taught us then."

In the *past*, God presented Himself before Moses, laying out those attributes that (from our viewpoint) must remain relevant in the *present*, because of an ancestral scene that committed God for the *future*.

What God gave on Yom Kippur so very long ago is indeed a sort of "abracadabra" for forgiveness, valid for all future Yom Kippurs. It is an almost magic formula that we need but say to leave God with no choice but to replay the primal scene of forgiveness from so long ago.

All is forgiven ... and that is the secret of Yom Kippur, for as the third line of this formulaic scene promises (v. 9b), "You will pardon [*v'salachta*] our sins and transgressions and take possession of us." God forgives because God committed Himself to do so before Moses on Mount Sinai.

There is still one more incredibly important detail to consider—a detail that is not really just a detail at all.

Our liturgical list of thirteen divine attributes is a truncated version of the original in Exodus 34. That original does not promise exactly what we have in our prayer books: "Adonai, Adonai, merciful and gracious God, endlessly patient, most kind and truthful, extending kindness to thousands, forgiving sins and transgressions and misdeeds, cleansing." Instead of "cleansing" it says just the reverse, "God will surely not cleanse," and then it adds, "He visits the iniquity of parents upon children and children's children, upon the third and fourth generation."

Is our omission of the "negative side" of God's attributes the work of a dishonest liturgist? No, it is rather an ancestral Rabbinic custom called *chutzpah*. Such is the talent of the Rabbis and their legendary nerve: God promises to forgive, but not entirely, and to enforce punishment, when due, throughout the generations. But this did not please the Rabbis, who dared amend the sentence to have God say that on this day the counters are reset to zero.

The Rabbis thereby force God's hand, and as their heirs we do the same. We make the text, and God, say something other than what God actually said. God will pardon us, we insist, not only because God said it and because on that one day long ago, God actually did it, but because we don't give God a choice.[2]

⚭

# Whose Attributes?

*Catherine Madsen*

Rigorously apprehended, the Mosaic God is inconceivable, incomprehensible, invisible, unattainable, in-human in the root-sense of the word. He is blank as the desert air. If there is a Jewish theology, it is negative.... Paradoxically, however, the distance to an imageless, unthinkable, unsayable God is also that of an unbearable nearness. Unseen, He sees all, He chastises to the third generation and beyond. Can there be a harsher observing and observance, one more alien to the animistic, iconic, pluralistic impulses of human nature, to the consoling ways in which we tell the stories of our being?

—GEORGE STEINER, *ERRATA*

And maybe God *is* in charge, it's just not the way we would do it.

—BARBARA E. THOMSON

What is unsaid is as important as what is said. According to the liturgy, God is merciful and gracious, slow to anger, abounding in kindness and truth, keeping mercy for thousands of generations, forgiving

Catherine Madsen is the author of *The Bones Reassemble: Reconstituting Liturgical Speech; In Medias Res: Liturgy for the Estranged;* and a novel, *A Portable Egypt.* She is librettist for Robert Stern's oratorio "Shofar" (on the CD *Awakenings,* Navona Records NV5878), and bibliographer at the Yiddish Book Center. She contributed to *Who by Fire, Who by Water—* Un'taneh Tokef; *All These Vows—*Kol Nidre; *We Have Sinned: Sin and Confession in Judaism—*Ashamnu *and* Al Chet; *May God Remember: Memory and Memorializing in Judaism—*Yizkor; *All the World: Universalism, Particularism and the High Holy Days;* and *Naming God: Our Father, Our King—*Avinu Malkeinu (all Jewish Lights).

iniquity, transgression and sin, and clearing the repentant. According to the source text (Exodus 34:6–7), God also does *not* clear the unrepentant, and visits the iniquity of the fathers upon the children and the children's children to the third and fourth generations. Where the liturgy offers the possibility of change, the biblical text suggests the impossibility of erasing the past. How can we ever come up with enough repentance to clear ourselves—to spare our children and our children's children and the third and fourth generations the consequences of what we are and what we do?

However abbreviated the text, the common tune for the Thirteen Attributes accurately conveys the uncertainty of God's mercy; it is serious, sober, ominous. It offers no placid assurance. In rational terms we may not altogether believe what we're singing, but we still feel it: the tune holds us, hides us, like Moses in the cleft of the rock on Sinai, to witness the passage of a dread and powerful God. We achieve—in Coleridge's words—"that willing suspension of disbelief for the moment, which constitutes poetic faith." Assert, proclaim, God's mercy; say it three times; render God merciful and the universe intelligible through sheer force of collective will.

In reciting the Thirteen Attributes we accept—for the moment—the fiction of a moral universe. God said to Moses, "I will make all my goodness pass before you"; the attributes of mercy serve as incentive and hope to the repentant sinner, and the (unmentioned but implied) attributes of justice show what happens if we refuse that incentive. But in our non-liturgical lives, and in the Bible as a whole, how consistently does God operate within the moral framework? How permanently can we extract God's attributes of mercy and justice from the general I-will-be-what-I-will-be of raw force, restless imagination, emotional volatility, and general unpredictability that characterize the Master of the Universe? Cause and effect is fairly reliable in the moral realm; it's even more reliable in the laws of physics; but there are always causes unknown to us and effects we discover only when it is far too late for repair. Ignorance and accident weigh as heavily in the scale of our errors as deliberate transgression, and often do far more damage. What are the attributes of a universe that works this way?

Only rarely do we hear from the *bimah* that God operates in the moral framework only as and when it pleases him. Poets and storytellers—and joke-tellers—know it perfectly well, but among writers and leaders of prayer, and among all but a few theologians, it's bad form to say what God himself says in Isaiah 45:7: "I form light and create darkness, I make peace and create evil, I the Lord do all these things." "Evil," in this passage, is not meant to imply existential evil but "adversity" or "woe" or "bad things"; but bad things do happen to good people. Job's comforters to the contrary, not all of our suffering can be traced to something we did to deserve it. Some of it happens for other reasons, or for none. In Exodus 34, the proclamation of God's attributes is part of a general remission of punishment for the making of the golden calf, and clearly does take place within the moral framework, but when God appeared to Job in the whirlwind he spread out the full moral conundrum. The world is vastly bigger than we are, and full of creatures that are on their own errands—and full of inanimate geological and hydrological and geomagnetic forces, all massively purposeful but without purpose as we understand it. We are not at the center of God's attention—or only in the sense that everything is at the center of God's attention. We are at the center of our own attention, but we have to know the difference.

There are people who don't want a God who creates evil, in either the existential or the practical sense. The earthquake that kills ten thousand, or the lonely suffering of one abused child, does and should shake one's faith in a benevolent God; but to say "I can't believe in a God who allows that to happen" is almost a non sequitur. So don't believe in him—who cares?—but the evil still happens, and is no less terrible for being unsupervised. You can divorce your religion, you can stop going to shul, you can use the word *God* only for swearing, but the Richter scale doesn't become obsolete or psychotherapy unnecessary because you stand on your principles. At one level, to say "I can't believe in a God who ..." is merely to say, "We get sick, we suffer, we die, our acts have unintended consequences—*I'm gonna go someplace where that doesn't happen.*" And where is that?

Well into the early modern period, the word "believe" did not indicate rational assent; it meant to trust in, to cleave to. Job's "though he slay me, yet will I trust in him" is a mistranslation—an attempt by the Rabbis to soften Job's mordant assessment of his position—but in spite of the Rabbis, the force of these words is as vast and wild as the great animals Behemoth and Leviathan that God shows to Job from the whirlwind. Even if what Job really says is "He will slay me, I have no hope," in both versions he immediately goes on, "but I will argue my case before him": he asserts his intention both to belong to and to contend with God. Hopelessness and the certainty of death make him stronger and more obdurate, not more resigned. What is it that we cleave to even when rational assent has failed, when we nurse no more illusions of God's benevolence? What stern and undeceived belief survives the collapse of faith?

To Moses, God proclaims his attributes while shielding him from the full force of his presence. He does not show him Behemoth and Leviathan. "I will cover you with my hand until I have passed by, and I will take away my hand and you shall see my back; but my face shall not be seen." In reciting the Thirteen Attributes on Yom Kippur we address the *hester panim*, the hidden face—"the trace," as Levinas calls it—which we cannot see and live; perhaps that face is like Medusa's and would turn us to stone. Perhaps what we trust in is that very danger, that lethal surplus of energy.

The "predicate theology" of thinkers like Mordecai Kaplan and Harold Schulweis proposes that defining the attributes of God is a dead end, and that instead we should consider the attributes of godliness. "The question for predicate theology," says Schulweis, "is not 'Do you believe that God is merciful, caring, peacemaking?' but 'Do you believe that doing mercy, caring, making peace are godly?'"[1] Rationally this approach is fairly satisfying; it puts the responsibility on us where it belongs, and discourages futile speculations. Even emotionally, it sets us the noble challenge of taking part in the operations of "earth and seed, water and sun, the human effort to prepare the soil, to weed and plough and plant, to harvest the field, to reap and winnow and grind the wheat, to knead and season the dough, to distribute bread for the sake of human life and health" that constitute "bringing forth bread from the earth."[2] But predicate theology only succeeds in realms where we have control. When there is too much water and no sun, or too much sun and no water, when distribution fails, when someone is gravely ill and we are not doctors or nurses but distressed onlookers, we are thrown back on a universe in which we are not in charge, in which perhaps no one is in charge. Then we yearningly invoke God's mercy, not because it is much in evidence but because we cannot do much else.

God's dare to Job—which may also be the dare of predicate theology—is this: Can we handle moral life against an amoral backdrop? Can we be merciful when God is unmerciful? Can we live with a universe that is not purely good, if there is an absence of good that we know how to fill? Within the compass of the whole world—and *towards* the whole world—we are bound to the moral framework; we have responsibilities and must fulfill them. The world (except, part-time, the human world) is not reciprocally bound to us. God's attributes of mercy are to that extent imaginary, the products of our gratitude and our longing. Ours have to be real.

☙

# A Love Letter from God

### Rabbi Jonathan Magonet, PhD

At the burning bush, Moses asks God to reveal the divine name. Reluctantly God first offers two ambiguous answers: the enigmatic "I am that I am" and the unhelpful "'I am'" sent me to you" (Exodus 3:14); and only then reveals the four-letter name *YHVH* that became the intimate expression of Israel's special relationship with the divine (3:14–15).

Later, after Israel's repeated wrongdoing and God's threat to abandon them, Moses requests to know God's *derekh*, God's "way" (Exodus 33:13), and God's *kavod* (33:18), a term derived from the word for "weight," often translated as "glory," but better understood as "presence in the world." Again Moses is met with reluctance on the part of God, who offers, instead, an ambiguous response: "I will make all my goodness pass before you and I will proclaim before you the name *YHVH*, and I will be gracious to whom I will be gracious and show compassion to whom I will show compassion" (33:19).

The caveat, as it were ("I will be gracious to whom I will be gracious and show compassion to whom I will show compassion"), implies God's

---

Rabbi Jonathan Magonet, PhD, is emeritus professor of Bible at Leo Baeck College in London, where he was principal (president) from 1985 to 2005. He is coeditor of three volumes of *Forms of Prayer* (the prayer books of the British Movement for Reform Judaism); editor of the eighth edition of *Daily, Sabbath and Occasional Prayers*; and editor of the journal *European Judaism*. He contributed to *Who by Fire, Who by Water—Un'taneh Tokef*; *All These Vows—Kol Nidre*; *We Have Sinned: Sin and Confession in Judaism—Ashamnu and Al Chet*; *May God Remember: Memory and Memorializing in Judaism—Yizkor*; *All the World: Universalism, Particularism and the High Holy Days*; and *Naming God: Our Father, Our King—Avinu Malkeinu* (all Jewish Lights).

determination to remain a free agent in deciding who deserves favor. But Moses's insistence again leads to a concession to be found in the following chapter (34:6–7), when God does provide a list of divine attributes—qualities that, with some omissions and one significant amendment, become the Thirteen Attributes of the Jewish liturgical tradition.

We will need to look in more detail at some of the words, but the biblical text according to a standard translation (not the one given officially in this volume, but the one that works best for my own purposes) reads as follows:

> The Lord [*YHVH*], the Lord [*YHVH*], God, loving and gracious, slow to anger and great in mercy and truth, showing mercy to a thousand generations, taking away transgression, rebellion, and sin but not holding people guiltless, visiting the transgression of the fathers upon sons and sons of sons to the third and fourth generation. (Exodus 34:6–7)

The Hebrew text contains two unusual word pairs: *rachum v'chanun* ("loving and gracious") and *chesed ve'emet* ("mercy and truth"). The first of the two, *rachum v'chanun*, is striking because of the similarity of vocalization. The parallelism of sound suggests that the combination of the words is a hendiadys, a composite form of words in which the meaning of the whole is greater than the sum of the parts. A similar example comes when Cain is punished by becoming a *na vanad* (from the verbs *no'a*, "to sway," and *nadad*, "to wander")—"a perpetual wanderer" (Genesis 4:12). Though very different in mode, our own cultural equivalent might be "Laurel and Hardy" or "Abbot and Costello." *Rachum*, by itself, means something like "compassionate love"; *chanun*, by itself, means "to act with grace, to give without expecting anything in return, a disinterested act of generosity." The combination of the two would give us a concept of "unbounded, limitless love."

This becomes particularly significant when we contrast it with the second verbal pair, *chesed ve'emet*. Again, both words have a similar vocalization, suggesting they too constitute a hendiadys. *Chesed* is the love that exists within a covenant, a kind of enduring faithfulness that goes beyond mere contractual legalism to include deep personal commitment, continuing even beyond the grave. Thus when Jonathan makes a covenant with David, he expects that after David becomes king, he will show *chesed* to Jonathan's family—even after he (Jonathan) dies (1 Samuel 20:14–15). Similarly, Ruth is praised for the *chesed* she has shown to the dead and the living (Ruth 1:8). *Emet*, the common word for "truth," is related to our familiar *amen*, meaning something that is firm, reliable, trustworthy. When we respond *amen* to someone's blessing, we assert our sense that it is reliably and firmly offered. So *emet* is "truth" in the sense of something experienced as utterly reliable. Together *chesed ve'emet* connotes reliable and faithful love as experienced within a covenantal relationship—a love that is trustworthy, but bounded, conditional, and constrained by the responsibilities of the covenant partners to one another.

We should recognize a paradox here: God's love is unbounded, unlimited, a matter of "grace," but also limited and bounded by the terms of the covenant. Actually, such a paradox is inevitable to explain how the God of the entire universe can enter into a binding relationship with a particular group of human beings. This is God's "love letter" to us.

Once this paradox is recognized, other elements in God's self-revelation become clearer. From the perspective of *chesed*, God's covenantal love is available to "a thousand generations." But the covenant requires limitations on the behavior of Israel as their part of the relationship. God is willing to forgive all manner of wrongdoing, provided a certain condition is met. This is expressed in the phrase *v'nakeh lo y'nakeh*, literally, "holding guiltless, does not hold guiltless." We need to look at a piece of biblical grammar to understand it.

The Bible regularly emphasizes statements by repeating the verb in two different grammatical forms. In the Garden of Eden, for instance, God warns Adam that on the day he eats the fruit of the tree of knowledge *mot tamut*, literally, "dying, you will die," meaning "you will surely die" (Genesis 2:17). The same combination can be expressed negatively by placing *lo* ("not") before the combined phrase, as when the snake tells Eve *lo mot t'mutun*, "you will surely not die" (Genesis 3:4). In our case, however, the negative *lo* comes after the verb "to hold someone guiltless" to emphasize that this is not always the case, that there are circumstances in which God does not hold someone guiltless! God definitely does not gratuitously declare people innocent—they must duly repent for pardon to arise.

However the liturgical version cuts the biblical text after the first word *v'nakeh*, thus deleting the negative and declaring everyone automatically innocent—just the opposite of what the Bible intended. This is a legitimate ploy by the Rabbis, given that the biblical text is unpunctuated, so one can insert a full stop wherever one wishes. The Rabbis have additional justification in emending the Exodus text because shortened and altered versions of it appear elsewhere in the Bible as well.[1]

This still leaves us with the problematic close to the biblical passage, the visiting of punishment onto subsequent generations. Here it is important to recognize who is addressed in this passage, and indeed in all the covenant laws, beginning with the Ten Commandments. The addressee is the adult Israelite male, to whom (in biblical society) belong wife, children, slaves, land, and animals. In the biblical mind-set, these are his possessions; they constitute his "self";[2] he is responsible for them throughout his lifetime, and whatever he does has consequences for them as well. The biblical world measures time not by an individual's own life alone but by generations—as we see from the way we hark back to the three generations of patriarchs, Abraham, Isaac, and Jacob, as if they are our own living father, grandfather, and great-grandfather. Conversely, a man in his lifetime may live to see his own children, grandchildren, and great-grandchildren, his own third and fourth generations. The punishment that is threatened here will thus affect all of these generations of his extended family, not in some future time, but those who are alive now, but only now, at this moment in time. Elsewhere in the Bible the prophets Jeremiah (31:29–30) and Ezekiel (18:20) argue against such an extension of answerability, but our Exodus passage still assumes it as normal.[3]

For liturgical purposes, the Rabbis have edited the attributes of Exodus to accent the forgiving nature of God—particularly on Yom Kippur, when we are assumed to have done the work of correcting our past wrongs and seeking reconciliation with those we might have harmed. At this crucial moment we want and need the reassurance of God's generous love and willingness to forgive.

In a broader theological context, we might say that the strictly bounded love of *chesed ve'emet* is balanced by the boundless grace of *rachum v'chanun*, so as to effect a restoration of relationship, mediated by acts of repentance. The covenant can be broken, but God's love can always restore it.

There is a further implication to the passage that moves me personally. If the covenant is reciprocal, then the same elements that are part of God's qualities in dealing with us must also be recognized in our dealing with God. It can be argued that the Shoah, the apparent abandonment of the Jewish People by God in our worst hour of need, represents a breaking of God's responsibility to us under the terms of *chesed ve'emet*—shattering of the covenant based upon trust. Indeed that is the lesson that leads so many to abandon God in return. Yet, for others, myself included, the Jewish People still seems willing to affirm the covenant despite all that has happened. That is our quality of *rachum v'chanun*, our own eternal, boundless love for God.

☙❧

# God Is a Long, Deep Breath

*Rabbi Jay Henry Moses*

Of all the spiritual challenges facing us today, none is more profound than the pace of change in our world. Advances in technology, transformations of society, and breakthroughs in communications have accelerated at a rate that was unimaginable only a couple of generations ago. The telephone was invented in 1876, and more than one hundred years later the rotary phone plugged into the wall was still the norm. In the last fifteen years phones have evolved exponentially from those clunky analog boxes to tiny wireless supercomputers in our pockets. Each of those fifteen years saw advances more significant than the entire previous century of telephone technology.

Our consciousness has not caught up to that pace of change. Ancient spiritual traditions like Judaism can play a crucial role in helping us adjust to the inevitable lag between the rapid acceleration of change in our surroundings and our slower natural pace of human evolution. Especially important in this regard is the concept of *erekh apayim*. *Erekh apayim* refers to the divine quality of "patience, long-suffering, and slowness to anger," but also to a human perspective on our own role in a universe of change.

---

Rabbi Jay Henry Moses is vice president of the Wexner Foundation, where he directs the Heritage Program. Previously, he served for five years as associate rabbi at Temple Sholom of Chicago. Rabbi Moses has taught at Hebrew Union College–Jewish Institute of Religion, the Jewish Community Center in Manhattan and its Makom: Center for Mindfulness, and in many other adult education settings. He contributed to *We Have Sinned: Sin and Confession in Judaism*—Ashamnu *and* Al Chet; *May God Remember: Memory and Memorializing in Judaism*—Yizkor; and *All the World: Universalism, Particularism and the High Holy Days* (all Jewish Lights).

On the High Holy Days—our annual spiritual check-in on the big questions of life and death—this concept of *erekh apayim* evokes profound questions and insights. This is particularly true for twenty-first-century Jews who are so caught up in the pace of change that we have difficulty even imagining God (much less ourselves) as *erekh apayim*: "patient, long-suffering, and slow to anger." Cultivating patience in an era of instant gratification is an important spiritual discipline—as the etymology of the phrase *erekh apayim* itself intimates.

*Erekh apayim* is a purely metaphorical idiom in Hebrew, far less accessible than kindness, truth, forgiveness, or others of the thirteen divine attributes of our texts. *Erekh* is simple enough: it means "long." But *apayim* is related to the word *af*, which has two meanings: "anger" and "nose." Start with the simpler meaning of *erekh apayim* from *af* as "anger." As *erekh apayim*, God takes a long time to get angry; hence the common rendering in English "slow to anger."

The subtler nuance of *erekh apayim* emerges from *af* as "nose"—the external body part most closely associated with breathing. Understood this way, *erekh apayim* means "long breath," or, more colloquially, "deep breath." In a way, the two meanings are linked: short, shallow breath is part of the physiological response to feeling anger (as well as fear). A long, deep breath connotes equanimity.

God is characterized here by the image of a long, deep breath. This action, which serves to calm us when we are angry, anxious, or frightened, is associated with God's very essence. How can this image enrich our spiritual experience of the High Holy Days?

My first meditation teacher, Sylvia Boorstein, likened the stream of thoughts that runs through our minds—the stories we tell ourselves, our guilt, self-doubt, and so on—to a spoonful of salt. If we pour that spoonful into a small cup of water, the water is thoroughly suffused with saltiness—unpleasant to the taste and overwhelming. So too, by analogy, when our consciousness is so focused on the ego that it becomes constricted; trapped in the loop of our thoughts, our mind becomes the small cup of water, dominated by the salt of our negative thought patterns.

But if you pour that same single spoonful of salt into a lake, its effect is diluted by the depth and volume of the water. Meditation is the act of expanding our consciousness from a small cup of water to a large, placid lake.

One time-tested and reliable practice for attaining expansive consciousness, then, is meditation: a practiced series of long, deep breaths. This turns out to be ideal preparation for the High Holy Days, because it establishes the state of being in which our sins, shortcomings, and guilt are absorbed by the infinite, eternal sweep of time.

This expanded consciousness is attainable not only through meditation; it may also serve as a worthy goal for our own High Holy Day prayer experience. Contemplating the meaning of God as *erekh apayim*, we come to see it as the divine oceanic perspective against which to measure our shortcomings. Praying the words of the Thirteen Attributes, we attempt to view ourselves from this perspective by widening the lens through which we view the world. This does not mean that our shortcomings disappear as negative behaviors for which we bear responsibility, but they are put into a perspective that allows us to be more patient with ourselves—and with others as well.

Recognizing our shortcomings without unduly burdening ourselves by the egoistic sense that we are the center of the universe allows us to face up to the deepest truth of the pain that we have caused. The emergence of this deeper truth also allows us to atone more thoroughly.

This perspective of *erekh apayim* also enables us to overcome our need for instant gratification. If clarity regarding the issues of our lives is not immediately forthcoming, we can live with the patient awareness that further meditation or prayer practice will eventually yield answers. In our age of limited attention spans and overstimulation, cultivating the expansive consciousness of *erekh apayim* becomes the key to a meaningful prayer experience and a life of integrity and truth.

But taking the long and patient view of our human condition is just one nuance of taking seriously the presence of God as *erekh apayim*. The other derives from the biblical meaning of God's *af* as "anger." In Exodus 32, the Israelites commit the quintessential sin of worshiping the golden calf. God directs Moses, "Now, therefore, leave Me alone, that my wrath may wax hot against them, and that I may destroy them" (32:10). The Hebrew for "my wrath" is *api*, "my *af*—my anger." We see here an image of God as just the opposite of the "long-suffering divine patience" of *erekh apayim*; here God instead is severe, reactive, and impatient.

When God reveals the thirteen divine attributes—in the very next scene—it is as if God is atoning by transmuting the blazing anger of *api* into "the long deep breath" of *erekh apayim*. God's deepest, truest essence, this text would seem to say, is not vindictive anger but abiding empathy with human imperfection. God endures our sins over the long haul, breathing deeply rather than lashing out in fury each time we transgress against the divine will. Responsibility and punishment for misdeeds remain inescapable features of Jewish theology. But so too does the comfort of *erekh apayim*—the perspective of eternity in which we encounter a God who is patient, long-suffering, and slow enough to anger to forgive our shortcomings.

It is especially fitting that the Thirteen Attributes appears in *N'ilah*, the service that marks Yom Kippur's close with the claim that the "gates of repentance" are slowly swinging shut. The plaintive urgency of *N'ilah* reminds us that our time for repentance is almost up. Just when we might be experiencing the anxiety of knowing that we have not yet truly atoned, the Thirteen Attributes with *erekh apayim* at its center reassures us: God takes the long view. Even if, God forbid, we miss the "deadline" and the gates lock before we have achieved High Holy Day closure, we need not despair. In a world where change moves at lightning speed and equanimity is elusive, the patient, slow-to-anger Long, Deep Breath of *erekh epayim* awaits us always.

௭௸௸

# "Adonai, Adonai"

## THE MESSAGE OF AWE BUT THE SOUND OF COMPASSION

### *Rabbi Sonja Keren Pilz, PhD*

Personally, I like theater. I like the moment when a script invades, conquers, and alters my consciousness for a few hours; and I like the dizziness with which I sometimes leave a theater after an experience that has caught my breath, evoked tears and laughter, touched my heart, and changed my soul.

The day of Yom Kippur is meant to be such an experience. Think of *Kol Nidre*, for example, or the reenactment of the high priest's ritual of old, as the rabbi, cantor, and (in some places) the entire congregation fall facedown on the floor to the diminishing tones of the *Alenu*. For that matter, we may well feel touched, changed, ecstatic, humbled, and forgiven—or at least dizzy—just because we have been fasting all day long. In the larger framework of our entire year's liturgy, the worship of Yom Kippur stands out indeed for dramatic enactment, awe-inspiring texts, and extraordinary experiences, making it a day like no other.

This is what Yom Kippur stands for. What it has meant to me. Until I began to think about the Thirteen Attributes—for this liturgy is so different!

In preparation for this essay, I went back to look at the music for the occasion.[1] Synagogue composers rarely wrote specifically High Holy Day music for the Thirteen Attributes. They settled instead for the familiar melody that they knew from other occasions in the yearly synagogue

---

Rabbi Sonja Keren Pilz, PhD, was ordained at the Abraham Geiger College in Germany in 2015. She has traveled, studied, and taught in Germany, Israel, and the United States. Her first book, *Food and Fear: Metaphors of Bodies and Spaces in the Stories of Destruction*, will be published in 2016.

cycle, especially the recitation of the Thirteen Attributes as the Torah is removed from the ark on the three Pilgrimage Festivals. People who attended services then knew how to sing or hum these lines: *Adonai, Adonai, el rachum v'chanun....* The melody is simple and easily repeatable, like a mantra, where we never go off track, get lost in the rhythm, or have trouble remembering the tune. It is sung not just once, moreover, but three times in succession—like a lullaby that our mother would sing to us or the lullaby we now sing to our children or grandchildren. It is simple and known, familiar and comforting, assuring and soothing.

Our familiarity with this music is only enhanced on the High Holy Days, when we sing it many times: before removing the Torah scrolls on Rosh Hashanah and Yom Kippur morning (*Shacharit*), during the *s'lichot* (penitential prayers) for Yom Kippur evening (*Ma'ariv*), and at the concluding service of *N'ilah*—all together, up to twenty-one times, depending on one's *machzor* and *minhag*, as Rabbi Margaret Moers Wenig teaches.

The lullaby-like melody adds a lighter and calmer tone to the overall solemnity of the High Holy Days. Yom Kippur is by far the most dramatic and awe-inspiring day of our year, the moment when we stand before God, requesting forgiveness for our sins. Yet we retain the soft and gentle festival melody for God's attributes.

A contradiction? Not so very much. Here's why.

For good reason, Yom Kippur is known as the Day of Awe par excellence. As the *Kol Nidre* service begins, we become acutely aware of our standing together in the gathering darkness of the night with the need to face our sins and repent. This is indeed the ultimate moment of truth when the Talmud itself recommends the Thirteen Attributes as the prayer that may induce God to forgive us. It is as if there were something magically potent about it, something giving it the power to remind God of all that is soft and merciful in the divine scheme of things. Maybe too, we may imagine, these same amazing lines will help us forgive both ourselves and others. We too need to feel all that is soft and merciful about them. In the midst of the dramatic turmoil of the highest of the High Holy Days, the Thirteen Attributes is a moment when we yearn to reach out for the tender, the forgiving, the soothing—and find it in the music.

The music for the Thirteen Attributes is, in most cases, influenced by the *nusach* (the traditional sound) of the *Amidah* for the three Pilgrimage Festivals—Pesach, Shavuot, and Sukkot. In traditional diaspora worship, which observes two days of these holidays, we get three additional repetitions of the Thirteen Attributes in the framework of the Torah services during *Shacharit* on each of the festival days—no small number. No wonder people know the sound rather well. The music for the Thirteen Attributes is part of this well-known liturgical-musical heritage that traditional Jews would know from their festival worship and then recognize when it came to Yom Kippur.

*Liturgically* speaking, the Thirteen Attributes probably began with the High Holy Days and then moved from there to the three Pilgrimage Festivals. As the Talmud indicates, they were already considered the way to obtain God's forgiveness, a quality that was necessary for the festivals as well. These three festivals, after all, were crucial agricultural moments that determined the life-or-death issue of harvesting a successful crop. But crops were not assumed back then to be matters of scientific determination. Rather, they were signs of God's judgment. It followed that we need repentance and pardon then as much as we do on the High Holy Days—how else might we hope to influence God's potentially evil decree and avoid famine and starvation?

But the *musical* motif moved in the opposite direction—from the festivals to the High Holy Days, thereby bringing the comforting sound of the three Pilgrimage Festival liturgy into the theologically and emotionally charged tension of the highest day of the year. New melodies for the Thirteen Attributes were not actually *invented* by, for example, Lewandowski and Wohlberg; rather, the old motifs were *preserved* as they had been, providing the lighthearted musical motifs of the three Pilgrimage Festivals, even at the dramatic peaks of the High Holy Days: the *Kol Nidre* service with which Yom Kippur begins and at *N'ilah*, Yom Kippur's end!

When Jewish musical motifs wander from one liturgical context to another, they mix the emotional associations and the theological statements of the two contexts. The music for the Thirteen Attributes is just one example of how words and a specific musical motif connect different occasions in the course of our liturgical year. Whenever this happens, we do not simply refer to the original day from which the music is borrowed; we add that day's tone and ambience to the prayer of the occasion that borrows it.

Yom Kippur marks the peak of the time of year when we turn to God as a king, a judge over our life and death, awaiting divine judgment over the quality of our lives. Imagining a situation as dramatic as this helps us put other things aside and reflect instead on the weightier matter of what God might actually think about us. What would God say to us, having read what our deeds of last year have inscribed in the pages of our book of life? How would we ourselves feel about those we know if we were given God's knowledge of their loneliest, saddest, meanest, angriest, most desperate and miserable moments of the last twelve months? And what might we think of ourselves, knowing, as we actually do, the same things about our own deepest selves?

We might get lost in our thoughts imagining this. We might feel ashamed and sad. We might feel like a child who needs to turn to her parents confessing that she has broken something she knows was dear to them. We might be afraid of getting judged instead of being forgiven. And then we hear and hum the simple tune of *Adonai, Adonai* ... and we feel comforted.

⟨◈⟩

# Cutting God Slack

*Rabbi Jeffrey K. Salkin, DMin*

An old friend, Jeremy, contacted me, and he told me the following tale of woe.

Quite by accident, he had discovered that his cousin Norma had been stealing money from the family business—hundreds of thousands of dollars.

At first, Jeremy was furious with Norma. "How could she have done this? How could she have financially endangered our family like that? My cousin is a thief and a liar. She must pay back every cent she stole—I won't be satisfied until she does."

Welcome to the mode of judgment, the demand for strict, uncompromising justice (*din*): people should get precisely what they deserve.

About a week later, Jeremy changed his tune.

"Poor Norma. I had no idea that she was so needy. Surely, that's the only reason why she would have done such a thing to our family."

Welcome to the mode of mercy, of compassion, of loving-kindness (*rachamim*): people should get the benefit of the doubt.

---

Rabbi Jeffrey K. Salkin, DMin, the senior rabbi of Temple Solel in Hollywood, Florida, is a noted author whose work has appeared in many publications, including the *Wall Street Journal, Reader's Digest*, and the *Forward*. He is editor of *The Modern Men's Torah Commentary: New Insights from Jewish Men on the 54 Weekly Torah Portions* and *Text Messages: A Torah Commentary for Teens*; and author of *Being God's Partner: How to Find the Hidden Link Between Spirituality and Your Work*, the best seller *Putting God on the Guest List: How to Reclaim the Spiritual Meaning of Your Child's Bar or Bat Mitzvah*, and *Righteous Gentiles in the Hebrew Bible: Ancient Role Models for Sacred Relationships* (all Jewish Lights), among other books. He contributed to *We Have Sinned: Sin and Confession in Judaism—Ashamnu and* Al Chet; *All the World: Universalism, Particularism and the High Holy Days*; and *Naming God: Our Father, Our King*—Avinu Malkeinu (all Jewish Lights).

Jeremy was experiencing the cosmic drama that plays out within us all—the battle between justice and mercy, between *din* and *rachamim*.

- A CEO has a loyal but aging employee who is becoming forgetful; his work has not been up to speed for quite some time. By rights (*din*), the boss should let him go. But still (*rachamim*) ...
- A teacher has a student with a failing grade average. If he fails the student (*din*), she will be prevented from going on to the next grade level, and besides, she has tried her best, so maybe a pass would be in order (*rachamim*).
- A policewoman pulls a driver over for going seventy in a fifty-mile-per hour zone. He deserves a hefty ticket (*din*). But he is on his way to the hospital to visit his father. Couldn't she just let him off with a warning (*rachamim*)?

Struggle is central to Judaism—every Jewish holiday centers on it. On Hanukkah, the Maccabees struggled against the Greeks and the forces of assimilation. On Purim, Mordecai and Esther struggled against Haman. On Pesach, Moses struggled against Pharaoh. On Tisha B'Av, Jews of the First and Second Commonwealth struggled against the Babylonians and (later) the Romans who destroyed the Temple in Jerusalem.

But these are conflicts with an obvious good against an obvious evil. They are *struggles*, certainly; but not *dilemmas*. The struggle on the Days of Awe is a dilemma because it pits two equally necessary goods, justice and mercy (*din* and *rachamim*), against one another. Significantly, on these most sacred of days, Judaism sides with *rachamim*. It didn't have to be that way. Infamously, our detractors have sometimes made the mistake of identifying Judaism as a religion of strict legal justice, and that's just not the case.

One of Israel's greatest public intellectuals is Amos Oz, born Amos Klausner, whose father was Yehuda Klausner.

In the 1940s, the Klausner family lived in Jerusalem. Yehuda Klausner dreamed of becoming a best-selling author of scholarly books, like his friend, Israel Zarchi, whose books always sold out within a few days of their printing.

Klausner would privately print his books, and he would take them to Achiasaph's bookstore on King George Street in Jerusalem. Klausner's books sat there in a pile, as he became depressed and discouraged.

Finally, one day he got a call from the bookstore. All of his books had been sold! Yehuda Klausner was elated, and this launched his modest career in scholarly writing.

A few years later, young Amos Oz was visiting Israel Zarchi in his cluttered apartment. Mr. Zarchi left the living room to get Amos a cup of hot cocoa. While Mr. Zarchi was in the kitchen, Amos Oz looked around, and he noticed something under the coffee table.

It was a pile of his father's books.

Israel Zarchi returned to the living room with the cup of cocoa. He saw Amos Oz looking at the pile of his father's books—and he held his index finger to his lips, as if to say: Please don't say anything to your father.

Israel Zarchi had secretly bought all of Klausner's books. And because of that, Yehuda Klausner had thought himself to be a minor commercial success, and because of that, he continued writing.

This is what Amos Oz has said about that incident:

> I have many close and dear friends. And yet, I am not sure that I could do for any of them what Israel Zarchi did for my father. Israel Zarchi was poor. He lived hand to mouth. At a certain moment, he must have said to himself, I can either buy some clothes that I need, or I can buy the three copies of Klausner's book.
>
> And he chose to buy my father's book.[1]

Consider the theology of *Les Miserables*. The poverty-stricken Jean Valjean has committed a minor crime. The policeman, Javert, spends his life hunting him down—the incessant and obsessive commitment to strict justice (*din*).

Jean Valjean, on the other hand, is a man of deep compassion and kindness (*rachamim*), which he demonstrates, over and over, to everyone.

Javert cannot bear the thought of such kindness even within himself. He does nothing that is, strictly speaking, "wrong." Indeed, as an officer of the law, he is the epitome of justice. But we find him despicable—precisely on that account. He refuses to struggle with the reality of a far more nuanced world where justice and mercy must coexist together.

Even God goes through that struggle. Unlike Javert, however, God seeks to keep the *midat hadin* ("attribute of justice") and *midat harachamim* ("attribute of mercy") in balance. The whole purpose of the Days of

Awe is to encourage God to get off the throne of justice and to shuttle to the throne of mercy. God's personality mirrors ours, we say (and vice versa). We are to be like God, not Javert.

This is a genuine struggle—a struggle for which, paradoxically, even God cannot guarantee victory.

> What does God pray? Rav Zutra bar Tuvia said in the name of Rav: "May it be my will that my mercy may suppress my anger, and that my mercy may prevail over my other attributes, so that I may deal with my children with the attribute of mercy and, on their behalf, stop short of the limit of strict justice." (Talmud, Berakhot 7a)

Why do we even come to synagogue on the High Holy Days? Why do we chant God's thirteen attributes—in a form that totally ignores God's "strict justice" side? And why do we focus singularly on God's compassionate side—before the open ark?

Because we hope that our prayers will remind God of who God really is—a God of mercy.

Lest God forget.

⌒⟋⟋⟋⟍

# Becoming God

*Rabbi Dennis C. Sasso, DMin*

Exodus 34:6–7 is, I believe, inappropriately called "the thirteen attributes"—inappropriately, because they are not really attributes. If we work our way through God's self-revelation in Torah, we discover God as a much more profound reality than a super-being with super-attributes like mercy and patience and so on. God is not an entity for which attributes can even be claimed.

It all begins in Exodus 3:14 when we encounter Moses at the burning bush hearing the divine name: *ehyeh asher ehyeh.* Tomes of interpretive literature have emanated from this cryptic statement, inquiring whether *ehyeh* denotes God's "essence" or God's "presence." Context implies the latter: God promises presence to and engagement with Israel—saying elsewhere explicitly, "I will be with you" (3:12). God is the promise of loyal companionship.

A few chapters later, God's ongoing presence is reaffirmed. "I am *YHVH.*" God says, "I appeared to Abraham, Isaac, and Jacob as *el shaddai,* but I did not make myself known to them by my name *YHVH.*... I have now heard the crying of the Israelites ... and have remembered the covenant" (Exodus 6:2–3, 6:5). As the chapter unfolds, God proposes "to free," "to deliver," "to redeem," "to take" Israel as God's people, and to

---

Rabbi Dennis C. Sasso, DMin, has been senior rabbi of Congregation Beth-El Zedeck since 1977. He lectures worldwide on Caribbean and Central American Sephardic Jewry and teaches about Reconstructionism and on interfaith relations. He serves on the board of directors for the United Way of Central Indiana, the Greater Indianapolis Progress Committee, and the Lake Family Institute for Faith and Giving of the IUPUI Center on Philanthropy. He is affiliate professor of Jewish studies at Christian Theological Seminary (Disciples of Christ). He contributed to *All the World: Universalism, Particularism and the High Holy Days* and *Naming God: Our Father, Our King—Avinu Malkeinu* (both Jewish Lights).

"bring them into the land" promised to the ancestors—five guarantees that inspire the custom of four cups of wine plus (eventually) the cup of Elijah at the Passover seder. The name *YHVH* evokes again the confirmation of divine loyalty, companionship, and the redemptive presence of God's covenantal love.

In Exodus 20 we encounter the consummation of all this in the Ten Commandments (literally, Ten Words). They begin with a preamble, proclaiming redemptive loyalty: "I *YHVH* am your God, because [*asher*] ..." (v. 2). *Asher* introduces the concept of "cause," the implication that God's presence follows logically from the covenant. Again, it is divine "presence" that is at stake.

We still know little about who or what God is beyond a loyal covenantal presence. So in Exodus 34:6–7, Moses returns to the mountain to find out more. This time, we get not only a reiteration of that redemptive presence, but also the attributes as, apparently, a set of divine qualities that have found their way into our liturgy. Whether we have here thirteen or, perhaps more accurately, twelve is a matter of punctuation and interpretation. The number thirteen comes from counting the initial *YHVH* twice. I am with those who believe that the first one is part of the introductory statement and not the beginning of the list of attributes proper. Hence, we would read verse 6 not as "*YHVH* passed before him and said, '*YHVH, YHVH* ...'"—but "*YHVH* passed before him and *YHVH* said, '*YHVH* ...'"[1]

Exodus 34 follows the account of the golden calf (chapter 32), where the people defy the prohibition against idolatry and try to reduce the God of Israel to a "thing." The thirteen attributes (*sh'losh esreh midot*)—known also as the "covenant of the thirteen" (*b'rit sh'losh esreh*)—confirm God's forgiveness and the renewal of the covenant even following Israel's infidelity. These words constitute one of the most powerful moments of our penitential season's liturgy. They become foundational for future reflection on the nature of God, and the Midrash sees them as a call to humans to emulate God's qualities: "Just as God is gracious and compassionate, you too be gracious and compassionate."[2]

The book of Jonah, which we read in the afternoon of Yom Kippur as a story of God's infinite will to forgive, reiterates the attributes: "For I know that you are a merciful and gracious God, endlessly patient, most kind ..." (Jonah 4:2). As is well known, our liturgy omits the ending attributes that promise punishment despite God's mercy, and so too does

Jonah, who prefers to conclude with an assertion that God "renounces punishment" (*nicham al hara'ah*). In Jonah, God's loyalty and compassion extend beyond Israel not only to the sinful Ninevites, but to all creation.

But the thirteen attributes are still not actually attributes, in the sense of saying what God *is*. Rather, they refer to God in *relational* terms, for we encounter the divine not as an "essence" but as a "presence"—through experience and in the process of relationship. The biblical and Rabbinic God is not the "Immutable Unmoved Mover" or the "Perfection of Being" that we get in Aristotelian philosophy and, from there, in medieval Muslim, Jewish, and Christian thought. Rather than a static, unmoved entity, the God of biblical and Rabbinic faith is an active, dynamic, changing, responsive reality. God is neither passive nor impassive; God is *compassive*. God is not absolute; God is relational, relevant, and responsive.

Regrettably, tradition has translated *YHVH* as *Adonai*, "my Lord" (*Kyrios* in Greek, *Dominus* in Latin). God thereby morphed into a superanthropomorphic and supernatural being, a mighty monarch and cosmic controller. Such an understanding undermines the best intentions of biblical and Rabbinic theology, where God is not a "being," but a "way of being"; not a "person," but an interactive "process."

All names for God are metaphors, partial expressions of our quest to apprehend and comprehend the divine reality. "Divinity is not in us but through us,"[3] says Rabbi Mordecai Kaplan, for whom God is "the process that makes for salvation"[4] in the universe and through us. This salvation is not a post-mortem, supernatural event, but the natural fulfillment of our human purposes as creatures in the divine image. Worship of God is the act of giving expression to these attributes, not only through word, but also through deed. Idolatry is the opposite—conformity and indifference, prejudice, intellectual and spiritual stagnation. Religion itself can become idolatrous when we think of it merely as a system of symbols, rituals, and practices, rather than an invitation to act in the world and relate to others in keeping with the attributes of mercy, love, trustworthiness, patience, and forgiveness.

Rabbi Harold Schulweis interprets his teacher Rabbi Mordecai Kaplan when he says we should think of God not as the "subject" but as the "predicate" of the sentence. Subjects are "substantive," but God is not a substance, an entity. God is not a noun, but a verb or an adverb, the active part of the sentence. Instead of affirming that "God is just" or "God is love," it is more appropriate to say "justice is godly," "love is godly." In the hymn *Adon Olam*, we say of God, *V'hu hayah v'hu hoveh v'hu yihyeh*, "God *was, is,* and *will* be."[5] Godliness is not a fixed and perfected entity, but a perfecting, life-giving process of constant surprise, possibility, and novelty.

Schulweis prefers to speak of God not in locational terms ("Where is God?"), but in experiential or existential terms ("When is God?"), for God is not a "fact" or "datum" of reality; God is the "factor," the ground of all reality. Questions like "What is God?" or "Who is God?" should be replaced by questions of purpose, "When is God?" and "What for is God?" The "why" of God is an intellectual distraction about putative origins rather than an exploration of divine purpose.

Emmanuel Levinas also speaks of God as other than being and beyond essence. Levinas believes that God is "a direction rather than an end point ... a process ... a mysterious eruption to be pursued but never [fully] possessed." For God is "co-present ... as one approaches the Other in responsibility, that is, in love, goodness and justice."[6]

*YHVH*, the God of the thirteen attributes, is the God of constant becoming and renewal, the God who invites us to live *with* the past, but not *in* the past. Schulweis explains the words *elohim* and *YHVH* as very much in the spirit of traditional Rabbinic thought. *Elohim* represents the world as it is, its actuality. *YHVH* represents the world in its ideality, as it ought to be.[7] The thirteen attributes invite us to become partners of God in transforming the world that is into the world as it ought to be, even as each of us continues the process of becoming from what we are into what we can yet be. That is, after all, the calling of forgiveness and renewal of the High Holy Days.

☙❧

# Anthropology— Encountering the Self

# The Common Thread of Judaism

## GOD'S CHARACTER AND OUR OWN

*Dr. Annette M. Boeckler*

" **A** new species was born: Homo globalis, the large class of people whose identity is strongly defined by their being plugged into global infotainment."[1] So says psychologist Carlo Strenger, in his suggestively labeled book, *The Fear of Insignificance*. "Lives are reduced to careers and the narrative of one's lifetime looks more like a series of achievement graphs ... than the biography of a human being with depth."[2]

Far from our human striving after meaning is the biblical God, whose portfolio has nothing to do with accomplishments and everything to do with character: "Adonai, Adonai, merciful and gracious God, endlessly patient, most kind and truthful, extending kindness to thousands, forgiving sins and transgressions and misdeeds, cleansing" (Exodus 34:6–7).

While Jewish liturgy ends God's *curriculum vitae* here, the actual biblical quotation whence it comes appends a kind of small print: "but by

---

Dr. Annette M. Boeckler is senior lecturer for liturgy at Leo Baeck College in London and manager of its library. She studied theology, Jewish studies, and ancient Near Eastern studies in Germany and Switzerland and *chazzanut* both privately (with Cantor Marcel Lang, *z"l*, and Cantor Jeremy Burko) and at the Levisson Instituut in Amsterdam. She contributed to *All These Vows—Kol Nidre*; *We Have Sinned: Sin and Confession in Judaism*—Ashamnu *and* Al Chet; *May God Remember: Memory and Memorializing in Judaism*—Yizkor; *All the World: Universalism, Particularism and the High Holy Days*; and *Naming God: Our Father, Our King*—Avinu Malkeinu (all Jewish Lights).

no means cleansing. He visits the iniquity of parents upon children and children's children, upon the third and fourth generation." To be sure, God's punishment extends only to the generations that a single person can experience in a single specific family—compared to the thousands of generations that experience God's kindness. But still—God's overabundant mercy is not a carte blanche for happy sinning in the presence of the anyway-always-merciful God.

People outside of Judaism, however, often tend to overemphasize the negativity. They ignore entirely the Rabbinic emphasis on mercy, and they get the biblical part wrong as well, as if the "God of the Old Testament" is altogether judgmental. They often rely here on a version of the thirteen attributes carried later (and selectively) by the prophet Nahum: "God passionate, avenging Adonai, vengeful is Adonai and fierce in wrath, Adonai takes vengeance on his enemies, He rages against his foes. Adonai is endlessly patient and greatly powerful but certainly not cleansing" (Nahum 1:2–3).

But this is a unique utterance by a prophet who is upset about Israel's overconfidence in God's so well-known mercy. Still, the fact that Nahum quotes it demonstrates just how well known the formula had become by his time. Probably no other biblical verse is quoted or alluded to as much as Exodus 34:6–7, where the attributes appear in their most complete form. These "character traits" of God, as it were, can be regarded as a common thread throughout the Bible and, later, a common thread throughout the prayer book, too.

## The Common Thread of Prayer

Citations of God's mercy abound in the Bible and are regularly cited in our liturgy. The daily evening prayer, for example, opens with Psalm 78:38: "He, being merciful, forgave iniquity and would not destroy" (*V'hu rachum, y'khaper avon v'lo yashchit*). *Ashrei* (Psalm 145) perhaps the best-known liturgical psalm of all, said traditionally three times daily, insists (verse 8), "Adonai is gracious and compassionate, slow to anger and abounding in kindness" (*chanun v'rachum Adonai, erekh apayim ug'dol chased*). The core text of the *tashlich* ceremony (for the afternoon of the first day of Rosh Hashanah) combines Micah 7:18 with an allusion to Exodus 34:6–7 itself: "Who is a God like You, forgiving iniquity and remitting transgression? [God] who has not maintained his wrath forever against the remnant of his own people, because He loves graciousness!" In the afternoon of Yom Kippur itself we read a parody in which a prophet quotes God's attributes as the justification of not doing God's will in the first place. Jonah explains to God, "I fled beforehand ... because I know that You are a compassionate and gracious God, endlessly patient, most kind, renouncing punishment" (*el chanun v'rachum erekh apayim v'rav chesed v'nicham al hara'ah*) (Jonah 4:2–3). After chanting *Kol Nidre* we quote the end of another Torah passage containing God's attributes— Moses's plea for mercy, after the sin of the scouts:

> "Adonai, endlessly patient, most kind, forgiving sins and transgressions, yet certainly not cleansing, but visiting the iniquity of parents upon children, upon the third and fourth generation: pardon, I pray, the iniquity of this people according to your great kindness, as You have forgiven this people ever since Egypt." And Adonai said, "I pardon, as you have asked." [*Adonai erekh apayim v'rav chesed nosei avon vafesha v'nakeh ... s'lach na la'avon ha'am hazeh k'godel chasdekha.... Vayomer Adonai salachti kidvarekha.*] (Numbers 14:18–19)

As with Jonah, Moses here quotes God to God—not as in Exodus 34 where God addresses Moses.

And these are just the prayer-book citations! Were we to cite biblical instances that did not make it into our prayers, the list would be even further enlarged. No fewer than twenty-eight times the Bible alludes to God's attributes of mercy, which had obviously become a liturgical formula from very early times.[3] Later biblical books even use them liturgically within the Bible itself, as in the post-exilic prayer (fifth century BCE) of Nehemiah 9:16–17:

> They—our ancestors—acted presumptuously; they stiffened their necks and did not obey your commandments.... But You, a God of forgiveness [*elo'ah s'lichot*], gracious and merciful, endlessly patient and most kind [*chanun v'rachum, erekh apayim v'rav chesed*], did not abandon them.

Here we find an early form of *vidui-s'lichot* (a confession with prayers for mercy) that eventually characterize the Yom Kippur liturgy of today.

## Exodus 34:6–7: The Paradigmatic List Itself

Of all these lists of God's mercies, however, the best known to Jews is Exodus 34:6–7 itself. It recurs at festival day worship throughout the year and in elevated liturgical circumstances that make it memorable: it is chanted and is repeated three times in front of the open ark itself. The list became a leitmotif of Yom Kippur especially, a regular feature of the *s'lichot* part of the service—the poetry celebrating God's mercy. Exodus 34:6–7 is usually sung movingly by the whole congregation or a choir.

Some features of Exodus 34:6–7 are extraordinary. Above all, Exodus 34:6–7 is presented as God's own words about Himself. This literary device of a self-revelation conveys to the words the highest truth and authority. The Talmud even accords them the status of a divine prayer!

> Rabbi Yochanan said: Were it not explicitly written in the verse, it would be impossible to say this, but it actually teaches that the Holy One, Blessed be He, wrapped Himself (in a *tallit*) like a prayer leader and showed Moses the order of prayer. He said to him: Whenever Israel sins, let them perform this procedure before Me [let the prayer leader put on a *tallit* and publicly recite the thirteen attributes of mercy] and I will forgive them. (Talmud, Rosh Hashanah 17b)

The recital of these words thus received a magical aura symbolic of certain redemption.

Exodus 34:6–7 is the most complete of all the Torah's lists of attributes—so complete, in fact, that (in the biblical original, although not in the liturgical citation of it) the attribute of justice is contained as if it were a part of God's mercy.

Stylistically speaking, Exodus 34:6–7 is akin to the Priestly Blessing (Numbers 6:24–26), in that both passages contain a growing number of words in each successive content unit: After the introductory repetition of God's name (*Adonai, Adonai*), Exodus 34 provides 3 words (*el rachum v'chanun*—in v. 6a), then 5 words (v. 6b) and 7 words (v. 7a). Numbers 6:24–26—the Priestly Blessing—builds similarly through 3-, 5-, and 7-word units, adding up to 15 words. The Exodus passage then concludes with a prose passage (which our liturgy omits). It too has 15 words, so that (not counting the introductory double *Adonai* ) we get a total 2 × 15 words, twice the Priestly Blessing, that is—the first 15 about God's mercy, the second 15 about God's justice. To count within these first 15 words of mercy 13 divine attributes connects God's signature with our daily statutory prayer, the weekday *Amidah*, which contains 13 blessings in its main middle part.

The very duplication of God's four-letter name, *YHVH* (pronounced *Adonai* in the situation of prayer), is interesting in that the Masoretic text prints it with a musical sign separating the two names. Tradition interprets the sign as an indication of intensity—like the calls elsewhere of "Abraham, Abraham" (Genesis 22:11), "Jacob, Jacob" (Genesis 46:2), and "Moses, Moses" (Exodus 3:4).[4] But they are also a reminder of the style used in prophetic books to convey comfort: Isaiah, for instance, where God says, "I, I" (*Anokhi, anokhi*—51:12); "Comfort, comfort!" (*Nachamu, nacham*—40:1); "Awake, awake!" (*Uri, uri*—51:9; 52:1); and elsewhere as well. The repetition calls for elevated attention—attention for a message of comfort.

Finally, Exodus 34:6–7 is directly linked with the second commandment:

> You shall not make for yourself a sculptured image, or any likeness of what is in the heavens above, or on the earth below, or in the waters under the earth. You shall not bow down to them or serve them. For I, Adonai your God, am an impassioned God, visiting the guilt of the parents upon the children, upon the third and upon the fourth generation of those who reject Me, but showing kindness to the thousandth generation of those who love Me and keep my commandments. (Exodus 20:4–6)

Incredibly enough, the Exodus 34 list follows immediately upon the sin of making a golden calf (Exodus 32), the prime biblical example of disobeying the second commandment! The commandment stresses God's justice, however, while Exodus 34:6–7 (after the actual event has occurred) highlights God's mercy!

## Mercy as Characteristic and Character

According to the prophet Joel, it is God's attribute of mercy that makes *t'shuvah* (the repentant "return" to God) possible. "Return to Adonai, your God," Joel says, "for He is merciful and gracious, endlessly patient, most kind, and renouncing punishment" (2:13). There would not be a people of Israel still today and no divine-human relationship altogether, for that matter, if God did not have exactly this kind of portfolio.

*T'shuvah* ("return") requires knowing the ideal to which one needs to return. Maimonides, therefore, taught:

> As God is called "merciful," you should be merciful; as God is called "gracious," you should be gracious.... Similarly, the prophets called God by other titles: "endlessly patient" [and] "most kind" ... to inform us that these are good and just paths. We are to accustom ourselves to these paths and resemble God to the extent of our ability."[5]

Maimonides labels this "the path of God" (*derekh Adonai*), insisting that by training ourselves to emulate these characteristics over and over again, they will "become a fixture of our character."[6] In the end, therefore, the discipline of approaching God means approaching ourselves as well, in the consummate human task of developing character.

◌⟩⟨◌

# Not What We Were
# but What We Will Be

*Rabbi Joshua M. Davidson*

When I read the Thirteen Attributes, what matters most to me is not what we know about God but what God seems to know about us. "You do not treat them according to their evil" (*Lo kh'ra'atam tigmol*), we say. Why not? What does God know about us that we ought to remember, ourselves?

It all begins with that book of life that we talk about so much when the High Holy Days arrive. *L'shanah tovah tikatevu v'techatemu*, we say, "May you be written and sealed for a good year." The passive voice "*be* written and sealed" makes it seem as if we ourselves have nothing to do with it all. But actually, as the *Un'taneh Tokef* makes perfectly clear, the record of our days is inscribed in our own hand! All year long, we write its entries, and then we even sign it (see Prayers of Awe, *Who by Fire, Who by Water*—Un'taneh Tokef, 29). Yom Kippur is the day we get to open it and leaf through its pages ... our childhood days of promise and new adventure; the growing-up years with opportunity but also uncertainty and self-doubt; and the dog-eared pages of adulthood, highlighted by joys and achievements, but also failures and disappointments, missteps and resentments. Satisfaction, love, and belonging; bitterness, loss, and loneliness ... the book of life recounts them all. On Yom Kippur we revisit them.

---

Rabbi Joshua M. Davidson is the senior rabbi of Congregation Emanu-El of the City of New York. Prior to his appointment in 2013, he served for eleven years as the senior rabbi of Temple Beth El of Northern Westchester and five as assistant and associate rabbi at New York City's Central Synagogue. He contributed to *Naming God: Our Father, Our King*—Avinu Malkeinu (Jewish Lights).

## Opening the Book of Our Days

Before Sting's musical *The Last Ship* opened on Broadway, the sixteen-time Grammy winner spoke about his career, and *New York Times* columnist David Brooks reflected on it: Sting had reached a period in his life and work where "the muse abandoned him ... for days, then weeks, then months, then years.... But [when Sting] went back and started thinking about his childhood in the north of England ... on a street that led down to a shipyard where some of the world's largest ocean-going vessels were built ... when Sting did this, his creativity was reborn." Most of us are no different, Brooks concluded; we too may "have an urge, maybe more as we age, to circle back to the past and touch the places and things of childhood." Over time we forget the dreams that launched us. "Life has a way of blowing [us] off course," Brooks writes.[1] When we can remind ourselves of what we had hoped for our lives, we reignite aspirations for what we might yet become—and we are always in the state of becoming.

Yom Kippur is the Day of Atonement. "Atonement" is a remarkably descriptive word. Its root, from Middle English, is "at one." It means to reconcile, to harmonize, to "make one," to make whole the disparate entries in our book of life—our joys *and* our regrets, all those seemingly disconnected, fragmentary experiences that, together (and *only* together), define our lives. God apparently "doesn't treat us according to our evil," but according to all that we are, our entire book of entries.

## At-One-Ment

Rabbi Steven Leder tells an insightful tale about his rabbinical school class in homiletics. One day, his professor cut the newspaper's obituary section into pieces and distributed them randomly to the students. Their task was to compose the eulogy for the person whose obituary they had received, to create a life story from the bare bones of information the paper provided. The students needed to imagine their subjects' life circumstances, their joys, mistakes, successes, and heartbreaks, everything that gives life substance and meaning. Leder later comprehended what he hadn't at the time: the essence of that assignment was to teach that "every day we are creating the details, acts of love, stories, visions, and legacy of our lives.... We write [them] with the pen of our lives."[2]

On Yom Kippur we take time out from writing, to reflect on the story we have composed so far. But with the shofar's final blast, we pick up the pen anew. We cannot rewrite the past. But we can begin a next chapter in which yesterday's missteps become the first steps to brighter tomorrows. The Talmud teaches, "Great is repentance, for through it [even] premeditated sins are accounted as though they were merits" (Yoma 86b). Every one of our mistakes can prompt us to become more compassionate and loving. Our repentance (if it is real), our *t'shuvah* (if it is heartfelt), can birth great acts of goodness. If we have caused pain, we can commit ourselves to soothing it. If we have done wrong, we can seek to make amends. The shofar beckons us to bridge estrangement, to reach out to those we have hurt ... and, except in extreme cases, to those who have hurt us.

Forgiving is not easy. Sometimes the hurt feels too great, the wounds too raw. And forgiving is especially difficult when we yearn for an apology that never comes. But repairing relationships cannot depend on having every offense explained. There are certain aspects of the people we love we will never understand. How often we are unaware even of our own mistakes, unable to fathom even our own motivations! Why should we necessarily expect more of others? Yom Kippur entreats us to forgive them.

And to forgive ourselves, which may be the greater challenge. Reading through the ledger in our book of life, our greatest regrets are often the mistakes, missed opportunities, and destructive behaviors that we perceive as self-inflicted wounds. God may not "treat us according to our evil," but we tend to define ourselves that way. And unlike God, we make the further mistake of doubting we can do any better.

Fred Shoemaker, a renowned golf instructor, wonders why golfers get so upset after hitting bad shots. And this is his explanation: "The ... reason people get upset after a bad shot is that they think they are going to do it again." And then he offers a bit of practical wisdom not only for golfers: "Just because you did something once [or even many times] does not mean that you will do it again. Your future is not determined by your past."[3]

Our future is not determined by our past. Judaism categorically rejects determinism. It insists on our embracing the power to change. Says the Yiddish proverb, "You are what you are, not what you were."[4] God treats us not according to our evil—*lo kh'ra'atam tigmol*—but according to our potential.

## Not What You Were but What You Will Be

Yom Kippur defies the commonplace notion that a fork in the road, once bypassed, can never be traveled. Yes, often enough, "way leads on to way,"[5] but we can always start anew. We all know people who become disenchanted with a first career but then bravely return to school, or who suffer devastating reversals in their businesses but manage to retrench and to rebuild. Who has not marveled at the heartbroken who pick themselves up from failed relationships, even marriages, to give life and love another chance, or been humbled by survivors who suffer sickness or loss but find the strength to carry on?

Having taken the wrong fork along life's complicated pathway need not doom us to remain in pain. Having been hurt by others, we need not remain embittered. But whether we shackle future dreams to past disappointments, that choice is completely ours.

As a young child Rachel Naomi Remen would make *Kiddush* with her grandfather. "*L'chaim!*—to life!" he would say, smiling.

Once she asked him, "Is it to a happy life, Grandpa?"

"It is just 'To life!' *Neshume-le*," he answered.

"Seeing the confusion on my face," Remen writes, "he told me that *L'chaim!* meant that no matter what difficulty life brings, no matter how hard or painful or unfair life is, life is holy.... *L'chaim!* is a way of living life ... of choosing life."[6]

At whatever page the book of life lies open, its message on Yom Kippur should be the imperative of hope; for Yom Kippur, writes Rabbi Jacob Rudin, "belongs with tomorrow and not with yesterday." It is the day the shofar calls: "Peace, peace be to your broken heart. Let it be put together again and made whole."[7]

According to an old custom, the fragments of the glass broken by the groom at a wedding are saved as good-luck amulets. Today, couples sometimes collect the pieces and include them in the design of a new ritual object: a *Kiddush* cup perhaps, or a mezuzah, or a set of candlesticks. The Day of Atonement—the day of at-one-ment—insists that God sees beyond what we were to what we still can be. Can we do any less? Believing in our own power to grow, to heal, and to be made whole, we can recast the broken fragments of our lives into new and powerful entries in our book of life—for the end of the story has yet to be written.

*ᏮᎥᎶ*

# A Divine Gardener, the Human Face, and a Thousand Acts of Mercy

## INNOVATIVE INSIGHTS FROM THE NEW REFORM *MACHZOR*

*Rabbi Edwin Goldberg, DHL*

When creating the current *machzor* for the Reform Movement (2015), the editors viewed the Thirteen Attributes as more than one more traditional text to be rendered; they saw it more centrally as the very heart of the High Holy Day message. In a single sentence, it focuses worshipers on God's compassionate side (and by extension, ours) over God's judgmental temperament. To get the *machzor* right is to get the Thirteen Attributes right.

---

Rabbi Edwin Goldberg, DHL, served as coordinator of the Central Conference of American Rabbis (CCAR) editorial committee on the CCAR *machzor Mishkan HaNefesh*, published in 2015. He has a doctorate in Hebrew letters from Hebrew Union College–Jewish Institute of Religion and is the senior rabbi at Temple Sholom of Chicago. He is author of *Saying No and Letting Go: Jewish Wisdom on Making Room for What Matters Most* (Jewish Lights). He contributed to *We Have Sinned: Sin and Confession in Judaism—Ashamnu and Al Chet; May God Remember: Memory and Memorializing in Judaism—Yizkor; All the World: Universalism, Particularism and the High Holy Days;* and *Naming God: Our Father, Our King—Avinu Malkeinu* (all Jewish Lights).

Throughout the *machzor* we find the theme of moving God from the throne of judgment to the throne of mercy. We plead for *malkeinu* (our distant ruler) to be *avinu* (our loving parent). We see God challenge Jonah to care for human beings as much as for a plant. Nevertheless, even in Reform liturgy (which omits so much of the penitential poetry added throughout the Middle Ages), the most commonly recited prayer remains the statement of our sins. They go together, of course. We sin, so we need divine compassion. But the traditional emphasis on human sinfulness sometimes overwhelms the message of God's compassion—and, therefore, of our own inherent nature that allows us, too (as made in God's image), to act compassionately in a world where we can be good as well as evil.

As is widely known, the thirteen attributes first appear not in the *machzor* but in the book of Exodus, after the instance of the golden calf and the following rapprochement between God and Israel. The words are declared as Moses is looking at God's back, as it were. Why God's back? Michael Lerner, in his book *Jewish Renewal*, has written that by looking at God's back, Moses effectively sees what God sees. And what does God see? God views the world through eyes of compassion and acceptance.[1] In short, the Days of Awe are about our seeing the world through the loving eyes of God.

How does our new Reform *machzor, Mishkan HaNefesh,* accentuate this approach? We begin with the title itself: *mishkan* is the place of God's dwelling. On the Days of Awe, the synagogue takes on a particularly sacred hew. The Torah scrolls are dressed in white, we expect sermons that change our lives, the music is especially lofty and deep, and the community as a whole assembles like no other time in the year. The synagogue may be many things on other days, but on Rosh Hashanah and Yom Kippur, one cannot miss the fact that it is a *mishkan*, a sanctuary, our modern equivalent to the desert Tabernacle where God came to dwell. As for *nefesh*, the *nefesh* is our individual inner soul, the part of us that is distinctively our own, knowable in all its depth only to ourselves and to God. The High Holy Days become the single moment in the calendar when we, personally, become aware of entering a sacred, communal space while at the same time creating equally sacred but personalized space for our own inherent loneliness. We enter the *mishkan* so we can see the world through God's perspective and then apply that perspective to our own lives. We remember what God finds most important and then we judge ourselves by that standard. Paradoxically, we are *judged* by our *compassion*.

How is this lesson conveyed by the *machzor*? Consider the Yom Kippur evening service. During the *s'lichot* (penitential prayers) section, we present the Thirteen Attributes with a refrain showing the gap between our shortcomings and God's benevolence.

> We are insolent—
> but You are compassionate and gracious.
>
> We are stubborn and stiff-necked—
> but You are slow to anger.
>
> We persist in doing wrong—
> but You are the essence of mercy.[2]

We then ponder what might happen if we could see God's face—not as God actually is (even Moses could not see that), but within our own hearts. It is a variation on a *piyyut* by Yehudah Halevi, who wondered, in his own well-known liturgical staple, "Where shall I find You?" (a poem we use elsewhere in the *machzor*, as part of the *Avodah* service.[3] But our poem here is original, one of many compositions in the *machzor* by Rabbi Sheldon Marder. It evokes another *piyyut* associated with Yom Kippur, the short conclusion to the confession that appears regularly throughout the liturgy of Yom Kippur, *Ki Anu Amekha* ("We are your people ...").[4] God appears there in a set of reciprocal relationships with Israel, for example: "We are Your people; and You are our God.... We are Your flock; and You are our shepherd." We introduce the image of a garden and its loving gardener. Like a garden, we are potentially in a state of growth, but requiring nurture lest we fill with weeds, forget how to blossom, or wither and die. As the poem progresses, however, its emphasis is not just on God. We need God's care, but equally, we need to be tender toward each other as well as toward ourselves.

> If I could see God's face within my heart ...
> I'd see the face of a Gardener—
> compassionate to weed and flower alike, patiently
> pruning, graciously planting,
> loving the endless hours of tending and nurturing the
> earth—seeds, roots, all that grows;

and true to the essence of the gardener's work:
forgiving the fallen branches, the withered petals, the
cracked stones, the broken stems.

If I could see God's face within my heart ...
I'd see the human face in a thousand acts of mercy—
the one who gives bread to the hungry and shelters the
lost, who hears the voice of grief
and makes room for the stranger;
who brings relief to the blind, the bent, the unjustly
imprisoned;
and is true to the essence of holy work:
defying evil, healing brokenness, easing pain;
and, in the end, forgiving ourselves as God forgives us.[5]

The movement from petitioning God for kindness to "forgiving ourselves as God forgives us" was the result of long and hard discussion, through which the *machzor* editors came to understand that tearing ourselves apart with remorse is actually detrimental to constructing better, repentant selves. Yes, an honest assessment and recognition of our moral failings must occur, but there should also be compassion and understanding for our imperfections. By the end of Yom Kippur, our *machzor* should have charted a path that acknowledges our errors, but also the goodness we have performed and our hope to grow in goodness in the year ahead.

One major innovation in *Mishkan HaNefesh* that reflects this approach is the section we introduce called *Hakarat Hatov*, "Recognizing the Good." It forms part of our *s'elichot* section for Yom Kippur morning (pp. 312–13) and Yom Kippur afternoon (pp. 424–25) and balances the accent on our sins by a list of the good acts we have performed as well.

Let us affirm the good we have done;
let us acknowledge our acts of healing and repair ...

For the good we have done
by acting with self-restraint and self-control;

For the good we have done
through acts of generosity and compassion;

> For the good we have done
> by offering our children our love and support....[6]

Worshipers used to the more traditional Yom Kippur focus on sin alone may find it jarring to see this balance between sin on one hand and virtue on the other. We were not the first, however, to recognize the fullness of human nature and the need to appreciate the good that is in us. As a model for our approach, we looked, in part, to Rav Nachman of Breslov, whose words we included:

> Always look for the good
> in yourself.
>
> And remember:
> Joy is not incidental to your spiritual quest;
> it is vital.
>
> For so it is written (Isaiah 55:12):
> "You will go out through joy,
> and be led forth in peace."
> Focus on the good in yourself;
> take joy in what is good,
> and you will be led forth from inner darkness.[7]

For the editors of the *machzor*, Rav Nachman captures not just a balanced view on our moral frailty and goodness, but also the essence of the thirteen attributes and their connection to the repentance of the day. We are chastened by guilt but vouchsafed by a loving God whose very insistence on divine compassion leads us toward showing our own compassion—to others and to ourselves.

Remember the old Rav Nachman parable? One year, in some mythical kingdom far away, the entire stock of grain became poisoned. Anyone who ate it would become insane. Grain had been stored from years past, but only a small amount. The king fell into a quandary. Should people eat and become crazy? Or starve to death? Finally the king decided to feed the people the contaminated grain. But he reserved a little of the unpoisoned grain for a trusted advisor, the king said, so someone will know the rest of us are crazy.

That mythical kingdom turns out to be not so far away after all. It could very well be ourselves. With their emphasis on mercy and gentleness, their awareness of human brokenness, their affirmation of vulnerability, and their ethic of forgiveness, the thirteen attributes are analogous to that unpoisoned grain. While everyone else seems to be living insane lives, filled with unhealthy competition, bruised egos, skewed values, and inappropriate feelings of shame, it is surely the task of religion in our time to preserve for our planet a vision of compassion and a visage of what God who personifies it would have us do.

With its single-minded focus on sin and punishment, the traditional *machzor* is akin to the poisoned grain. On the day when we starve for repentance, we do indeed require reminders of our sins and the regrets that such awareness ought to occasion. But too much of that poisons us; we become overly soured on who we, personally, are—as on human nature itself. We grow insane with a jaundiced view of humanity at large and ourselves as part and parcel of it. So God insists on the attributes of mercy as the antidote. It is, I think, the innovative genius of *Mishkan HaNefesh* that leads us to apply the lesson of these attributes to the larger perspective on human nature as a whole. The Days of Awe inevitably leave their mark on how we see the human condition. We proclaim God's attributes not just for what they say about God, but for what they imply about us, God's creatures. At our best, we too are compassionate, gentle, and good. We should avoid the inevitable madness that too much self-incrimination evokes.

To be sure, the issue is *too much* recrimination. The thirteen attributes don't just let us off the hook; we remain responsible for our actions; there are consequences for wrongdoing, and even the best of us approaches the High Holy Days knowing we are guilty as much as we are good. But after centuries of overemphasizing guilt, it is time to balance the picture. Our relationship with God, when healthy, is not about castigation and guilt alone. It is about love and support. It is about holding ourselves responsible but never giving up on ourselves as able to reach the moral heights that God intends. It is about the garden reaching for the sun and the gardener who cares about our doing so.

✺

# Like God

## NOT PERFECT, BUT LIVING UP TO OUR BEST SELVES

*Ruth W. Messinger*

Regularly during the High Holy Day services we recite the enumerated attributes of God, perhaps because we *ourselves* need regularized reminders of the many ways in which the mysterious world force whom we call divinity cares for and tends to us.[1] The world does not always testify to such kindness after all! Nor, for that matter, does the Bible itself. Both nature and human behavior, on one hand, and our sacred literature, the Bible first and foremost, on the other, are much less sanguine in their observation of the way things really are. But here, at least, in our prayer book, the vindictiveness of God that we know much of from elsewhere in our text is not in evidence. Rather, we speak on this holy day of the positive attributes of God and of a God who is compassionate and caring—a God, as it were, trying to live up to the best.

This God is powerful, kind, merciful, gracious, and forgiving—and so, presumably, are we when we too are at our best. These, we recognize, are the qualities that we need more of when we fail to become our very best selves, when we do not manage to offer proper care and compassion. Especially on Yom Kippur, we make a point of rehearsing what we (like God) ought to strive to become, because this is the day when we atone for

---

Ruth W. Messinger is the president of American Jewish World Service (AJWS). She contributed to *Who by Fire, Who by Water*—Un'taneh Tokef; *All These Vows*—Kol Nidre; *We Have Sinned: Sin and Confession in Judaism*—Ashamnu *and* Al Chet; *All the World: Universalism, Particularism and the High Holy Days*; and *Naming God: Our Father, Our King*—Avinu Malkeinu (all Jewish Lights).

those moments when we fall short of such a goal. With our lesser selves in mind, we hear that God, at least, comes through, for when we need it most, God is slow to anger, ready to pardon, and righteous in dealing with us.

There are times when others depend on us to come through similarly for them. If we are made in God's image, we too should live up to our best when called upon to exercise our partnership with God in repairing the world through the higher form of justice that demands a perspective, above all, of mercy. If God did not manage to complete creation but left it up to us to carry on where God left off, then we too should not be dismayed by the thought that we cannot so easily do all that must be done; but (again, like God) we must do *what* we can, and all *that* we can, to improve the world. We should at least live up to our best, as we say God does.

If, indeed, we are God's partners in this enterprise, then these are attributes that we should want to adopt and mirror as enhancements of "the best" of who we are, of what we do, and of how we make a difference. How distinctively divine—and thus, how distinctively human as well—is the capacity to be gracious to others, to be patient in our work with them, and to be forgiving if they are not always with us in our endeavors. What a gift it is to have power—yes, power—and to employ it personally for good; to summon up the qualities of patience and mercy that we have recognized in God and to engage others in this work of world construction.

Two sides to the very same coin are at stake here. From God's perspective, we human beings are asked to strive to be more than what we sometimes are. From the human reading of the record we call the Bible, we see that God too must struggle to live up to the divine better self. How alike we are, then, we humans and our God. The reading of the attributes becomes very personal. This is how God is, yes, but more importantly, this is how we can be—how we should be. We are to mirror the merciful attributes of God and apply them to make our own positive and everlasting difference in the world. It is our own kindness, not just God's, that is at the heart of these thirteen attributes of the divine.

We are told that God is merciful in acting "like a father to his children, to prevent them from falling." We should, accordingly, be ready to hold up others—individuals and communities—when they are in danger of falling themselves. Especially when others do not respond with immediate gratitude, say, or when they do not come through as we wish, despite our greatest efforts to help, then we, like God, must be gracious in reaching out again and again and be patient and kind in nurturing them until they are capable of responding.

For American Jewish World Service (AJWS), these attributes, the specific words that compose them, and the overall lesson for human nature that they convey, have special resonance. It is our intention as representatives of the Jewish People to rally what is best within us—the best, that is, that is in God and that has been given now to us as our most precious qualities—and to act, therefore, with constant respect for the humanity of those who lack the power and privilege that we enjoy. We employ our own privilege and power to support them in their own development; we show kindness and patience to those who are trying to make their own way. We strive for the compassion, grace, and forgiveness that we have identified as attributes of God because we see ourselves as partners to God who share the possibility of those same attributes ourselves.

We at AJWS identify these attributes as simply the way we should be in the world. We believe that each of us, always, whether personally or in our work, should be like God: striving for compassion, kindness, and forgiveness as we face the ongoing challenge of taking up where God left off.

These sentiments are powerfully present in this observation by Rabbi Lord Jonathan Sacks:

> We are here to make a difference, to mend the fractures of the world, a day at a time, an act at a time, for as long as it takes to make it a place of justice and compassion where the lonely are not alone, the poor not without help; where the cry of the vulnerable is heeded and those who are wronged are heard.... We know God less by contemplation than by emulation. The choice is not between "faith" and "deeds," for it is by our deeds that we express our faith and make it real in the life of others and the world.[2]

ᏯᏘᏂᎾᎧ

# Mercy

## WHO NEEDS IT?

*Rabbi David A. Teutsch, PhD*

Before we can sincerely acknowledge wrongdoing out loud, we must admit it to ourselves. Such self-acknowledgment is painful, so most of us undertake it only if something positive can be accomplished by our doing so. If we look at offenses against other people, for example (as opposed to those we commit against God), we see that they involve a three-step process: acknowledging our error, trying earnestly to repair the damage, and seeking forgiveness from those we have hurt. The incentives for undertaking this task include restoring damaged relationships, building a more harmonious community, salvaging our reputation, and reestablishing trust—all of which makes it possible to work together, to achieve collaboratively what we cannot accomplish alone, and to mitigate the pain of loneliness and broken ties with those whose company we enjoy. We have all experienced at least some of these benefits at work or school and with families, colleagues, and friends. This sort of reconciliation happens

---

Rabbi David A. Teutsch, PhD, is the Wiener Professor of Contemporary Jewish Civilization and director of the Center for Jewish Ethics at the Reconstructionist Rabbinical College, where he served as president for nearly a decade. He was editor in chief of the seven-volume *Kol Haneshamah* prayer book series. His book *A Guide to Jewish Practice: Everyday Living* won the National Jewish Book Award for Contemporary Jewish Life and Practice. He is also author of *Spiritual Community: The Power to Restore Hope, Commitment and Joy* (Jewish Lights) and several other books. He contributed to *Who by Fire, Who by Water*—Un'taneh Tokef; *All These Vows*—Kol Nidre; *We Have Sinned: Sin and Confession in Judaism*—Ashamnu *and* Al Chet; *May God Remember: Memory and Memorializing in Judaism*—Yizkor; *All the World: Universalism, Particularism and the High Holy Days*; and *Naming God: Our Father, Our King*—Avinu Malkeinu (all Jewish Lights).

regularly, not just on Yom Kippur, and even though it involves owning up to one's inner failures, it is primarily interpersonal.

By contrast, the effort at *t'shuvah* ("repentance") that is at the heart of Yom Kippur is within the self—we are addressing the divine within ourselves. Only in theory is it "interpersonal," because the other "person" involved is now God, and unlike human beings whom we have hurt, God does not engage in obvious dialogue with us as we go about saying we are sorry, though if we listen carefully, we can hear the whispered voice of the divine within ourselves. Although Jewish tradition imagines Yom Kippur to be a matter between the self and God as king, shepherd, and judge, I experience *t'shuvah* as reconnecting to the divine within myself. From that perspective, repentance on Yom Kippur is an internal thing, a matter of personally owning up to the shortcomings that we may have hidden from ourselves for a very long time.

What makes the process hard is that we can never achieve moral perfection no matter how hard we try. According to Rabbinic tradition, if we were to be measured solely by the standard of *din* ("strict justice"), we would be adjudged inadequate. We depend on *rachamim* ("mercy") to be judged worthy. But here, too, acknowledgment of moral failure generally requires the prior belief that we have something to gain through the process. We speak as if forgiveness from the judge and reconciliation with the king were the gains, as indeed, in theory, they are. But only in theory, since these changes are internal to the self rather than external. They are hardly as measurable or as concrete as the changes in relationship that *t'shuvah* can bring when it comes to other human beings. What, we should ask, are the perceived benefits that accrue from repentance over sins against God?

The answer is that they are matters of our inner lives, of what we might call our souls. To begin with, we simply feel better about ourselves. Doing our best when no one else is looking requires virtue, or moral character; acknowledging failure and resolving to do better *builds* moral character. Atonement leads to newfound self-respect and a fresh sense of wholeness. It puts an end to avoidance and denial that close off part of the self. It brings a sense of renewal, of return to a path of goodness, of inner peace.

However, we can attain those benefits only if we are able to forgive ourselves, and that is far easier said than done.

Paradoxically, we often find it harder to forgive ourselves than to forgive others. We have high expectations of ourselves and become deeply distressed when we have to face the fact that we have failed to meet those expectations in some way. It is easier to take a more contextualized, gentler view of others' failings than of our own. The *t'shuvah* process requires seeing some inherent good in ourselves so that we can own up to the bad and still be left with a balanced and constructive overall view of ourselves.

The Rabbis of old were familiar with this issue. They dealt with it by projecting it onto God. The Talmud thus pictures God praying, "May it be my will that my mercy [*rachamim*] suppress my anger and prevail over my other attributes so that I deal with my children out of mercy and stop short of strict justice [*din*]" (Berakhot 7a). God seeks the capacity to forgive within the divine self, just as we do in our human selves, because we are made *b'tzelem elohim*, "in God's image"—which I understand as meaning "with a spark of the divine within us." We can properly reclaim the Talmudic projection as our own internal aspiration; God's prayer is really our prayer: "May it be my will that my mercy [*rachamim*] suppress my anger and prevail over my other attributes so that I deal with *myself* out of mercy and stop short of strict justice [*din*]." That is to say, "May I find the capacity within myself to acknowledge my inner failings, do *t'shuvah*, forgive myself, and reconcile myself with the divine aspect within me."

So *t'shuvah* requires that we see ourselves as mostly good, as mostly doing worthwhile things with our lives. Jack Kornfield tells about an African tribe called the Balemba. When someone in the tribe behaves irresponsibly or unjustly, the tribe is called together, the person is put in the middle, and everyone in the circle takes a turn telling all the good things that person has done and been over his or her lifetime. When the recounting is complete, a feast is held to welcome the person back into the tribe. When we are in touch with the good in ourselves and have hope about our capacity to face our wrongdoing and return to wholeness, we are ready to do *t'shuvah* within ourselves and between ourselves and God.[1]

It should be clear by now that I do not imagine God to be a personal being "out there" somewhere. For me, God is the unifying force of the universe, which Rabbi Mordecai Kaplan described as the life of nature, and the divinity within us that moves us toward living harmoniously with each other and with that greater life. How fully we live in the light of the divine depends in part upon how effectively we do *t'shuvah*, removing the barrier of alienation that prevents us from awareness of the divine presence working within us and around us.

The Thirteen Attributes occurs in the Yom Kippur liturgy as part of the buildup to the principal litanies of sins, *Ashamnu* and *Al Chet* (see Prayers of Awe, *We Have Sinned: Sin and Confession in Judaism—* Ashamnu *and* Al Chet). The Thirteeen Attributes prepares us for confession, *explicitly* by invoking God's mercy and slowness to anger—but as I have said, *implicitly* by urging us to practice divine compassion upon ourselves. It holds open the possibility not only of forgiving sin but also of returning to a state of purity, of full inner reconciliation and reconnection to the divine flow in the world. That possibility is itself enough potential gain to give us the motivation needed for confession. The melody only emphasizes this function of the Thirteen Attributes, through its plaintive and almost beseeching simplicity. We seek the capacity to experience God (within ourselves) as merciful, to look honestly at ourselves and to be self-forgiving.

The Thirteen Attributes assures us that kindness and mercy infuse the world, a perspective that is reflected in the translation by Joel Rosenberg that appears in the Reconstructionist *machzor Kol Haneshamah*:

> Adonay, Adonay, God loving and gracious,
> patient, and abundant in kindness and truth,
> keeping kindness for a thousand ages,
> forgiving sin and rebellion and transgression,
> making pure!
> May you forgive our sins and our wrongdoing,
> may you claim us as your own!
> Forgive us, our creator, for we have done wrong,
> grant pardon to us, sovereign, for we have transgressed,
> for you, Eternal One, are good and merciful,
> abundant in your steadfast love
> to all who call on you![2]

This is not an all-encompassing description of God. Quite the reverse—it is a functional description of how we hope to experience God when we do *t'shuvah*. We hope that we will be graciously and kindly received, that our failures will be forgiven, that we will attain a state of purity, and that we will experience ourselves as being favored as children of God. The divine is always accessible when we are ready for that encounter. Actually doing *t'shuvah*—facing ourselves, confronting our failures, and purging ourselves of what within us leads us astray—does bring us back toward purity. The daily morning prayer *Elohai N'shamah* reminds us that the soul within us is pure. If the *t'shuvah* process works, we will reconnect to that purity.

The Thirteen Attributes also appears in the Torah service when a festival falls on a weekday. In that location, the recitation is not connected to *t'shuvah*. But in their own way, the holidays in question all mark instances of divine benevolence toward Israel: Pesach's Exodus, Shavuot's giving of the Ten Commandments, Sukkot's protection of the Israelites in the desert; but also the re-enthronement of God on Rosh Hashanah and the purification rituals of Yom Kippur. Chanting the Thirteen Attributes during the Torah service invokes our awareness of God's presence throughout the holiday cycle and draws us consciously nearer to living in the divine presence.

The setting for Exodus 34, the original location of the thirteen attributes, is precisely about the divine presence. The accessibility of the divinity in the universe is an unimaginably enormous gift to each of us. The hope flowing from that gift not only encourages us to do *t'shuvah*. It sustains our lives every day.

⌒ഗ∞ഗ⌒

# In Whose Image?

## YOM KIPPUR'S ANNUAL CHOICE

*Rabbi Daniel G. Zemel*

The High Holy Days expose us to moral nakedness. We face nothing but ourselves and God with nothing behind which to hide. With nothing to otherwise entertain or engross us, there is just this simple but life-changing decision: will we be seekers after the one true God or will we be idolaters? There is no other choice. Things are just naturally set up that way. The text, the calendar, the ritual—they all come down to this. It happens only once a year, when life comes to a temporary standstill. Everything flows from this single moment of truth.

The Jewish calendar for the rest of the year protects us from this stark reality, which, if faced too often, would simply drive us away. Other holidays are saturated with healthy diversion—history, ritual, and story—all important, all demanding, and all real, but not the stuff of the High Holy Days, which strip us of all pretense and force the single most demanding choice any human being can make.

On Sukkot, we build and decorate a sukkah, select just the right *etrog*, and assemble our *lulav*. We consider our historic desert wanderings and rejoice in the "season of happiness." We might pause briefly to read Ecclesiastes and consider our lot in life—a last great gasp of the Days of

Rabbi Daniel G. Zemel is the senior rabbi of Temple Micah in Washington, DC. He contributed to *Who by Fire, Who by Water—Un'taneh Tokef; All These Vows—Kol Nidre; We Have Sinned: Sin and Confession in Judaism—Ashamnu and Al Chet; May God Remember: Memory and Memorializing in Judaism—Yizkor; All the World: Universalism, Particularism and the High Holy Days;* and *Naming God: Our Father, Our King—Avinu Malkeinu* (all Jewish Lights).

Awe, as I think of it. Ecclesiastes does indeed consider life's absurdities, but we quickly retire to our decorated sukkah and the bounty that the autumn harvest celebrates.

Passover sends us scurrying to prepare the seder, *kasher* our homes, then gather to discuss the story of slavery and freedom. There is, again, so much to preoccupy us, from seder plates to matzah covers, from Miriam's cup to Elijah's, and now, for many, even the feminist orange. America loves Passover.

Shavuot has us hunting down our favorite recipes for cheesecake or blintzes. We confront the Sinai moment, reiterate the Ten Commandments, and study Torah all through the night. The story of Ruth, Naomi, and Boaz inspires us to acknowledge the power of conversion and the miraculous American phenomenon of Jews by choice in ever-burgeoning numbers. Shavuot asks us now how we are all Jews by choice.

The post-biblical so-called "minor" holidays of Hanukkah and Purim have their own ways of deflecting us from ourselves. Candles, *chanukiyot*, dreidels, latkes, hamantaschen, Purim *spiels*, *Megillah* readings, and *groggers* all entice us in different ways. We revel. We party. We enjoy.

These are the celebrations that come round annually and consume our attention. We may glide thoughtlessly right through them or be meticulous in observing them, but either way, there is plenty to keep us busy. Whether celebrating, studying, or cooking, we are doing—always doing.

There is, of course, Shabbat, our weekly day to rest from all that doing, but still, there is the business of the preparation: cooking, inviting guests, making the Shabbat table beautiful, and then basking in *z'mirot* while munching on extra bits of lovingly braided challah. Shabbat is the relaxation from the drumbeat of our week, the spiritual metronome that measures our soul's timelessness. But precisely because of its "time-out" quality, Shabbat is not and cannot be the time for taking stock of who and what we are.

These other calendrical occasions make their own demands and invite their own participation, without, however, forcing us to encounter God. Not these days. Not now. On Rosh Hashanah and Yom Kippur there is no turning away.

Rosh Hashanah serves as introduction. There is no historical event to consider, no heroes to celebrate. There is only the creation of the world, the dawn of humanity—of us! The Torah portion that most grabs our attention is a story of life and death, father and son. Will the giver of life be also the taker of life? On Rosh Hashanah too, we open the book of life, in the spirit of mortal judgment. The creator God of the universe, the very source of life itself, turns out also to be God who threatens the possibility of no life. That sets us thinking about our own mortality—whence we came and where we are going. If we successfully follow these clues to their deeper message, we reach the ultimate and unanswerable questions that are the end of all thought: Why are we here? Who are we and to what purpose?

It all comes to a dramatic head on Yom Kippur, the sole day on the Jewish calendar with nothing else to consider—no story, no historical event, no hero, deed, or special ritual food. Yom Kippur is the blank slate of the soul. With the onset of *Kol Nidre*, the ark is emptied of its usual Torah scrolls, making us read ourselves into it. Without us there is no holiness, no text, no day.

There is only the question of what we are: seekers of God or of idolatry. Yes, idolatry, a word not overly encountered nowadays. Let me tell you what I mean.

The Torah tells us that we are created in the image of God. This should be no truism that we spout with blissful ease; it should give us pause. Each year, inevitably with the onset of Yom Kippur, I confront what this really means through the words of Solomon Goldman, a great rabbi in his time, and my grandfather:

> The Book of Genesis is the great clearing which the fashioners of the Jewish saga made in the jungle of primitive folklore.... In the myths, the gods were portrayed as vulgar, spiteful, cantankerous, perverse, and cruel—all as men made after them after the likeness of their own weak and erring flesh. And since the worshipper is rarely better than the object of his worship, such distorted notions of deity were bound to have a deleterious effect on behavior. In Genesis, God is perfection, as perfect as the noblest tendencies of the human heart could make him. And since, again in Genesis, man is created in God's image, it may be supposed to have been assumed that his highest aspirations were to emulate his creator.[1]

This says it all. On Rosh Hashanah we are presented with creation—our very being. Through Yom Kippur we are given the chance to decide: do we see ourselves in the image of God, or do we create some God in the paltriness of our own image?

To be sure, this God in whose image we are made is not portrayed—even in our own literature—as being beyond struggle. But God is never depicted as innately, determinedly, and hopelessly vulgar, perverse, or cruel. Abraham can protest the destruction of Sodom and Gomorrah because he assumes that God has a better nature to which he can appeal. On our holiest days of Rosh Hashanah and Yom Kippur, we encounter our God who wants mercy to win out over justice. This, according to the Talmud (Berakhot 7a), is God's own prayer for Himself. God wants to be a God of mercy.

I want to make clear the choice here—God or idolatry. Idolatry means a God made in our image. Idolatry means letting ourselves off the hook. Idolatry means being content with who we are. The honest embrace of Yom Kippur is an annual attempt to cast off idolatry, to cleave to our endlessly compassionate God and to recommit ourselves to living in God's image.

That is why we open the *machzor* and read words proclaiming God as merciful, overflowing with grace and understanding, loving, and forgiving. This is the God we could learn to long for and seek in our lives. This is the God who so gently challenges us to be better than we are, more than what we have been. This is the God in whose image we seek to find our own, as the community of Israel, and as our own individual selves. We want to be better. We want our communities to be better—more loving and forgiving, more prayerful, filled with grace and embrace.

This is what Rabbi Joseph B. Soloveitchik calls covenantal community. The rest of the year is for doing: observing, keeping, and preparing. Rosh Hashanah and Yom Kippur open up the door of being, human being in loving community:

> Friendship—not as a social-surface relation but as an existential in-depth relation between two individuals—is only realizable within the framework of the covenantal community, where in-depth personalities relate themselves to each other ontologically and total commitment to God and fellow man is the order of the day. In the majestic community, in which surface personalities meet and commitment never exceeds the bounds of the utilitarian, we may find collegiality, neighborliness, civility, or courtesy—but not

friendship, which is the exclusive experience awarded by God to covenantal man, who is thus redeemed from his agonizing solitude.[2]

All Israel is given a choice each year.
    If not now, when?

⟨ΠΠΟ⟩

# "Communology"—
# Encountering
# Community

# Loose Ends Can't Always Be Tied

*Rabbi Lawrence A. Englander, CM, DHL, DD*

The *N'ilah* service has just begun, and I look up from my *machzor* to take a peek outside. The sky is getting dark—a sure sign that we're now in the homestretch. I'm looking forward to that first taste of honey cake and coffee. Even more, I anticipate walking out of the sanctuary back into the world, knowing that I have been forgiven for all my failings of the past year. I feel bathed in the warmth of the setting sun.

As the *machzor* tells me, the gates of repentance are about to close, beckoning me to walk through. The circle of liturgy also comes to a close, as we repeat the same prayer that we said the night before: *El melekh yoshev*—"Sovereign God, who sits on the throne of mercy ... who forgives all your people's transgressions."[1] Suddenly there is a catch in my throat. I can't say the words. The warmth in my body has dissipated, and I even begin to shiver. Is it really that simple? Can God really wave a magic wand so that every nasty insult, every act of betrayal, simply disappears into thin air?

Yes, I know the Mishnah (Yoma 8:9) teaches that Yom Kippur can atone for sins between us and God. But it also says that sins between us and our fellow human beings require reconciliation from those we've wronged before asking for God's forgiveness. So I look back to the page: apparently

---

Rabbi Lawrence A. Englander, CM, DHL, DD, has been rabbi of Solel Congregation of Mississauga, Ontario, since its inception in 1973. He is author of *The Mystical Study of Ruth*, former editor of the *CCAR Journal*, and a contributor to *We Have Sinned: Sin and Confession in Judaism—Ashamnu and* Al Chet; *May God Remember: Memory and Memorializing in Judaism—Yizkor; All the World: Universalism, Particularism and the High Holy Days*; and *Naming God: Our Father, Our King—Avinu Malkeinu* (all Jewish Lights).

the *El melekh* prayer is telling me that God is far easier to appease than people. What about that insensitive comment I made to someone at a meeting? Even though I apologized, I can't blame her if she still bears a grudge. Or what about my good friend who suddenly turned on me? I know that it's not entirely his fault, that I bear some share of the blame for what happened—but our relationship will never be the same. Truth be told, I sadly realize, when I walk out of the sanctuary, I'll still be carrying all the old scars. And no amount of praying will heal them entirely.

I remember an experiment performed by a fellow rabbi over the High Holy Days. On Rosh Hashanah, he handed out cards inscribed with the words *Al chet shechatati*—"For the sin that I have committed by ..."; he then invited his congregants to finish the sentence and submit their cards (anonymously, of course), so that he might read aloud a random sample during the Yom Kippur *s'lichot* (penitential prayers) service. The responses were overwhelming; they moved him deeply:

"For the sin that I have committed by cheating on my husband."
"For the sin that I have committed by stealing from my business partner."

It was not revealed whether the adulterous wife told her spouse; but even if she did, and even if he forgave her, her behavior had to inflict a lasting wound on their relationship. And likewise, even if the business partner confessed and returned the cash, could he in turn regain the trust of his associates? Not every loose end of life can be tied up, even by spending an entire day in prayer. If that's the case, I ponder, as I struggle to bring my attention back to the service, why do we bother with all this liturgy anyway?

Just before I give in completely to depression, I remember a story in the Talmud (Ta'anit 20a–b) about two men who committed acts of violence through their words. Rabbi Elazar ben Rabbi Shimon, riding on a donkey, was returning home from his teacher's house, basking in a "scholar's high," proud of himself for the new knowledge he had learned. Along the road he chanced upon a man who was extremely ugly.

Staring down at the man from his perch on the saddle, he said, "Empty one! Are all the people of your town as ugly as you?"

The man replied, "I don't know. But go and tell the artist who made me, 'How ugly is this vessel you have made!'"

Shocked into realizing the insult he had inflicted, Rabbi Elazar dismounted, bowed low to the ground, and begged the man for forgiveness. But the injured party, intransigent, repeated his demand.

The rabbi said nothing in reply and decided to travel a few paces behind the man. By coincidence, the man headed straight into Rabbi Elazar's hometown. His neighbors flocked to greet him, saying "Shalom, Rabbi. Shalom, Master."

The man walking in front demanded indignantly, "Whom are you calling rabbi and master?"

They replied, "The one who is walking behind you."

"If so," the man rejoined, "may there be no one else like him among our people!" And he then related what the rabbi had said to him. The two men remained locked in a standoff.

It was the neighbors who broke the silence. "Please forgive him anyway," they implored, "for he is deeply learned in Torah." The man eventually agreed to do so, providing that Rabbi Elazar refrain from behaving this way again.

Evidently Rabi Elazar learned his lesson, for in the next day's class he taught, "One should always be gentle as the reed, not unyielding as the cedar. Because of its softness, the reed is privileged to be used for the making of the pens that write Torah scrolls, tefillin, and mezuzot."

Here we have a case in which two individuals harm each other. Asking forgiveness from each other did not help, nor did invoking God. The two would have remained at loggerheads were it not for a third party entering the discussion: the *community*.

It is no accident that the documents written by the reed all involve the community. The Torah is studied in the *bet midrash*, tefillin are worn in the synagogue, and mezuzot welcome the community into one's home. In all three cases, God's will becomes manifest only when the *community* puts their teachings into practice. This is exactly what happens in the Talmudic story. The *community* has to teach the two men to exchange the stiffness of a cedar for the pliability of a reed. Only then do they learn that the wounds they have inflicted on each other may not vanish, but their *attitude* toward them can soften. It is the nurturing community that raises individuals to the level of holiness.

As I return my attention to the sanctuary, the cantor is leading the singing of God's thirteen attributes. Members of the congregation—many of them friends whom I have known for a long time—surround me with song. This community in prayer is giving me the opportunity to place my loose ends in God's hands. So as the community continues to sing, I focus on prayer and give it a try. I find, somehow, that I am able now to deal more capably with my doubts and insecurities. I think: if God can be "endlessly patient, most kind, cleansing," then I can try harder to approximate these qualities. I can't take back my thoughtless words to others, nor can I forget their insults leveled at me, but I *can* change my attitude toward them and, like the reed, soften their lasting impact on me. If I can perceive the divine image in my fellow human beings—see them, that is, as God sees them—then the scars may persist in my memory, but they will hurt less to the touch.

The service has come to an end. People give each other a hasty hug and rush for the door to get home and break the fast. As I leave the synagogue, I don't experience the sense of calm that I had hoped for. My life has not become a clean slate; I still have lots to think about and even more to act upon. But my immersion in a community at prayer has helped me along; I know now that my attitude toward certain people is undergoing a change. And so is my attitude toward myself.

So maybe all those prayers were worth it after all.

౸౸౸

# A Dual Message to the Jew in the Pew from the Throne of Mercy

*Rabbi Aaron Goldstein*

As a rabbi who has studied the liturgy, I know that the prayer book is actually not just one liturgy but two: the printed liturgy before us and a liturgy that is not there but that might have been. I refer to the fact that the Rabbis who bequeathed us the prayers had before them some biblical prototypes that they deliberately misquoted and selectively misread, so as to give us a liturgy that said what they believed it ought to rather than what their biblical forebears might have recommended in an earlier era. Much of the liturgy's force depends on appreciating these "misreadings" as the carefully crafted Rabbinic artistry that has stood us in good stead over the centuries and that resonates still for us today.

The "ostensive" or "actual" liturgy is just the "straightforward" prayer-book readings—what the words actually say. Hidden from view is the second liturgy (what we do not have but what lies invisibly below the surface)—an "edgy" reading that reveals a more complex analysis of the issues that the liturgy silently addresses.

As a rabbi with a large and diverse membership in attendance on the High Holy Days, I know also that I have not one congregation but two: some people relish knowing the edgy complexities of the creative

Rabbi Aaron Goldstein is the senior rabbi of Northwood and Pinner Liberal Synagogue, London; lecturer in practical rabbinics at Leo Baeck College, London; and previous outreach director for Liberal Judaism, UK. His rabbinical studies at Leo Baeck College and Hebrew Union College–Jewish Institute of Religion in New York fostered a love for applying meaningful liturgy to the congregational setting.

misreadings; others find their lives complex enough and prefer the sim-
plified comfort of the straightforward prayers as they are—the ostensive
and actual liturgy, that is, without the backdrop of what the liturgy might
have been had the Rabbis settled for the biblical models that they ultimately rejected instead.

The thirteen attributes of God are part of the ostensive and actual
liturgy: they are simply there, to be straightforwardly read and sung for
what they are and what they say. As such, they speak to the second congregation, the folk who appreciate the service for what it is and require
nothing deeper. But those same attributes are equally a profound example
of selective Rabbinic misreading, precisely what the first congregation—
those looking for edgy complexity—are likely to appreciate.

At stake is the ending of Exodus 34:7, the part of the biblical thirteen attributes that the prayer book deliberately omits. We get the first
part—the promise that God is merciful and compassionate, but not the
follow-up assurance that "Adonai certainly does not cleanse, but visits
the iniquity of parents upon children and children's children, upon the
third and fourth generation." The whole thing follows the introductory
setting of the scene, a courtroom, where "God is a king seated on a throne
of mercy, governing graciously, pardoning the sins of his people, removing the first, first, extending pardon to sinners and forgiveness to transgressors, dealing generously with all living beings." One can see why the
inclusion of the missing biblical material about God's ultimate justice,
not just God's mercy, would rather change the tone of this introduction,
to the point, even, of negating its main assertion.

One can find this liturgical device similarly employed elsewhere.
We read in a prayer preceding the morning *Sh'ma* that God "forms light
and creates darkness, makes peace and creates all things." Only when I
went to rabbinical school did I learn of the deliberate Rabbinic misquota-
tion here. The original (Isaiah 45:7) has God say, "I form light and create
darkness, I make peace and create evil."

Here, too, we get the possibility of reading the liturgy in two ways.
A straightforward approach tells us simply that God creates everything.
Knowing the Isaiah prototype, however, suggests the edgy possibility of
wrestling with the brute fact that God must also, then, in some way, be
responsible for the world's evil as well.

Selective quotation—for this is surely what this amounts to—is
considered a present-day scourge because what is not quoted is generally

unknown by the audience. The originator's intentions are at the mercy of the manipulating editor, usually misquoting to support a particular political perspective. To some extent, the Rabbis did just that—with theology, not politics, in mind. But they were more akin to legal interpreters of an ancient constitution, updating their age-old biblical mandate. The original was there for all to see; their interpretive finesse was an art form, the expected way to make old texts yield new meanings. The Sages were creating no deception; cognizant instead of the needs of their community and their relationship with God, they were reinterpreting divinity as what they thought the Bible itself would have done had it been composed in their own era.

So much for the dual message of the liturgy. What about the dual character of today's congregations? As I say, some of those attending services on the High Holy Days require nothing more than the straightforward message of a God who is all-merciful; others prefer the option of wrestling with a complex, even edgy, relationship with God.

For the majority of our congregants, the reassurance that God's throne is purely a seat of mercy reflects their fundamental need for this season. Taking seriously the larger liturgical message of the day, they may be somewhat overwhelmed by consciousness of sin and guilt. All of us are guilty of something, we all know; the prayers quite naturally focus our conscience on some aspect of our behavior or character from the year past. The confessions of the day weigh heavily upon us.

The fundamental notion of the ten days of repentance would fail these people if they were left to wallow in their guilt with no opportunity or expectation of absolution. So, for them, the entire force of the day addresses the straightforward message of forgiveness. From the opening *S'lichot* (poems of pardon) to the closing service of *N'ilah*, we get the repetitive image of God on the throne of mercy guaranteeing pardon. The thirteen attributes are just what they are—a redundant insistence on God's compassionate essence, set evocatively to music—for us, here, in the United Kingdom, a composition arranged by Robert Barrington Jay.

The extent to which this audience within our congregation wishes no edginess to their Yom Kippur experience can be estimated from the following. One of my colleagues had delivered a challenging sermon relating to Israel. More than a handful of enraged congregants confronted us. Apart from complaints against real or perceived criticism of the State of

Israel—for some of the complainants an activity that is taboo—the other argument went (and I paraphrase it, of course), "How dare you ruin my peaceful, comfortable, annual rite of coming to shul?"

This is a problem for those of us who consider it our task to discomfort congregations in hope that they may act more justly in the world. Yet, unless the sole aim of our rabbinate is social activism, we must recognize the duality of the congregation we face. There is nothing wrong with those who come seeking only comfort and hope from their worship during the *Yamim Nora'im*. This might be a sole source of unadulterated comfort in a life that is otherwise filled with difficulties. There are other moments and means to catalyze social activism.

But there is also that other audience, the "edgy" folk who welcome complexity on what may otherwise seem to them to be a rather monotonous day of redundant liturgical reading and singing. They may welcome a sermon with a challenge in it. And they love the idea of deliberate liturgical misquotes and selective citations. Intellectual or moral complexity is the spice that brings the liturgy to life for these congregants. They revel in the knowledge that there is a secret, a mystery; a key that unlocks a glint of deeper understanding, a momentary glimpse into the deeper nature of God, perhaps.

When I glance out on the sea of bowed heads during the repetition of the thirteen attributes, I see both congregations: the people invested in examining their own conscience in the light of a merciful God; and the edgy crowd as well, the folk who enjoy the euphoric moment of getting behind a prayer's ostensive wording and appreciate the struggle that it hides by its selective perception of what to say and what to suppress.

The faces of the edgy may not be replete with happiness, for inherent in the knowledge of a selective citation or misquote is an awareness that life is not all good, all light, all peace, all atonement. The ambiguity of the text reflects the ambiguity of life itself—the fact that any given year has its personal tragedies; that occasionally it does seem as if we are being punished; that we find it hard to believe in a rose-tinted promise of pure divine goodness or of human kindness and altruism performed necessarily by us all.

We have two liturgies, then; and two congregations, one for each of them; but also two goals for the High Holy Days. The same person may shift from one to the other in a single day or from year to year. But we congregational rabbis need to keep them both in mind—they are of equal value. Our earliest Rabbinic ancestors created the duality: a straightforward message of God's inherent compassion; but also the edginess of a world that is not as simple as it looks: comfort and agitation—Yom Kippur provides them both.

☙

# Who Knows Thirteen?
## JEWS DO

*Rabbi Julia Neuberger*

For me, the thirteen attributes of God are inextricably linked to the significance of the number thirteen in Jewish tradition. I was brought up, like many of us, in a society in which thirteen was thought to be unlucky. But not in Judaism! Take Maimonides's Thirteen Principles of Faith, which we sing on Erev Shabbat as *Yigdal*, or recite and sing as *Ani Ma'amin*, announcing with each one, "I believe with perfect faith ...":

> [1]... that the Creator, Blessed be His Name, is the Creator and Guide of everything that has been created; He alone has made, does make, and will make all things.
> [2] ... that the Creator ... is One, and that there is no unity in any manner like His, and that He alone is our God, who was, and is, and will be.
> [3] ... that the Creator ... has no body, and that He is free from all the properties of matter, and that there can be no (physical) comparison to Him whatsoever.
> [4] ... that the Creator ... is the first and the last.

---

Rabbi Julia Neuberger (properly known as Rabbi Baroness [Julia] Neuberger DBE) is senior rabbi of West London Synagogue, a cross bench (independent) member of the House of Lords, and a trustee of the Van Leer Foundation and Van Leer Jerusalem Institute. She was Bloomberg Professor at Harvard Divinity School in 2006 and is a former Harkness Fellow. She has advised the UK government on end-of-life care and on diversity in the judiciary and was volunteering champion for former prime minister Gordon Brown. She is particularly concerned with social issues, especially health care, asylum and refugee issues, housing, and old age. She is the author of many books and articles and a regular broadcaster on the BBC.

[5] ... that to the Creator ... and to Him alone, it is right to pray, and that it is not right to pray to any being besides Him.

[6] ... that all the words of the prophets are true.

[7] ... that the prophecy of Moses our teacher, peace be upon him, was true, and that he was the chief of the prophets, both those who preceded him and those who followed him.

[8] ... that the entire Torah that is now in our possession is the same that was given to Moses our teacher, peace be upon him.

[9] ... that this Torah will not be exchanged, and that there will never be any other Torah from the Creator....

[10] ... that the Creator ... knows all the deeds of human beings and all their thoughts, as it is written, "Who fashioned the hearts of them all, Who comprehends all their actions" (Psalm 33:15).

[11] ... that the Creator ... rewards those who keep His commandments and punishes those that transgress them.

[12] ... in the coming of the Messiah; and even though he may tarry, nonetheless, I wait every day for his coming.

[13] ... that there will be a revival of the dead at the time when it shall please the Creator ... and His mention shall be exalted for ever and ever.[1]

I am not at all sure that I do personally believe even the majority of these to be true. I do not, for instance, for good scientific reasons, believe the Torah is the same now as was given to Moses—I am not even sure it was given to Moses at all, in any sense that we would understand! I do not believe in the coming of a personal Messiah, but in a messianic age that human beings will help to create. I remain pretty unconvinced about physical resurrection. And so on ...

But what is significant for me is that Maimonides chose to cite thirteen principles, not twelve or fourteen or ten (as in the Ten Commandments, for example)—I even suspect he had the thirteen attributes in mind as his model. Maimonides may not have known the negativity surrounding the number thirteen in Christian and Western culture, but as time went on, and as that Christian culture became the norm for more and more Jews, the positive Jewish accent on thirteen stood out as unique. Maimonides must also have known that the age of majority for Jews (originally boys, now girls too, in progressive movements) is thirteen. And eventually, years after Maimonides (although it is hard to say how many), we chose even to sing a Passover seder song, *Echad Mi Yode'a* ("Who Knows One?"), that counts the numbers up to thirteen—citing none other than God's thirteen attributes at that point, as if nothing could be a higher value than that.

> Who knows thirteen? I know thirteen.
> Thirteen is the attributes.
> Twelve is the tribes.
> Eleven is the stars [of Joseph's dream].
> Ten is the commandments.
> Nine is the months of birth.
> Eight is days of circumcision.
> Seven is the days of the week.
> Six is the orders of the Mishnah.
> Five is the books of the Torah.
> Four is the matriarchs.
> Three is the Patriarchs.
> Two is the tablets of the covenant.
> One is our God in heaven and on earth.[2]

The number thirteen thus stands out dramatically in Jewish tradition as just the opposite of the way it functions elsewhere as the quintessential example of bad luck. Most hotels have no thirteenth floor. Airplanes often omit row thirteen. People get nervous on the thirteenth of the month, especially if it is Friday the thirteenth, a reflection, possibly, of the fact that there were thirteen present at the Last Supper—including the betrayer—and Friday was the day of the crucifixion. It may even be that as the solar calendar trumped the lunar calendar in many civilizations, the thirteen lunar menstrual cycles/months per year were suppressed as unlucky. In ancient Persia, and even now in modern Iran, the thirteenth (and last) day of the Persian New Year Nawrooz, Sizdeh Bedar, is considered so unlucky in some interpretations that people decamp to the countryside for the day.

Knowing the thirteen attributes, then, Maimonides saw the positive value of thirteen. And that positivity continued even after Jews became aware of the negative valence accorded the number in Christian and in Western lore. In so doing, Jews insisted on remaining differentiated from everyone else.

In Leviticus 19:2, "You shall be *k'doshim*, because I, Adonai, am *kadosh*," the Hebrew does not mean "holy," as usually translated, but "separate, distinct, different." So the thirteen attributes of God reflect difference, God's difference and ours. The deliberate use of thirteen for God, for the principles of our faith, and even for how we like to count reminds us that we Jews are different. Our various lists of thirteen become mnemonics of Jewish distinctiveness. Chief among them are the thirteen attributes of God that we say liturgically in shortened form (but still calling them "thirteen"!) on the High Holy Days and on festivals, year after year, to remind us not just of God but also of ourselves—of our Jewish difference.

So, when I read and sing the thirteen attributes of God, I reflect on the fact that there are thirteen of them—symbolizing Jewish difference.

And yet, they do mean something, and the meaning does command my attention. The attributes are shortened in our prayer book so that only the merciful ones are included there. We sing of mercy, therefore, but have often suffered and may well wonder why. We understand God as forgiving sin and iniquity, yet we believe that human justice matters—we train as lawyers to be part of an earthly legal system. If God shows mercy to thousands of generations, why do millions of innocent people suffer in war, famine, and natural disasters? And so on. We find the theology hard—and yet we say it, even as we doubt its truth.

And so we do not just say it; we sing it! As the whole congregation joins in the singing, we manage somehow to turn to God in *t'shuvah*, "penitence," as if God were all the things we sing about. Theological difficulties pale, and we are able to act "as if" we believe. Standing with our fellow Jews on these days, in all of our difference, we seek spiritual renewal, forgiveness, and reconciliation.

And in so doing, we may just recall that "magic" number thirteen, recognizing that our use of thirteen for all that we *wish* were true (the divine attributes of Torah and Maimonides's principles as well) underscores the fact that we are different. Hard as it may be to believe them all in those rational moments when the song ends, they convince us somehow to revel in our Jewish commitment to forgive and be forgiven in this life, and to confess our sins to God, for this life and for any other that may come.

# I Show Up

## MY UNEXPECTED GIFT
## OF COMPASSION

*Rabbi Sandy Eisenberg Sasso, DMin*

"Adonai, Adonai, merciful and gracious God, endlessly patient, most kind." On Yom Kippur, the holiest day of the year, these comforting words are chanted while we stand before the ark. We prepare to remove the Torah scrolls and bear witness to the covenant. The attributes are recited not just once, but three times. They also appear twice again in the liturgy, at the beginning of Yom Kippur (on the night of *Kol Nidre*) and at the end of the sacred day (at *N'ilah*).

We are invited to encounter the divine as full of compassion. Yet this is not the face we often meet. Natural disaster and human tragedy have us questioning, challenging, even denying such a God.

Some years are harder than others. Personally, this has been a hard year. My mother has been suffering from progressive Alzheimer's for four years, each month a further descent into unknowing. This is no gentle decline, but a turbulent falling out of time. Every day brings new

Rabbi Sandy Eisenberg Sasso, DMin, is rabbi emerita of Congregation Beth-El Zedeck in Indianapolis, where she has served for thirty-six years, and director of the Religion, Spirituality, and the Arts Initiative at Butler University in partnership with Christian Theological Seminary. She is the author of award-winning children's books, including *God's Paintbrush*, *In God's Name*, and *Shema in the Mezuzah: Listening to Each Other*, winner of the National Jewish Book Award (all Jewish Lights); *Creation's First Light*, a finalist for the National Jewish Book Award; and *Anne Frank and the Remembering Tree*. She is also the author of *Midrash: Reading the Bible with Question Marks* and coauthor with Peninnah Schram of *Jewish Stories of Love and Marriage: Folktales, Legends and Letters*.

challenges, confusion, anger, fear. There are little moments of lucidity, and I think, "There you are. There's my mom." But those times don't come very often. It's like a game of hide-and-seek. She keeps hiding and I keep seeking, but more and more I can't find her.

Memory is at the core of who we are as a people. So I wonder who we are when our memory is gone, when all that we knew and felt has disappeared, when all that made us cry and laugh has vanished. I wonder who we are when the body is strong, when breath-rhythm and heartbeat keep regular pace, but the mind stops working. I wonder who we are when we can't form new memories or retrieve old ones, when everything passes like water through a sieve.

Rosh Hashanah is called the Day of Remembrance. Metaphor tells us that God writes our name in the book of life, but what if we do not know our name? Who cares if God remembers if my mother can't? What good is God's compassion if she doesn't know it and I don't feel it? What good is compassion if our fragmented world too infrequently experiences it?

The poet Yehuda Amichai says every person is a dam between past and future but I don't know what to do when the dam breaks. All I know is how the heart breaks.

The last place I want to be is standing before the open ark, Torah scrolls in white garb, a full congregation, listening to the chanting of these words. I do not want to call God *el rachum v'chanun* ... "merciful and gracious God, endlessly patient, most kind."

We repeat the attributes three times, trying to convince ourselves of their truth. We chant again and again, "Merciful and gracious God, endlessly patient, most kind." I heard it said that if you speak something often enough it becomes true. I wish it were so. I love the power of words, but I do not believe you can make true what is false.

Here I am in the congregation as I have always been. I am a rabbi; where else would I be? Sunset arrives on Yom Kippur evening and I show up. I know I am not alone. There are others with greater pain and deeper loss and more to complain about life's unfairness.

I am retired from my congregation, so I am not leading the service. Instead, I am thinking of the biblical patriarch Jacob and his ladder dream. It happens in the least likely of locations, at Mount Moriah. On Rosh Hashanah the Torah reading takes us there, to be with Abraham and Isaac on the mountain. This is the place of Jacob's father, Isaac's binding. But Jacob doesn't want to be at Moriah. He's heard enough from his dad, seen enough of the consequences of that moment. Better to avoid the mountain at all costs, better not to meet this God, to confront the fear of Isaac. Who wants to encounter this terror, this face of the divine? But Jacob couldn't pass by, even though he tried. Midnight surprised the day, and he couldn't go on; he had to sleep.

I always wondered how he could do that, how Jacob could sleep on that frightening mountain where his father had once lain bound, face-to-face with the sacrificial knife, and with the angel late in coming. But Jacob did. He put his head on that rock and made it a pillow. For a moment, Jacob stopped fleeing, stopped deceiving, stopped fighting, and surrendered. And that moment birthed a dream, a ladder with angels ascending and descending, more promising and gentler than Isaac's tardy savior.

Between two setting suns, the liturgy of atonement murmurs on. As if in a dream, like Jacob, I let go. I stop analyzing every prayer. Is it gender inclusive? Is it intellectually credible? For a moment, the words float away. For a moment, feeling trumps thinking. I stop arguing with divine notions of reward and punishment, with anthropomorphic images of God with which I disagree. If Jacob could stop at Moriah to face the God who made Isaac tremble, then why was I so resistant to stand before the ark and encounter the face of compassion? Unlike the rock that Jacob had made a pillow, compassion was more like a pillow that my resistance made a rock, too hard to rest upon.

I let the music's ebb and flow carry me. I am too tired and hungry to fight any longer. And just then I see it—a ladder! It is formed from community. Each rung lets me ascend and descend without harm. Someone is there to catch me, to hold my hand, to listen quietly without judgment. There are some, call them angels if you will, to weep with me and make me laugh, to pour me a glass of wine in the evening and welcome me home. I recall that Jacob ends up calling Moriah by a different name. He calls the place Beth El, "divine home."

The last recitation of the Thirteen Attributes catches me by surprise. Nothing changes and everything does. The world outside is the same as before I began the fast. It is only the world inside that has begun to change. I forgive others; I forgive myself. In the last rays of Yom Kippur's light, neither day nor night, I find what I need: the gentle gift of compassion; I am home.

❦

# PART IV

# Secularism and God

## The Case of Israel

# Israeli "Secular" Poets Encounter God

*Rabbi Dalia Marx, PhD*

A friend of Franz Kafka, Gustav Janouch, once asked him if "poetry tends toward religion."[1] "I would not say that," Kafka replied, "but certainly to prayer."[2] This response testifies to the intimate affinity between poetry and prayer and to the way poetry touches the sacred while bypassing institutionalized religion. This poetry-prayer similarity becomes particularly important for many Israelis who are likely not to attend synagogue regularly. This does not mean they find the search for God irrelevant, however. For many Israelis, the encounter occurs through nontraditional ways, such as poetry.

Prayer and poetry do indeed have much in common. Both communicate beyond literal meaning; both rely on the power of metaphor. Yet they are different. Prayer, at least in the classical sense of the word, requires an addressee: in a Jewish context—God. Not so poetry. Prayer

Rabbi Dalia Marx, PhD, is a professor of liturgy and midrash at the Jerusalem campus of Hebrew Union College–Jewish Institute of Religion and teaches in various academic institutions in Israel and Europe. Rabbi Marx earned her doctorate at the Hebrew University in Jerusalem and her rabbinic ordination at HUC–JIR in Jerusalem and Cincinnati. She is involved in various research groups and is active in promoting progressive Judaism in Israel. Rabbi Marx contributed to *Who by Fire, Who by Water*—Un'taneh Tokef; *All These Vows*—Kol Nidre; *We Have Sinned: Sin and Confession in Judaism*—Ashamnu *and* Al Chet; *May God Remember: Memory and Memorializing in Judaism*—Yizkor; *All the World: Universalism, Particularism and the High Holy Days*; and *Naming God: Our Father, Our King*—Avinu Malkeinu (all Jewish Lights). She writes for academic journals and the Israeli press and is engaged in creating new liturgies and midrashim.

uses words to praise, acknowledge, give thanks, and petition. Poetry need not do so.[3] Modern poetry, anyway, usually concentrates on the personal and the idiosyncratic, while classical Rabbinic prayer stresses the k'lal, the entire people of Israel and prayer that is public. It is composed of relatively fixed texts recited at designated times; poetry has no such regularity. The more ancient a prayer is, the more it is considered sacred, and the lack of a known composer is what endows it with holiness and authority. Poems, by contrast, are generally products with a known context and author. Prayer is generally anything but subversive, while poetry may be just the opposite, And yet, the affinity between these two literary genres is undeniable.

In Israel, it has frequently seemed that any given individual was either "religious" (meaning "Orthodox" or even "ultra-Orthodox") or "secular," meaning "non-observant." But Israeli secularism has always been unique. It has remained faithful to Jewish peoplehood and nationhood and has never been totally detached from the Jewish past. Even the fiercely secular Zionist pioneers sometimes demonstrated aspects of spirituality, a longing for the transcendent, and a high regard for abandoned tradition itself. Early kibbutzim, for example, wrote Haggadot for the Passover seder, but with new meanings and values, such as freedom and justice.[4] Even when rejecting religion, they identified themselves as part of the Jewish People, and when it came to God, rather than speaking of the "death of God," as was the case in other Western cultures,[5] they expressed rage toward the very God they did not worship and in whom they did not believe. Poetry was often the means to express this desire for the sacred, a way to engage in discourse that was unorthodox but still (in its own way) religious.

For Sephardi-Mizrachi Jews, moreover, this dichotomy—which was true specifically of the earlier Ashkenazi setters—did not exist. These Jews from Mediterranean lands, rather than from eastern and central Europe, maintained Jewish tradition to one degree or another without seeing any need to choose between religion and modernity. In recent years the rigid dichotomy between the two has eroded for Ashkenazi Jews as well.

If we discount the arbitrary identification of "religious" with "Orthodox," the very categories of "secular" and "religious" begin to seem artificial—incongruent with such genuinely religious notions as faith and commitment to holiness. Even traditionally Jewish literature does not necessarily express sweet piety or blind faith; it sometimes articulates doubt, despair, or defiance. In like manner, Hebrew literature, and especially poetry, becomes the heir of the traditional love-hate relationship with the divine. According to Ariel Hirshfeld (b. 1953), a literary critic and professor of Hebrew literature, "faith, the love of God, God's existence, contact with God and God's forms of revelation in the world, in the life of the individual and in the life of the community, religious experience—mystic and non-mystic—these are what inform the great, most influential pages" of such founding authors as Bialik, Agnon, and others, that tradition has continued to our own time. Hirschfeld adds:

> It was modern Hebrew literature that took upon itself the committed spiritual engagement with the question of Jewish faith. It did so for two reasons: it aimed to inherit the mantle of Jewish scholarly tradition.... And more importantly, because for over a century, the traditional Jewish world did not manage to produce any spiritual creativity, whether philosophical or literary, that would ... offer the Jew and the Israeli reader a serious treatment of questions of their existence and faith.[6]

Religious coercion and lack of religious freedom may make many Israelis shy away from any form of organized religion; yet these same Israelis, many poets among them, may seek holiness and the nearness of God nonetheless. Religious poetry, says Mizrachi scholar and poet Havivah Pedaya, may have "little or nothing to do with poetry written by those who observe the commandments. And that's because religious experience per se doesn't really concern them.... [It is] poetry in which the presence of God exists, a poetry whose trials and joys are linked to the thirst for the Divine and a longing for metaphysical grace and consolation."[7]

    I do not go as far as some scholars do when they argue that the mere use of the Hebrew constitutes holiness and, therefore, cannot be secular. I reject the notion that Hebrew is essentially and inevitably a religious language.[8] Yet, in many cases, it is. Simply by using the age-old language of Jewish aspiration, Hebrew poetry may weave together, at least symbolically, the many segmented parts of the painfully fragmented Israeli reality—tradition and religion included.

Apart from the so-called secular Israeli poetry, there is also the category of *shirah emunit* ("religious" or "faith poetry"), which has thrived in the last few decades.[9] Poets of this genre write within the framework of traditional (if not strictly Orthodox) Judaism.[10] My interest here, however, is how so-called *secular* poetry deals with the desire, defiance, and despair regarding the encounter with God.[11]

My examples here are three female poets, each with a different literary style and aesthetic, and each from a different poetic generation: Leah Goldberg (1911–1970), Yona Wallach (1944–1985), and Orit Gidali (b. 1974). Together, they provide a modest prism through which to rethink the ways Israeli writers may seek out the spiritual and develop ways to encounter God.

## Leah Goldberg

Leah Goldberg (1911–1970) was a literary scholar, theoretician, journalist, editor, and author of children's books, but first and foremost, she is remembered for her poetry. Goldberg was born in Königsberg and was raised in Kaunas (Lithuania). She studied in the universities of Kaunas, Berlin, and Bonn, where she received a doctorate in Semitic linguistics. Upon arriving in Israel in 1935, she settled in Tel Aviv and became active in a modernist poetry circle called Yachdav ("Together"). In 1950 Goldberg moved to Jerusalem, where she lectured at the Hebrew University and, later, became a professor of comparative literature. Despite her authorship of children's books, she never married or had children of her own. Until her death (at age fifty-nine), she lived with her mother, who outlived Leah by more than a decade after Leah succumbed to cancer and who received the Israel Prize on her daughter's behalf after Leah passed away.[12]

Goldberg's prose as well as her scholarly, theoretical, and ideological writings are essentially secular.[13] She was active in the Labor Party and in Zionist Socialist institutions; she routinely contributed to its daily newspaper, *Davar*, coedited its weekly children's edition, and also published in *Al Hamishmar*, the daily of MaPaM (the United Workers' Party).[14] Nevertheless, she has been aptly called a "praying poet":

> Much of her poetry consists of prayers and negotiation with the desperate need and the quest to pray. Many poems are

explicit prayers to God, very commonly referred to as "my God": in other praying-poems the Divine addressee is less explicit, and somewhat intertwined with earthly, human addressees. Some poems take prayer [*tefilah*] as their theme; in many others, across the entire range of themes addressed by her poetry, she simply prays.[15]

The three Goldberg poems below all deal with God, faith, and prayer: the first, though not actually a prayer, is nevertheless addressed to "my God"; the second, also to "my God," is now a famous prayer as well; the third is a prayer put into the mouths of wandering birds.

| [I Saw My God at the Café] | [אֶת אֱלֹהַי רָאִיתִי בַּקָּפֶה] |
|---|---|
| I saw my God at the café.<br>He revealed Himself to me<br>  through a cigarette smoke<br>gloomy, remorseful, and frail<br>He signaled me: "life goes on"! | אֶת אֱלֹהַי רָאִיתִי בַּקָּפֶה<br>הוּא נִתְגַּלָּה לִי בַּעֲשַׁן סִיגָרִיּוֹת.<br>נְכֵה־רוּחַ, מִסְתַּלֵּחַ וְרָפֶה<br>רָמַז לִי: "עוֹד אֶפְשָׁר לִחְיוֹת"! |
| He did not look anything<br>  like my lover:<br>He was closer than him,<br>  and miserable,<br>like a translucent shadow<br>  of starlight.<br>He hardly filled the void. | הוּא לֹא הָיָה דוֹמֶה לַאֲהוּבִי:<br>קָרוֹב מִמֶּנּוּ, וְאֻמְלָל,<br>כְּצֵל שָׁקוּף שֶׁל אוֹר הַכּוֹכָבִים<br>הוּא לֹא מִלֵּא אֶת הֶחָלָל. |
| To a pale-reddish twilight<br>as if confessing a sin before<br>  death,<br>He kneeled down to kiss<br>  the feet of man[16]<br>and to beg his forgiveness.[17] | לְאוֹר שְׁקִיעָה חִוֵּר וַאֲדַמְדַּם<br>כְּמִתְוַדֶּה עַל חֵטְא לִפְנֵי מוֹתוֹ,<br>יָרַד לְמַטָּה לְנַשֵּׁק רַגְלֵי אָדָם<br>וּלְבַקֵּשׁ אֶת סְלִיחָתוֹ. |

This poem was published in Goldberg's first anthology *Taba'ot Ashan* (*Smoke Rings*) in 1935, the year of her arrival in Israel. The speaker in the poem meets God as if bumping into an acquaintance in a café. Cafés were important institutions for poets in those years, and Goldberg would have spent much time there socializing and writing. The God she meets suffers guilt over human suffering. He is "gloomy, remorseful and frail." Another possible translation of the first line is "I came across my God in the coffee," as if the speaker were a fortune-teller, reading coffee, like tea leaves, and encountering her God there.

This poem contains at least three ironic shifts. God appears first as a forlorn, anguished individual. Instead of the smoke and fire that accompanied revelation in days of old, we get the grotesque diminuation into the fire and smoke of the cigarettes. This is not the God whose "glory fills the universe"; here, "He hardly filled the void." The second irony is that in the world of our poem it is God who sinned against humanity, not (as in traditional religion) the other way around. It is not worshipers who prostrate themselves seeking divine pardon, but God who "kneeled down to kiss the feet of man / and to beg for his forgiveness." In this final line, the personal encounter with God at the café ("I met *my* God") becomes generalized as God kneels to seek forgiveness from all humanity.

From her diaries and testimonies of her friends, we know that Goldberg saw herself as a woman unworthy of love. Often she referred to herself as "ugly"—undesirable to men. Her diaries relate tales of unrequited love.[18] Not only did she never marry, but she never enjoyed an ongoing romantic relationship with a man and, as mentioned, was childless. Her childhood traumas, especially her father's mental illness (for which he was institutionalized), haunted her. In this poem Goldberg blames God, and yet—in the poem's third ironic shift—God is closer to her than her unattainable lover. God's revelation is not in glory and splendor (as a lover might have been), but He is nonetheless present. Hardly almighty, however, Goldberg's God does not even fill the void (the void, also, in her own heart?), but He owns up to responsibility and begs forgiveness "as if confessing a sin before death." In a dramatic reversal of roles, God here is not all-powerful but frail, requesting (rather than granting) compassionate forgiveness of sin.

The next poem, part of a short collection published in 1954, explores the meaning of life, especially from the perspective of old age (although Goldberg was only forty-three at the time). It addresses God directly—a prayer in form and content:

## The Poems of the End of the Journey, 3

Teach me, my God, to bless
  and to pray
Over the secret of the withered leaf, on the glow
  of ripe fruit,
Over this freedom: to see,
  to feel, to breathe,
To know, to wish, to fail.

Teach my lips blessing
  and song of praise,
Renewing your time each
  morning, each night,
Lest my day today be
  as days gone by
Lest my day become for me
  simply habit.[19]

## שירי סוף הדרך [ג]

לַמְּדֵנִי, אֱלֹהַי, בָּרֵךְ וְהִתְפַּלֵּל
עַל סוֹד עָלֶה קָמֵל,
עַל נֹגַהּ פְּרִי בָּשֵׁל,
עַל הַחֵרוּת הַזֹּאת:
לִרְאוֹת, לָחוּשׁ, לִנְשֹׁם,
לָדַעַת, לְיַחֵל, לְהִכָּשֵׁל.

לַמֵּד אֶת שְׂפָתוֹתַי בְּרָכָה וְשִׁיר הַלֵּל
בְּהִתְחַדֵּשׁ זְמַנְּךָ עִם בֹּקֶר וְעִם לֵיל,
לְבַל יִהְיֶה יוֹמִי הַיּוֹם
כִּתְמוֹל שִׁלְשׁוֹם,
לְבַל יִהְיֶה עָלַי יוֹמִי הֶרְגֵּל.

This poem, initially published in the women workers' newspaper, is one of the best known by Goldberg. It is often recited in ceremonies and prayer services and even appears in several liberal prayer books, both in Israel and in the Diaspora.[20] It has attracted several musical compositions. The compassionate (and even patronizing?) attitude toward a disempowered God reflected in the previous poem is completely missing from this one. Here, the speaker looks at the world with awe and asks for a proper language "to bless and to pray" what she sees around her; she asks for the ability to behold the wonder in nature and learn not only to speak of the sublime but also of "the secret of the withered leaf" that she might pray over it.

Faith is problematic for Goldberg, who seeks it and reflects upon it in its absence. Here and there in her writing, we find her soul yearning for contact with a living God. A diary entry from December 12, 1927 (when she was only sixteen), for instance, declares:

How happy is the person who has his God; he does not have to look for Him. How happy also is he who believes that there is no God, and indeed that he has no need of Him. I, I know nothing. I am miserable. I need some faith. I shall not be able to live without such. However, I am skeptical and, therefore, feel cold.[21]

Our poem presupposes this possibility of a cold world—where days slip by as habits. The poet seeks the language of prayer to connect with a God who can deepen her consciousness of wonder.

Traditional prayers are a manifestation of faith; this one is a supplication for faith to arise. She negotiates with the living God from whom she feels alienated. Yet she refers to this God with whom she struggles as "my God."

The last Goldberg poem that will be discussed here, "Journeying Birds," concludes a series of four poems called *Mishirei Tziyon* (*From the Songs of Zion*). The first of the four, *La'ilah* ("Night"), demands, *Shiru lanu mishirei Tziyon*, "Sing for us a song of Zion," a reiteration of Psalm 137:3, the mournful psalm, in which Babylonian conquerors tauntingly demand songs of Zion from their Levite captives. The Levites respond bitterly, "How shall we sing Adonai's song in a foreign land?" (Psalm 137:4). In Goldberg's poem, the speaker is at home in the Land of Israel but is alienated from childhood memories of a more traditional milieu. Her response becomes, "How can we sing Zion's song on Zion's soil / when we have not begun to hear?" Songs cannot be sung when newcomers do not feel at home, "hearing" the land. The next three poems in the series provide answers to this challenge. The fourth one puts the missing words in the mouths of the wandering birds:

| | |
|---|---|
| **Journeying Birds** | **צִיּפּוּרֵי מַסָּע** |
| That spring morning<br>heaven grew wings.<br>Wandering westward,<br>the living heavens recited<br>*T'fillat Haderekh*:[22]<br>"Our God,<br>bring us in peace<br>beyond the ocean<br>beyond the abyss, | אוֹתוֹ בֹּקֶר אָבִיב<br>צָמְחוּ לַשָּׁמַיִם כְּנָפַיִם.<br>וּבְנוּדָם מַעֲרָבָה<br>אָמְרוּ הַשָּׁמַיִם הַחַיִּים<br>אֶת תְּפִלַּת הַדֶּרֶךְ:<br>"אֱלֹהֵינוּ,<br>הֲבִיאֵנוּ בְּשָׁלוֹם |

and return us in fall
to this tiny land,
for she has heard our songs."[23]

אֶל מֵעֵבֶר לַיָּם
אֶל מֵעֵבֶר לַתְּהוֹם,
וּלְעֵת סְתָו הַחֲזִירֵנוּ
אֶל הָאָרֶץ הַקְּטַנָּה הַזֹּאת,
שֶׁשָּׁמְעָה אֶת שִׁירֵינוּ".

Unlike Goldberg's other poems discussed here, "Journeying Birds" reflects no distance from God—who appears like the God of tradition and who is addressed in a heartfelt prayer for a safe journey. Yet the prayer emanates from the mouth of birds, not the poet's. What is impossible for her, who does not possess the language of prayer, can be uttered freely and naturally by the birds.

This is not a typical poem for Goldberg in the sense that she uses a familiar liturgical phrase, *T'fillat Haderekh*, even drawing upon its contents, which, traditionally, asks God "to bring us to our destination for life ... and peace ... and to return us to our homes in peace." Like traditional Jewish prayer too, the birds speak in the first person plural.[24] Goldberg, by contrast, could only address "my God," not the "traditional God" of common Jewish prayer.[25]

"Journeying Birds" answers the question presented in "Night," the first poem in this series, in a positive and hopeful way. Goldberg herself frequently traveled to Europe lecturing and teaching; so too the birds leave "this land" intentionally—not as captives—knowing they may return at will. In "Night" the speaker mourns the fact that she cannot sing the song of the land because "we have not begun to hear [the land's song]." The land, however, has heard the birds' songs. Goldberg often writes about birds, who symbolize, for her, joy and freedom.[26] In this very native and local poem she allows the birds to address the ineffable with a joyful prayer that she cannot make herself.

## Yona Wallach

Yona Wallach (1944–1985) was born in Kfar Ono (today Kiryat Ono); she moved to Tel Aviv in her twenties, where she became a productive poet, with a unique voice, known also for her bohemian lifestyle. She reached national prominence in 1982, with "Tefillin," a poem that treated this sacred ritual object as a vehicle for sexual sadomasochistic arousal and led to major public controversy. Twenty-eight years after her untimely death, Wallach reemerged as a cultural phenomenon (from 2013 to 2015, for example, three films were made about her life and legacy).

Wallach had little or nothing to do with organized religion and was never a student of Jewish (or any religious) matters. Yet her writing reveals profound mystical yearning for the divine.[27] In keeping with her minimal Jewish education, she employs few Jewish idioms in her poetry and does without such common Jewish themes as Shabbat, the festivals, the Land, or the people of Israel. Some critics claim that her poetry (which is described as "highly idiosyncratic, mystical, religious and poetic") contains "hints and shards of kabbalistic concepts and terminology."[28] But if so, her use of Kabbalah is intuitive rather than being rooted in systematic knowledge or adherence to any mystical school.

Shortly before Wallach succumbed to cancer, she spoke about her encounter with God to fellow poet Hillit Yeshurun:

> I heard Him from a very tender age. I heard Him and felt Him from a very tender age. I loved Him tremendously. I was truly in love with Him, it was the love of my life. He has been calling me ever since I was a little girl.[29]

This intimate familiarity with God is reflected in "Never Will I Hear the Sweet Voice of God" (1976), a poem that laments the absence of an intimate encounter with a God who is presented as embodied by an actual voice and a physical and even sensual presence:

### Never Will I Hear the Sweet Voice of God

Never will I hear the sweet
  voice of God
never again will His sweet voice
  pass under my window
big drops will fall in the wide
  open spaces a sign
God doesn't come anymore
  through my window

לְעוֹלָם לֹא אֶשְׁמַע עוֹד אֶת קוֹלוֹ
הַמָּתוֹק שֶׁל הָאֱלֹהִים
לְעוֹלָם לֹא אֶשְׁמַע אֶת קוֹלוֹ
הַמָּתוֹק שֶׁל הָאֱלֹהִים
לְעוֹלָם לֹא יַעֲבֹר עוֹד קוֹלוֹ
חַלּוֹנִי תַּחַת
טִפּוֹת גְּדוֹלוֹת יֵרְדוּ בַּמֶּרְחָבִים אוֹת

how again will I see
  His sweet body
dive into His eyes not descend
  anymore to pull out
glances that pass by in the
  universe like wind
how will I remember this
  beauty and not weep
days will pass in my life like
  spasms in the body
near shards of touch remembered shattered from weeping
the form of His motion when
  He moved enchanting the air
never will the voice of longing
  pass the threshold
when man will revive like the
  dead in memory, like being
if only His sweet glance
  would stand by my bed
and I weep.[30]

אֵין הָאֱלֹהִים בָּא עוֹד בְּחַלּוֹנִי
אֵיךְ אוּכַל עוֹד לִרְאוֹת
אֶת גּוּפוֹ הַמָּתוֹק
לִצְלֹל בְּעֵינָיו לֹא אֵרֵד עוֹד לִשְׁלוֹת
מַבָּטִים יַחְלְפוּ בַּיְּקוּם כְּמוֹ רוּחַ
אֵיךְ אֶזְכֹּר אֶת הַיֹּפִי הַזֶּה וְלֹא אֵבְךְ
יָמִים יַעַבְרוּ בְּחַיַּי
כְּמוֹ רְטָטִים בַּגּוּף
לְיַד רְסִיסִים שֶׁל זִכְרֵי מַגָּע
נִשְׁבָּרִים עוֹד יוֹתֵר מִבֶּכֶה
מַקְסִימָה אֶת הָאֲוִיר צוּרַת
תְּנוּעָתוֹ בְּנוּעוֹ
לְעוֹלָם לֹא יַעֲבֹר קוֹל הַגַּעְגּוּעִים
אֶת הַסַּף
עֵת אָדָם יִחְיֶה כְּמוֹ מֵתָיו
בִּזְכְרוֹנוֹת, כְּמוֹ הֱוָיָה
וְלוּא יַעֲמֹד מַבָּטוֹ הַמָּתוֹק
לְיַד מִטָּתִי וְאֶבְכֶּה.

The poem's decisive second line, "never *again* ..." assumes prior intimate
encounters with the divine. The poem draws on these memories, describing the many forms of such encounter in an increasing crescendo of
intensity. At first, it is just God's "voice" that passed under her window,
but later, she beholds "His sweet body" and, more intimately, mentions
diving "into His eyes." Toward the end she even refers to a tangible communion—the "shards of touch remembered." From this touch, this most
intimate form of encounter, she withdraws, renouncing the possibility of
a future encounter and substitutes "the voice of longing" for the initial
"voice of God" that she may never experience again. She settles for the
hope of God's "sweet glance" in place of the real presence, standing by
her bed that she may weep the loss.

Some have speculated that the death of her father when she was only four (he was killed in the War of Independence in 1948) left Wallach in search of a positive and beneficial male figure. Whatever the case, one cannot fail to be struck by the absence of such a godlike figure here and in the next poem as well.

"When You Come to Sleep with Me Like God" (1983) should be read in the context of a group of poems beginning with the words "When you come to sleep with me like ..." (or, simply, "Come to sleep with me"), in which she describes taboo-breaking fantasies of sexual intercourse with male figures, usually in authority and power—a policeman, "my father," a judge, and even God.[31] Wallach wrote these poems when she was already very ill, perhaps reflecting her despair at imminent death. Some understand these poems as an attempt to shock the reader. Others find in them a protest of the weak and the powerless against the authoritative and powerful. I see these poems—especially the one that follows—as reflecting a desire for an impossible union, or even communion.

| When You Come to Sleep with Me Like God | כשתבוא לשכב אתי כמו אלוהים |
|---|---|
| Come sleep with me like God | תָּבוֹא לִשְׁכַּב אִתִּי כְּמוֹ אֱלֹהִים |
| only in spirit | רַק בָּרוּחַ |
| torment me with all your might | עֲנֵה אוֹתִי בְּכָל שֶׁתּוּכַל |
| be unattainable forever | הֱיֵה לֹא מֻשָּׂג לְעוֹלָם |
| let me go in my suffering | הַנַּח לִי בְּסִבְלִי |
| I'll be in deep waters | אֶהְיֶה בְּמַיִם עֲמֻקִים |
| I'll never reach the shore. | לְעוֹלָם לֹא אַגִּיעַ לַחוֹף. |
| Not even in a glance | גַּם לֹא בְּמַבָּט |
| not in a feeling | לֹא בְּהַרְגָּשָׁה |
| or in flood | אוֹ בְּמַבּוּל |
| waters beneath and above | מַיִם לְמַטָּה וּמִלְמַעְלָה |
| never any sky open air | לְעוֹלָם לֹא שָׁמַיִם אֲוִיר פָּתוּחַ |
| the open place most closed in the world | הַמָּקוֹם הַפָּתוּחַ הֲכִי סָגוּר בָּעוֹלָם |
| an open place | |
| always a closed open place | |
| not open not closed | |
| that is, closed open | |
| that is, not closed and not open | |

never I shall imagine
seeing everything from above
seeing from above the landscape
Be only spiritual
a pain clean and alone like
  the sound of pain
never shall I touch
never shall I know
never shall I really feel
not ever really
like all those of yours
always on the way.[32]

מָקוֹם פָּתוּחַ
תָּמִיד מָקוֹם סָגוּר פָּתוּחַ
לֹא פָּתוּחַ וְלֹא סָגוּר
כְּלוֹמַר סָגוּר פָּתוּחַ
כְּלוֹמַר לֹא סָגוּר וְלֹא פָּתוּחַ
לְעוֹלָם שֶׁלֹּא אֲדַמֶּה
לִרְאוֹת מִלְמַעְלָה אֶת הַכֹּל
לִרְאוֹת מִלְמַעְלָה אֶת הַנּוֹף
הֱיֵה רַק רוּחָנִי
כְּאֵב נָקִי וּמְבֻדָּד כִּצְלִיל כְּאֵב
לְעוֹלָם שֶׁלֹּא אֶגַּע
לְעוֹלָם שֶׁלֹּא אֵדַע
לְעוֹלָם שֶׁלֹּא אַרְגִּיש מַמָּש
אַף פַּעַם לֹא מַמָּש
כְּמוֹ כֹּל הָאֵלֶּה שֶׁלְּךָ
תָּמִיד בַּדֶּרֶךְ.

Unlike many poems that depict God as human (like Goldberg's "I Saw My God at the Café"), Wallach asks her human lover to act like God, thereby aspiring to the impossible: no lover can "play" God adequately. She begins with a call for her lover to sleep with her like God "only in spirit" and later requests, "Be only spiritual." But the poem expresses a clear visceral experience—the lover is to torment her; she wants to be engulfed in "deep waters," in pain "clean and alone." Yet she knows, "Never shall I touch / never shall I know / never shall I really feel."

In "Never Will I Hear the Sweet Voice of God," Wallach mourns her distance from God but at least relates past experiences of communion with him. Here, however, she does not even allude to that possibility. The poem is presented as an "*imitatio Dei* manual" for her human lover—he should strive to imitate God—which means, of course, that he will be unattainable. On another level, one may detect great anger toward God: He exists but is absent and that absence is painful precisely because of his omnipresence. It is a desperately negative evaluation of the potential for the sacred in the relationship among humans and with the divine itself; there can be no real encounter—it may come "only in spirit" and "always on the way."

## Orit Gidali

Orit Gidali is an Israeli-born poet and an instructor of creative literature with a master's degree in Hebrew literature from Beer Sheva University. Unlike both Goldberg and Wallach, Gidali is married and the mother of four children. Her poems often deal with home and children, which take on political significance. Her translator, Marcela Sulak, writes:

> Orit Gidali was born in Israel in 1974, months after the simultaneous surprise attacks on the country from the north and the south that initiated the Yom Kippur War and revived acute existential fears linked to the Holocaust twenty-five years before. She was born into a society skeptical of its leadership and into a culture that was beginning to shift its focus from the collective to the individual.... In Gidali's work, the domestic sphere is the stage on which the drama of the geopolitical is revealed on an individual scale.[33]

The following poem takes us into the house, a painful domestic realm, and is phrased as prayer. The title, *Elohei Imahot Hakash*, "God of the Straw Mothers," explores the vulnerable state of the mothers who, like straw, are disempowered but have to take on the role of God in the world.

### God of the Straw Mothers

God of the straw mothers, who are ready to burn, for they have no real blood, just true saliva, and truthful hands, and truthful heart palpitations. God, who sends them into house-battle, the living room field of conflict, the wars of the fragments. God, who sets them where there are no bulletproof

### אלוהי אמהות הקש

אֱלֹהֵי אִמָּהוֹת הַקַּשׁ הַמּוּכָנוֹת
לְהִשָּׂרֵף כִּי אֵין בָּן דַּם אֱמֶת, רַק
רַק אֱמֶת וִידֵי אֱמֶת וְהַלְמוּת־לֵב
אֱמֶת. אֱלֹהֵי הַשּׁוֹלֵחַ אוֹתָן אֶל
קְרָב הַבַּיִת וְזִירַת הַסָּלוֹן וּמִלְחֲמוֹת
הַשְּׁבָרִים. אֱלֹהֵי הַמַּעֲמִיד אוֹתָן
בִּמְקוֹם שֶׁבּוֹ אֵין אֲפוֹדִים וְאֵין

vests, no steel helmets, and where language is the tip of a spear that cannot be thrown far from the body, and where everything is naked in the face of the daughter's horses who gallops through her words, to see what is left standing this time after she strikes.

God of the distance between two bedrooms, like that between two fingers giving a V-sign, God of defeat, God of the one who will let no-one touch her because she once was touched, God of hope which is sung like a private anthem and then snuffed out, God of the insult spoken only inwards, God of silence.

You who formed the mother and her suffering from a rib might also have formed from the outstretched hand with which I reach toward her face each morning, to shift a rebellious hair or to stroke her as she moves, then immediately withdraw and retreat, afraid to be proven wrong.[34]

קַסְדּוֹת פֶּלֶד, וְהַלָּשׁוֹן הִיא קְצֵה
חֲנִית שֶׁלֹּא נִתָּן לְהָטִיל הַרְחֵק מִן
הַגּוּף, וְהַכֹּל עוֹמֵד חָשׂוּף אֶל מוּל
סוּסֵי הַבַּת הַדּוֹהֶרֶת בְּמִלּוֹתֶיהָ,
לִבְדֹּק מַה יַעֲמֹד הַפַּעַם אַחֲרֵי
שֶׁתַּהֲלֹם.

אֱלֹהֵי הַמֶּרְחָק שֶׁבֵּין שְׁנֵי חַדְרֵי
הַשֵּׁנָה, כְּמוֹ בֵּין שְׁתֵּי אֶצְבָּעוֹת
הַמְּסַמְּנוֹת נִצָּחוֹן, אֱלֹהֵי הַתְּבוּסָה,
אֱלֹהֵי זוֹ שֶׁלֹּא תִּתֵּן שֶׁיִּגְּעוּ בָּהּ
כִּי פַּעַם נָגְעָה. אֱלֹהֵי הַתִּקְוָה
שֶׁמּוּשֶׁרֶת כְּמוֹ הִמְנוֹן פְּרָטִי וְאָז
כָּבָה, אֱלֹהֵי הָעֶלְבּוֹן הַמְּדֻבָּר רַק
פְּנִימָה, אֱלֹהֵי הַשְּׁתִיקָה.

אַתָּה שֶׁעָשִׂיתָ מִן הַצֵּלָע אֵם עַל
עִצְבוֹנָהּ, יָכוֹל לַעֲשׂוֹת גַּם מִן
הַיָּד הַשְּׁלוּחָה, שֶׁאֲנִי שׁוֹלֵחַ אֶל
פָּנֶיהָ כָּל בֹּקֶר כְּדֵי לְהָזִיז שַׂעֲרָה
סוֹרֶרֶת אוֹ כְּדֵי לְלַטֵּף אַגַּב תְּנוּעָה,
וּמִיָּד מְשִׁיבָהּ וְנָסוֹגָה, פּוֹחֶדֶת
שֶׁאֶתְבַּדֶּה.

The invocation of the phrase "God of the straw mothers" echoes the first blessing of the *Amidah*, the central prayer of the Jewish worship service: "God of our fathers." But while the traditional prayer then specifies the names of the patriarchs, Gidali invokes anonymous mothers; and while the *Amidah* refers to the love that God has bestowed upon those patriarchs, Gidali pictures powerless mothers who must fight endless battles alone. And while the invocation of the fathers of faith empowers the worshipers, who liken their relationship with God to that of the ancestors, Gidali's reference to a "God of defeat" testifies only to God's connection to pain and loss. In this defiant but dispirited poem, identifying with the mothers is not empowering; anger is directed not just at God's absence (as in Wallach's poem) but also at God's uselessness in the world. The mothers are more defenseless even than soldiers in the battlefield, since they have "no steel helmets." Their tongue is their only weapon, and it is so near the body that it may harm its owner no less than the foe.

Gidali's lonely mothers are in constant struggle for survival; they suffer the pain and insult of difficult marriages and harsh motherhood. Gidali takes the wars of God into the unheroic domestic realm where home is utterly alienated territory and mothers are homeless in their own home. The domestic battle field becomes a realm created by God, however; so that one must question God's providence in the world He created.

"God of the Straw Mothers" is a prayer. Gidali passes over questions of whether God exists or may hear prayer. She simply addresses God as real (albeit, impotent). More than two-thirds of it is an address to God (the phrase "God of ..." appears nine times). Only the last sentence is a petition, and even it is very tentative. It does not dare to ask directly for help; it only reminds God that He "formed the mother and her suffering from a rib," but might equally have done so "from the outstretched hand with which I reach toward her face each morning." At best, God may collaborate with the poet—a woman herself (a friend? a sister? an angel?), who will provide aid. The redemptive help from God can at best just ease the pain. God is but an auxiliary entity to the human, who will ease the suffering.

This short journey through the work of three female poets, each representing a generation of Israeli poetry, shows that religiosity and engagement with God are not limited to classical forms of prayer and to "religious" circles. Hesitancy, tentativeness, aspiration, desire to hear the voice of and to be heard by the divine, anger, and even defiance are reflected in these poems that reveal a world of vivacious religious sentiment, which is far richer and more bountiful than initially expected. In light of the stagnation of many religious expressions on one hand and the lack of engagement on the other, one may hope to see the fulfillment of the call of the poet Avot Yeshurun that "Hebrew literature should renew prayer."[35]

ᑯᗰᎧ

# Facing God's Face and God's Back

## HEBREW POETRY AS PRAYER

*Dr. Wendy Zierler*

The thirteen attributes of God are revealed to Moses in the context of a series of biblical chapters rife with references to faces and backs. Moses has just received the first set of tablets from God, but the people are impatient with his absence and importune Aaron for gods "that can walk before us" (*l'faneinu*; Exodus 32:1). The golden calf ensues, with God declaring the people "a stiff-necked people" (*am k'sheih oref*; Exodus 32:9), defined by the inflexible back of their necks, betokening an unwillingness to bend and accept the yoke of heaven. Moses and the Levites smite the sinners, after which Moses seeks (and gets) divine forgiveness for the remaining people, but with the proviso that they are too stiff-necked for God to accompany them into the Promised Land.

---

Dr. Wendy Zierler is Sigmund Falk Professor of Modern Jewish Literature and Feminist Studies at Hebrew Union College–Jewish Institute of Religion, New York. She is editor with Rabbi Carole Balin and translator of *To Tread on New Ground: The Selected Writings of Hava Shapiro* and *Behikansi atah* (Shapiro's collected writings, in the original/Hebrew). She is also author of *And Rachel Stole the Idols* and the feminist Haggadah commentary featured in *My People's Passover Haggadah: Traditional Texts, Modern Commentaries* (Jewish Lights), a finalist for the National Jewish Book Award. She contributed to *Who by Fire, Who by Water*—Un'taneh Tokef; *All These Vows*—Kol Nidre; *We Have Sinned: Sin and Confession in Judaism*—Ashamnu *and* Al Chet; *May God Remember: Memory and Memorializing in Judaism*—Yizkor; *All the World: Universalism, Particularism and the High Holy Days*; and *Naming God: Our Father, Our King*—Avinu Malkeinu (all Jewish Lights).

Eventually, the pillar of cloud visits Moses, and Moses speaks with God "face-to-face [*panim el panim*], as one speaks with his friend" (Exodus 33:11). As a seeming result of these intimate discussions, God decides to accompany the people into the Promised Land after all: "My presence [literally, my face] will walk with you" (*panai yelekhu*), God says (Exodus 33:14).

Just as we learn of Moses's ability to speak "face-to-face" with God, we discover that maybe he cannot! When he asks to see God's glory, God offers only to pass "all my goodness before you"—literally, "upon your face" (*al panekha*; Exodus 33:19)—but insists, "You cannot see my face [*panai*], for no one can see Me and live.... You shall see my back; but my face shall not be seen" (Exodus 33:20, 33:23). The presentation of the thirteen attributes in the next chapter, with God passing before Moses's face, is thus linked to a revelation of "God's back." It is a potent enough revelation, however, that when Moses descends from Sinai, "the skin of his face sent forth beams" (Exodus 34:30) such that the people feared looking directly at his face. From then on Moses wore a veil in their presence (Exodus 34:33).

Why all these references to (covered) faces and backs? How can Moses speak "face-to-face with God, as if with a friend," but then need to be tucked away from God's face in the cranny of a rock, getting a glimpse only of God's back—an experience, however, that renders his own face unbearably radiant? To what extent are the thirteen attributes of God merely a distant, anterior glimpse of God? Are these spoken attributes of mercy instances of conversation face-to-face or just a theological retrospective from behind?

The Talmud (Rosh Hashanah 17b) depicts the episode as an anterior view. According to Rabbi Yochanan, God wrapped himself (as in a *tallit*) like a prayer leader, then showed Moses the thirteen attributes as an order of prayer that the people should recite to request forgiveness. If one considers the traditional position of a *sh'liach tzibbur* (a prayer leader) at the front of a congregation, his face toward the ark and his back to the people, Moses's view of God in this Talmudic passage is both literally and figuratively from behind—Moses and the people forever trailing God, pursuing God's mercy at a hierarchical, liturgical remove.

In contrast to Exodus 31–34, with its emphasis on backs, we get Psalm 27, which focuses on faces. It too is associated with the High Holy Days, in that it is traditionally recited throughout the penitential season from the beginning of Elul on. Like Moses (in Exodus), the psalmist (of Psalm 27) requests instruction in God's ways (v. 11) and seeks God's face: "I seek your face, Adonai" (*et panekha Adonai avakesh*; v. 8). In Exodus 33, God had promised Moses, "I will make all my goodness pass before you" (v. 19), but then shown him only God's back (v. 23). Psalm 27, therefore, beseeches God not to hide "your face from me" (v. 9), hoping to see the "goodness of Adonai in the land of the living" (v. 13).

Over the past few decades, a flowering of secular Israeli Hebrew poetry has reinvigorated Psalm 27's quest for this hidden but living reality of God. "Poetry, like religious belief," says Israeli scholar Avi Sagi, "assumes that manifest, immanent reality does not represent everything; there is a hidden foundation to existence, that which poetry reveals and to which faith turns (or faces)."[1] Some of this contemporary prayer poetry specifically evokes Exodus 31–34, albeit with Psalm 27's determination to seek God's face.

Against the grain of Exodus 33, poet Yehuda Amichai (1923–2000) insists that Moses actually saw God's face, albeit once, but then, tragically, forgot what it looked like. Moses didn't desire to see the desert or the land God promised, only God's face.[2]

According to Amichai, Moses's failing memory of the moment leads to a desperate attempt at retrieval, akin to a manhunt. Moses creates a facial composite of God, cobbled together from various visual images, including the image of the burning bush and the face of Pharaoh's daughter leaning over him in the basket. He distributes the composite in the hope that someone will lead him to the missing face of God. But Exodus itself declares, "No one can see Me and live" (33:20), so no such luck. Amichai's Moses dies on Mount Nebo—only then (as a sort of deathbed gift?) finally seeing—and receiving a kiss from—God's face.

If Amichai's poem depicts the quest for God's face, poet Rivka Miriam (b. 1952) details the dangerous consequences of seeing God's back. The poem, incredibly, appeared in her debut collection, published when she was only fourteen years old!

### For Man Shall Not See Me and Live, by Rivka Miriam

And Moses saw His back
Brownish-whiteness
And saw a wrinkle in His thirsty,
stiff neck, filled with astonishment.

And smelled yellow incense
Like the scent of bare footsteps
Promenading between
Clouds at night....
Moses saw His footsteps
That remained imprinted in the sand
And sprouted grass
As if to cover an old man's grave.
And a tear fell from Moses's eye
That became one with the sand,
With the sprouted grass
Upon the all-knowing footsteps.
Moses wanted to kneel
And offer hyssop
And be buried with an ancient god
In the wet dust.[3]

Rivka Miriam's depiction of revelation includes hints of clouds and incense, evocative of worship at the desert Tabernacle. What Moses actually saw was God as an old man, as wizened, stiff-necked, and inflexible as God's inflexible people. Whereas Amichai has Moses die as a consequence of seeing and being kissed by God's face, Miriam, a young girl, presents God as a proud, bent-over old man, an image that she then lays to rest in an "old man's grave." Unable to revivify this buried God, Miriam's Moses seeks only to kneel and be buried alongside its remains.

In yet another poem (in this same collection), however, Rivka Miriam's poetic speaker herself brings new life to the revelation:

### Still, by Rivka Miriam

God knocked on my window
And the skin of my face shone.
His spirit passed my threshold
And my eyes opened wide in his direction
He left his fingers impressed
In the mist of my window
The scent of his breath remained
In my room.
His shadow remained hidden

> Behind my curtain's silk
> And his deep song echoes
> From inside my floor....[4]

The poet has Exodus 31–34 in mind. Like Moses's face (34:29), the skin of the speaker's face shines after encountering God. The tablets were written with the finger of God (31:18), and the speaker's windowsill is imprinted similarly ("his fingers impressed in the mist of my window"). But God's "shadow remained hidden behind [*achorei*] my curtain's silk," recalling God's insistence that Moses see only God's "back" (*achorai*; 34:23).

In contrast to the biblical account, however, this revelation is no shadowy view from a stony desert crag; it occurs with eyes wide open and in a domestic, everyday context, the speaker's own room. In the second part of the poem (not reproduced here), God actually inhabits the room but finds it "too narrow" and flees to the fields. Still, the encounter leaves behind its multisensory impact: God's song "echoes from inside the floor" beneath her feet; God's "scent" still remains; God's finger leaves an imprint not only in the mist of her windowsill (as we see here) but also on her forehead, that is, in her mind and spirit. Completely absent from this poem are references to the biblical divine attributes or the Talmudic revisiting of the encounter from the perspective of seeking forgiveness. Instead, the poem focuses on the experience of encountering God in everyday life, with poetry its representation and result.

The notion of everyday revelation appears even more prominently in *Higanu l'Elohim* ("We Reached God"), the title poem of a 1998 collection by Admiel Kosman (b. 1957). The revelation here occurs on a mountainside, as in the biblical text, but accidentally, and to a group, not an individual:

> We reached God
> Completely by accident. In effect, we stumbled upon
> Him.
> We were at the halfway there, by the slope of the
> mountain
> With all the laden-down donkeys,
> And suddenly, by the curved path, when we inclined to
> look,
> We stumbled upon Him.

> He was looking for us too,
> Like a precious stone, He said, like a pearl,
> Precisely like something lost.
> Completely by happenstance, we were halfway there,
> when we reached
> The appointed land,
> That is, we reached God.
> And we found complete rest from life....[5]

The reference to finding "complete rest" may reflect the commandment to keep Shabbat, which appears later in Exodus 34 (v. 21)—albeit detached from the ritual context. Halfway through their mountain hike, this group of people experiences an unexpected epiphany in broad daylight, they and God together, seeking, finding, and speaking to one another face-to-face.

"The craving for God has never subsided in the Jewish soul," writes Abraham Joshua Heschel. "Despite the warning, 'Thou canst not see my face, for man shall not see Me and live' (Exodus 32:20), there were many who persisted in yearning."[6] Contemporary Israeli poetry reveals this persistence even in so-called secular Hebrew poetry, albeit in a more prosaic context. In the midrashic collection *Avot D'rabbi Natan*, Rabbi Shimon warns against making prayer a conversation; rather, prayer should offer "supplications before the Holy One Blessed be He, as it is said, for He is a merciful and gracious God, endlessly patient, most kind and will repent of the evil decree."[7] These contemporary Israeli poets searching for God prefer conversation over a formulaic recitation of attributes; they seek God's inspirational face through the medium of words and poetry, their own form of contemporary prayer.

⟨⟨⟨⟩⟩⟩

# Appendix

# Thirteen Attributes Elsewhere in the Bible

Numbers 14:18: Adonai is endlessly patient, most kind, forgiving sins and transgressions, [certainly not] cleansing....

Deuteronomy 4:31: For Adonai your God is the merciful God.

Joel 2:13: [Return to God who is] merciful and gracious. He is endlessly patient, and most kind.

Jonah 4:2: For You are the merciful and gracious God, endlessly patient and most kind....

Nahum 1:3: Adonai is endlessly patient and greatly powerful, [certainly not] cleansing.

Psalm 78:38: [God] is merciful, pardoning sins.

Psalm 86:5: For You, Adonai, are good and forgiving, most kind to all who call on You.

Psalm 86:15: You, Adonai, are the merciful and gracious God, endlessly patient, most kind and truthful.

Psalm 103:8: Merciful and gracious is Adonai, endlessly patient and most kind.

Psalm 111:4: Adonai is merciful and gracious.

Psalm 112:4: [God] is gracious and merciful and righteous.

Psalm 116:5: Adonai is gracious and righteous.

Psalm 145:8: Adonai is gracious and merciful, endlessly patient and very kind.

Nehemiah 9:17: [You, God of forgiveness] are gracious and merciful, endlessly patient, and most kind.

Nehemiah 9:31: ... for You are the gracious and merciful God.

2 Chronicles 30:9: ... for Adonai your God is gracious and merciful.

# *Notes*

## About This Book, by Rabbi Lawrence A. Hoffman, PhD

1. Peter E. Fink, ed., *The New Dictionary of Sacramental Worship* (Collegeville, MN: Liturgical Press, 1990), 382.

## The God of Grace in Judaism, by Rabbi Lawrence A. Hoffman, PhD

1. *Prayer of Manasseh, verse 7*, in James M. Charlesworth, ed., *The Old Testament Pseudepigrapha*, vol. 2 (Peabody, MA: Hendrickson, 2010), 634. Cf. commentary by Esther G. Chazon, "Prayer of Manasseh," in *Outside The Bible: Ancient Jewish Writings Related to Scripture*, vol. 3, ed. Louis H. Feldman, James L. Kugel, and Lawrence H. Schiffman (Philadelphia: Jewish Publication Society, 2013), 2143–2147.
2. *Tosafot*, Rosh Hashanah 17a, d.h. *sh'losh esreh midot*.
3. Cited from *Hamanhig*, in Daniel David Steinberg, *Sefer Sh'losh Esreh Middot* (Brooklyn: Hamatik Printing, 2005), 17–18.
4. See Steinberg, *Sefer Sh'losh Esreh Middot*, 59–60, 49–50, 71–73.
5. Ibid., 17.
6. The lyrics of "Amazing Grace" are by John Newton, who had graduated from impressed servitude as a sailor in the Royal Navy to become captain of his own ship transporting slaves across the Atlantic. The fact that he left the slave trade in 1754/1755, plus his support of William Wilberforce, the primary force behind the abolition of the slave trade in the British Empire in 1807, has led to the widely held assumption that "Amazing Grace" derived from Newton's shame at his former life as a slaver. That etiology may not be true, as Newton joined the abolitionist movement only in 1780, a year after the hymn was written and some twenty-five years after abandoning his career in slavery. He himself, moreover, never claimed the connection. More likely, the hymn came about because Newton had slowly experienced his own internal conversion to Christianity, from the time that his ship capsized in 1748, and he spent time on land reading, among other things, a fifteenth-century classic, *The Imitation of Christ*, by Thomas à Kempis. By 1754/1755, he had been married for five years and was forced to leave shipping when he collapsed aboard ship at sea. Upon returning home, he taught himself enough theology, Latin, and Greek to enter the Church of England as a curate in the small village of Olney, where he wrote his hymn. Only in 1835 did hymn writer William Walker match it to a song already known as "New Britain," the melody so well known today.

7. William James, *The Varieties of Religious Experience* (1902; repr. New York: Random House Modern Library, 1994), 470.
8. See Lawrence A. Hoffman, ed., *My People's Prayer Book*, vol. 5, Birkhot Hashachar—*Morning Blessings* (Woodstock, VT: Jewish Lights, 2001), 157–158.
9. Ibid.
10. See Lawrence A. Hoffman, ed., *Naming God: Our Father, Our King—Avinu Malkeinu* (Woodstock, VT: Jewish Lights, 2015), 58.

### Encountering God: Can God Be Known?, by Rabbi Lawrence A. Hoffman, PhD

1. Mishnah Rosh Hashanah 1:2; Cf. liturgy of *Un'taneh Tokef* and translator's commentary in Lawrence A. Hoffman, ed., *Who by Fire, Who by Water—* Un'taneh Tokef (Woodstock, VT: Jewish Lights, 2010), 38–39, n. 10.
2. See, e.g., Rudolf A. Makkreal, *Dilthey: Philosopher of the Human Studies* (Princeton, NJ: Princeton University Press, 1975), 305–342. Cf. summary discussion in Robert Audi, ed., *The Cambridge Dictionary of Philosophy* (Cambridge: Cambridge University Press, 1995), s.v., *Verstehen*, 834–835.
3. See, e.g., Jeffrey C. Alexander, *The Classical Attempt at Theoretical Synthesis: Max Weber*, Theoretical Logic in Sociology 3 (Berkeley: University of California Press, 1983), 30–31.
4. Stephen Burt, "Ice for the Ice Trade," *New Yorker*, November 23, 2015, 90.
5. Emile Durkheim, *The Religious Forms of Religious Life*, trans. Karen E. Fields (New York: Free Press, 1995), 386–387.
6. Max Bennett and Peter Hacker, *The Philosophical Foundations of Neuroscience* (Oxford: Blackwell, 2002), pt. 1, chap. 3; cited by Roger Scruton, *The Face of God* (London: Continuum Publishing, 2012), 42, n. 19.
7. Roger Scruton, *The Soul of the World* (Princeton, NJ: Princeton University Press, 2014), 10.
8. Scruton, *Face of God*, 33.

### Seeing God through the Metaphoric Imagination, by Rabbi Andrea L. Weiss, PhD

1. This list recurs with slight variations in sixteen other biblical passages: Numbers 14:18; Deuteronomy 4:31; Joel 2:13; Jonah 4:2; Nahum 1:3; Psalms 78:38, 86:5, 86:15, 103:8, 111:4, 112:4, 116:5, 145:8; Nehemiah 9:17, 9:31; 2 Chronicles 30:9. See the appendix.

### How the Bible Became the Prayer Book: Not Threats of Punishment but Rabbinic Promises of Forgiveness, by Rabbi Margaret Moers Wenig, DD

1. See Lawrence A. Hoffman, ed., earlier volumes in the Prayers of Awe series: *All These Vows—Kol Nidre* (Woodstock, VT: Jewish Lights, 2011); *Who by Fire, Who by Water—*Un'taneh Tokef (Woodstock, VT: Jewish Lights, 2010).

2. *High Holiday Prayer Book*, trans. Philip Birnbaum (New York: Hebrew Publishing Company, 1951), 527, 539, 987, 995, 1001.

3. Because *s'lichot* are considered a *seder t'fillah*, *Kaddish Titkabal* follows the recitation of *s'lichot* as it would usually follow an *Amidah*. Some stand for the thirteen attributes in *s'lichot* (though the ark is closed) as they would stand for the *Amidah*.

4. To be sure, punishment is not absent from the Yom Kippur liturgy. The martyrology (*Eleh ezk'rah*) explains the Hadrianic persecution following the Bar Kokhba revolt of 135 CE as punishment due Joseph's brothers and carried out, finally, with the martyrdom of the ten great rabbis of Bar Kokhba's day; see Birnbaum *machzor*, 837ff. The Long Confession (*Al Chet*) in both Ashkenazi and Sephardi traditions concludes with a listing of sins "requiring a burnt offering ... corporal punishment ... forty lashings" and so forth; cf. Birnbaum *machzor*, 555; and Lawrence A. Hoffman, ed., *We Have Sinned: Sin and Confession in Judaism—Ashamnu and Al Chet* (Woodstock, VT: Jewish Lights, 2012), 106–107. The *piyyut Un'taneh Tokef* imagines that on Rosh Hashanah it is written and on Yom Kippur it is sealed: who shall live and who shall die, and so on. That threat or warning, however, is immediately softened by the reassurances that "Turning, Prayer, and Righteousness [usually translated "Repentance, Prayer, and Charity"] temper the severity of the decree" and that God is slow to anger and easy to appease, does not wish us to die [for our sins], and will wait for us to return until the very day of our death; see Birnbaum, *machzor*, 361–363.

5. During the *S'lichot* service that precedes Rosh Hashanah, there is no confession by the individual—only confessions by the congregation as a whole. Those confessions are preceded by four recitations of the Thirteen Attributes. In every service of Yom Kippur, however, confessions are recited silently by the individual and then aloud by the congregation. When the confessions are recited by the individual, they are *not* preceded by the Thirteen Attributes. When recited by the congregation, on Yom Kippur evening and in *N'ilah*, the confessions are preceded by the Thirteen Attributes. Rabbi Joseph B. Soloveitchik describes the difference in tone between the silent/personal confession and the public/voiced one: "The individual does not sing the confession, he weeps.... Not so the community because it does not come to plead for atonement. It claims it as its right.... The communal confession is recited with a sense of confidence, even rejoicing. This is confession in the presence of a loyal ally, a most beloved one.... In many communities it is customary for the whole community to sing *Al Chet* [and *Ashamnu*] in heartwarming melodies"; see Pinchas Peli, ed., *Soloveitchik on Repentance: The Thought and Discourses of Rabbi Joseph B. Soloveitchik* (New York: Paulist Press, 1984), 119. Unlike the tradition to which Soloveitchik is referring, Reform liturgy has not preserved this same distinction between private and public confession, and Reform *machzorim* actually place the confessions prior to the Thirteen Attributes rather than following it.

6. Birnbaum *machzor*, 987, 991, 991, 993, 995, 997, 999, 1001. In contrast to the multiplicity of recitations of the Thirteen Attributes in Orthodox *machzorim*, the *S'lichot* service published by the Reform Movement in 1980 contained not even one recitation of the Thirteen Attributes and the 1993 edition included only one recitation. Similarly, the Reform *machzor* of 1978 (*Gates of Repentance: The New Union Prayerbook for the Days of Awe* [New York: Central Conference of American Rabbis]) omitted all recitations of the Thirteen Attributes from both Yom Kippur evening and *N'ilah*. A reclaiming of tradition is evident in its 2015 *machzor*, in which the Thirteen Attributes is included in the *s'lichot* of Yom Kippur evening and of *N'ilah*; see *Mishkah HaNefesh: Machzor for the Days of Awe*, vol. 2, *Yom Kippur* (New York: CCAR Press, 2015), 100, 105, 107, 644, 646, 648.

7. Of the eight times that the Thirteen Attributes is recited during *N'ilah*, only once does the cantor sing it alone. That comes in the midst of the *piyyut Enkat M'saldecha* (Birnbaum *machzor*, p. 997). The other seven times, the congregation recites it along with the cantor.

8. While the recitation of the Thirteen Attributes increases by 100 percent from Yom Kippur evening to *N'ilah*, the recitation of litanies of confession follows the very opposite trajectory. As our recitations of the attributes of divine mercy increase in number, our confessions decrease. While *Ashamnu* is common to all services, *Al Chet* is omitted at *N'ilah*. In its place, we find "You [God] reach out your hand [*atah noten yad*] to transgressors, your right hand extended to receive repentant sinners.... I do not want the sinner to die [from his sin]. Return to me and live."

9. This is *piska d'yoma*, the verse announcing the day recited on Yom Kippur evening.

## Thirteen Attributes or Ten *Sefirot*? The God of Medieval Mystics, by Dr. Sharon Koren

1. Talmud, Rosh Hashanah 17b; *Midrash T'hillim* 83; *Pirkei D'rabbi Eliezer* 45.

2. Elliot Wolfson, "Metatron and Shi'ur Qomah in the Writings of Hasidei Ashkenaz," in *Mysticism, Magic, and Kabbalah in Ashkenazi Judaism*, ed. Karl Erich Grozinger and Joseph Dan, 85 (Berlin: Walter van Guyter, 1995).

3. See Moshe Idel, *Kabbalah: New Perspectives* (New Haven, CT: Yale University Press, 1988), 112–116. For a different approach, see Elliot B. Gerstel, "S'firot, Middot, and Stars: The Zohar's Biblical Mandate," *Conservative Judaism* 63 (2012): 77–91.

4. *Sefer Y'tzirah* (*SY*), chap. 1. When necessary (see below), I supply precise pages, using the Hayman translation: A. Peter Hayman, trans. and ed., *Sefer Yesira, Texts and Studies in Ancient Judaism* 104 (Tuebingen: Mohr Siebeck Verlag, 2004).

5. Ibid., chap 4.

6. Ibid., 76.

7. Ibid., 70.

8. Gershom Scholem, *Origins of the Kabbalah*, (Princeton, NJ: Princeton University Press, 1991), 347–354; Mark Verman, *The Books of Contemplation: Medieval Jewish Mystical Sources*, (Albany, NY: State University of New York Press, 1992), 79–86, 211–227.
9. Scholem, *Origins of the Kabbalah*, 347–354; Moshe Idel, "The Sefirot above the Sefirot" [in Hebrew], *Tarbiz* 51 (1982): 239–280.
10. *Zohar* (*Idra Zuta*) 3:288b.
11. *Zohar* (*Idra Rabba*) 3:136a–b, translated by David Matt in *The Zohar: Pritzker Edition*, vol. 8 (Palo Alto, CA: Stanford University Press, 2014), 385.

## "By the Grace of God"—A Biblical Idea?, by Dr. Marc Zvi Brettler

1. *Oxford English Dictionary*, s.v. "grace."
2. Ibid.

## The Single, Solitary Self That Isn't, by Rabbi Jonathan Blake

1. See Nahum Sarna, *The JPS Torah Commentary: Exodus* (Philadelphia: Jewish Publication Society, 1991), 216.
2. *Mishkan T'filah* (New York: CCAR Press, 2007), 243.
3. As paraphrased in Lawrence Kushner, "Reading Music," in *I'm God, You're Not: Observations on Organized Religion & Other Disguises of the Ego* (Woodstock, VT: Jewish Lights, 2010), Kindle edition, loc. 2545.
4. See Primo Levi, who describes the journey of a carbon atom in the final chapter, "Carbon," of his celebrated memoir *The Periodic Table* (New York: Schocken Books, 1984), 224–233.
5. See also Neil Shubin, "Vision," chap. 9 in *Your Inner Fish* (New York: Pantheon, 2008). And on television, *Cosmos: A Spacetime Odyssey*, episode 2, "These Are Some of the Things That Molecules Do," first aired March 16, 2014.

## The Son of Truth Meets the God of Compassion, by Rabbi Shoshana Boyd Gelfand

1. For a rich analysis of this and other literary comparisons between the stories of Noah and Jonah, see chapter 1 of Judy Klitsner, *Subversive Sequels in the Bible* (New Milford, CT: Maggid Books, 2011), 1–34.

## Truth: Cast Down and Resurrected, by Rabbi Elie Kaunfer, DHL

1. *Genesis Rabbah* 8:5 (ed. Theodor-Albeck, 60). Translation from Hayim Nahman Bialik and Yehoshua Hana Ravnitzky, eds., *The Book of Legends*, trans. William Braude (New York: Schocken Books, 1992), 13.
2. Numbers 14:18; Joel 2:13; Jonah 4:2; Nahum 1:3; Psalms 86:15, 103:8, 145:8; Nehemiah 9:17.
3. This is at least as bold as the Rabbinic move to cut off the list of attributes in the middle. See Jacob Milgrom, *The JPS Torah Commentary: Numbers* (Philadelphia: Jewish Publication Society, 1990), 393.

4. Talmud, Shabbat 55a.
5. Ibid.
6. He echoes almost word for word Joel 2:13, which may point to a larger relationship between these books. See Uriel Simon, *The JPS Bible Commentary: Jonah* (Philadelphia: Jewish Publication Society, 1999), xxxix, 37.
7. Devora Steinmetz, "Jonah, Son of Truth," in *Beginning Anew: A Woman's Companion to the High Holy Days*, ed. Gail Reimer and Judith Kates, 308–324, esp. 319 (New York: Touchstone, 1997).
8. Ibid.
9. See Steinmetz, "Jonah, Son of Truth," 312, for a different model of truth, embodied in the widow of 1 Kings 17: "The widow's definition of *emet* stands in contrast with the one that Jonah and the early Elijah seem to hold: *emet* characterizes the prophet who brings change; mercifully and boldly challenging fate is what a prophet does who has God's word of truth in his mouth."
10. Elie Kaunfer, "*Aval Chatanu* ('But / In Truth We Have Sinned'): A Literary Investigation," in *We Have Sinned: Sin and Confession in Judaism—Ashamnu and Al Chet*, ed. Lawrence A. Hoffman, 181–185 (Woodstock, VT: Jewish Lights, 2012).
11. See Reuven Kimelman, "Psalm 145: Theme, Structure, and Impact," *Journal of Biblical Literature* 113, no. 1 (1994): 37–58, here 51, n. 69. See in addition to the sources listed there: Avraham Yosef Wertheimer and Avraham Liss, eds., *Piskei Ha-Ri'D Le-Rabbi Yeshaya DiTrani Ha-Zaken Le-Berakhot Ve-Shabbat* (Jerusalem: Makhon Ha-Talmud Ha-Yisraeli Ha-Shalem, 1964), 7–8.
12. The medieval authorities read into this a clue that this psalm should be recited every day (cf. Talmud, Berakhot 4b).
13. Cf. *Leviticus Rabbah* 17:1; *Sifrei B'midbar* 42; and others.
14. Daniel Goldschmidt, *Machzor Layamim Hanora'im*, vol. 1 (Jerusalem: Koren, 1970), 79.
15. Ibid., 168.

## Inviting God Back to the Garden, by Rabbi Angela Warnick Buchdahl

1. Abraham Joshua Heschel, *Who Is Man?* (Stanford: Stanford University Press, 1965).

## God—Still All-Good and All-Powerful, by Rabbi Walter Homolka, PhD, DHL

1. Hans Jonas, "The Concept of God after Auschwitz: A Jewish Voice," *Journal of Religion* 67, no. 1 (January 1987): 1–13.
2. Ben Sirach 17:3, 17:6–7, 15:14.
3. Ibid., 15:11–20.
4. *Genesis Rabbah* 9:7.

5. Ben Sirach 15:20.
6. Jonas, "The Concept of God," 12.
7. David Patterson and John Roth, eds., *Fire in the Ashes: God, Evil, and the Holocaust* (Seattle: University of Washington Press, 2005), 189–190.
8. Jenni Frazer, "Wiesel: Yes, We Really Put God on Trial," *The Jewish Chronical London*, September 19, 2008; www.thejc.com/news/uk-news/wiesel-yes-we-really-did-put-god-trial (accessed February 28, 2016).

## God Forgives Because He Has No Choice, by Rabbi Delphine Horvilleur

1. Technically, *v'salachta* is a second-person perfect verb, what the Bible customarily uses for our past tense. It is preceded, however, by the Hebrew letter *vav*, which converts references to the past into projections of the future.
2. This essay was translated from the original French with assistance from Robert Ley.

## Whose Attributes?, by Catherine Madsen

1. Harold Schulweis, *Evil and the Morality of God* (Cincinnati: Hebrew Union College, 1984), 122.
2. Ibid., 123–124.

## A Love Letter from God, by Rabbi Jonathan Magonet, PhD

1. Psalms 86:15, 103:8–10, 145:8; Joel 2:13; Jonah 4:2.
2. This is the broader meaning of "self" in the familiar phrase "You shall love your neighbor as your*self*" (Leviticus 19:18), that is, the fullness of who you are as an adult Israelite male.
3. It is not inappropriate in such circumstances to quote the popular creation of Stan Lee, "With great power comes great responsibility."

## "Adonai, Adonai": The Message of Awe but the Sound of Compassion, by Rabbi Sonja Keren Pilz, PhD

1. Cf. Moshe Nathanson, ed., *Zamru Lo*, vol. 3, *Congregational Melodies for the Shalosh R'galim and the High Holidays* (New York: Cantors Assembly, 1974), 58, for the congregational melodies of I. Rice and A. M. Bernstein; and Jeffrey Shiovitz, ed., *Zamru Lo: The Next Generation*, vol. 2, *Congregational Melodies for the High Holidays* (New York: Cantors Assembly, 2006), 69–71, for the compositions of M. Kotlowitz and L. Lewandoski—the melodies most commonly used—and Sol Zim.

## Cutting God Slack, by Rabbi Jeffrey K. Salkin, DMin

1. Amos Oz, *A Tale of Love and Darkness* (New York: Mariner Books, 2005).

## Becoming God, by Rabbi Dennis C. Sasso, DMin

1. Another possibility is Umberto Cassuto's reading, by which the repetition is meant to connote "The Lord, He is the Lord"—i.e., "*YHVH* [who is] *YHVH*." Umberto Cassuto, *Commentary on Exodus* (Jerusalem: Magnes Press, Hebrew University, 1967), 439.
2. See, e.g., *Sifrei D'varim, Ekev.*
3. Mordecai Kaplan, *Not So Random Thoughts* (New York: Reconstructionist Press, 1966), 144.
4. Mordecai Kaplan, *The Meaning of God in Modern Jewish Religion* (New York: Reconstructionist Press, 1962), 40–103.
5. Harold M. Schulweis, *Evil and the Morality of God* (Cincinnati: Hebrew Union College Press, 1984), 115–145.
6. Paul Marcus, *In Search of the Good Life: Emmanuel Levinas, Psychoanalysis, and the Art of Living* (London: Karnac Books, 2010), 182–83.
7. Harold M. Schulweis, *For Those Who Can't Believe* (New York: Harper Collins, 1994), 106–118.

## The Common Thread of Judaism: God's Character and Our Own, by Dr. Annette M. Boeckler

1. Carlo Stenger, *The Fear of Insignificance: Searching for Meaning in the Twenty-First Century* (Basingstoke, UK: Palgrave Macmillan, 2011), 1.
2. Ibid., 23.
3. Exodus 34:6–7 is alluded to in Exodus 20:5; Numbers 14:17-19; Deuteronomy 4:31, 5:10; Hosea 1:6–7; Joel 2:13; Jonah 4:2; Micah 7:18–20; Nahum 1:2-3; Psalms 51:3, 57:11, 69:16–17, 77:8–9, 78:38, 86:5, 86:15, 103:8, 108:4, 111:4, 112:4, 119:156, 145:8; Lamentations 3:22; Daniel 9:4; Nehemiah 9:17, 9:31; 2 Chronicles 30:9.
4. Abraham ibn Ezra to Exodus 3:4.
5. Maimonides, *Mishneh Torah*, Laws of Personal Development 1:6.
6. Ibid., 1:7.

## Not What We Were but What We Will Be, by Rabbi Joshua M. Davison

1. David Brooks, "Going Home Again," *New York Times*, March 20, 2014.
2. Rabbi Steven Z. Leder, "The Pen of Our Lives," in *The Extraordinary Nature of Ordinary Things*, (Springfield, NJ: Behrman House, 1999), 130–131.
3. Fred Shoemaker, *Extraordinary Golf: The Art of the Possible* (New York: Penguin Putnam, 1996), 9–11.
4. Rabbi Chaim Stern, ed., *Day by Day* (New York: CCAR Press, 1998), 164.
5. Robert Frost, "The Road Not Taken." in *The Poetry of Robert Frost: The Collected Poems, Complete and Unabridged* (New York: Henry Holt, 1979).

6. Rachel Naomi Remen, "Choosing Life," in *Chicken Soup for the Jewish Soul,* ed. Jack Canfield, Mark Victor Hansen, and Dov Peretz Elkins (Deerfield Beach, FL: Health Communications, 2001), 52–54.
7. Rabbi Jacob Philip Rudin, "Shofar Voices," in *Very Truly Yours* (New York: Bloch, 1971), 8.

## A Divine Gardener, the Human Face, and a Thousand Acts of Mercy: Innovative Insights from the New Reform *Machzor*, by Rabbi Edwin Goldberg, DHL

1. Michael Lerner, *Jewish Renewal: A Path to Healing and Transformation* (New York: HarperCollins, 1994), 114.
2. *Mishkan HaNefesh: Machzor for the Days of Awe*, vol. 2, *Yom Kippur* (New York: CCAR Press, 2015), 107.
3. Ibid., 455.
4. E.g., ibid., 106.
5. Ibid., 108.
6. Ibid., 313.
7. Ibid., 312.

## Like God: Not Perfect, but Living Up to Our Best Selves, by Ruth W. Messinger

1. This chapter was written with the thoughtful help of Joshua Fried, Rachel Gorosh, and Gabi Hersch.
2. Jonathan Sacks, *To Heal a Fractured World: The Ethics of Responsibility* (New York: Schocken Books, 2005), 5.

## Mercy: Who Needs It?, by Rabbi David A. Teutsch, PhD

1. Jack Kornfield, *The Art of Forgiveness, Lovingkindness and Peace* (New York: Random House, 2008), 42.
2. *Kol Haneshamah: Prayerbook for the Days of Awe*, ed. David A. Teutsch (Wyncote, PA: Reconstructionist Press, 1999), 811.

## In Whose Image? Yom Kippur's Annual Choice, by Rabbi Daniel G. Zemel

1. Solomon Goldman, *In the Beginning* (New York: Harper Brothers, 1949), xi.
2. Joseph B. Soloveitchik, *The Lonely Man of Faith* (New York: Doubleday, 1965), 66.

## Loose Ends Can't Always Be Tied, by Rabbi Lawrence A. Englander, CM, DHL, DD

1. In our official translation here, "God is a king seated on a throne of mercy, governing graciously, pardoning the sins of his people...."

## Who Knows Thirteen? Jews Do, by Rabbi Julia Neuberger

1. Translation from David Birnbaum, *Jews, Church & Civilization: An Integrated Historical Timeline*, vol. 3, 185–1499 CE (New York: Harvard Matrix, 2005), 157.
2. Translation by Joel M. Hoffman, in *My People's Passover Haggadah: Traditional Texts, Modern Commentaries*, vol. 2, ed. Lawrence A. Hoffman and David Arnow (Woodstock, VT: Jewish Lights, 2008), 202.

## Israeli "Secular" Poets Encounter God, by Rabbi Dalia Marx, PhD

1. I thank Rabbi Shelton Donnell and Rabbi Lawrence A. Hoffman, the editor of this volume, for their many helpful comments and their abundant help editing this essay. A more comprehensive version of this essay will be forthcoming. Every effort has been made to trace and acknowledge the copyright holders for the material included in this chapter. The contributor apologizes for any errors or omissions that may remain and asks that any omissions be brought to her attention so that they may be corrected in future editions.
2. Gustav Janouch, *Conversations with Kafka*, trans. G. Rees (New York: New Directions, 1971), 47.
3. John L. Austin, *How to Do Things with Words* (Cambridge: Cambridge University Press, 1962).
4. See an online permanent exhibition of Passover Haggadot from the kibbutz movement in the Israel National Library website: web.nli.org.il/sites/NLI/English/gallery/of-israel/passover/Pages/kibbutz.aspx.
5. Martin Heidegger, "The Word of Nietzsche: 'God Is Dead,'" in *Holzwege*, trans. J. Young and K. Haynes (Cambridge: Cambridge University Press, 2002), 53–112.
6. Ariel Hirshfeld, *Hashirah Ha'ivrit v'yetser Hara* ("Hebrew Poetry and the Evil Inclination"), *Ha'aretz*, June 2, 2004; see also Ariel Hirschfeld, "The Return of the Divine: God's Place in Modern Hebrew Literature," in *A Century of Israeli Culture*, ed. I. Bartal (Jerusalem: Hebrew University Press, 2002), 165–176. See discussion in Shachar Pinsker, "And Suddenly We Reached God," *Journal of Modern Jewish Studies* 5, no. 1 (2006): 22–23.
7. Cited in Shachar Pinsker, "'Never Will I Hear the Sweet Voice of God': Religiosity and Mysticism in Modern Hebrew Poetry," *Prooftexts* 30, no. 1 (2010): 128–146.
8. In a famous letter to Franz Rosenzweig (1926), Gershom Scholem described the power of modern secularized Hebrew: "Fraught with danger is the Hebrew language!" He explains that the immense religious power contained in it can cause the Hebrew language to turn against its speakers.
9. Among these poets are Admiel Kosman, Miron Izakson, Hava Pinchas-Cohen, the poets of the Mashiv Haru'ach group, and Sephardi-Mizrahi *payetanim*.
10. Cf. Hamutal Bar-Yosef, *Mysticism in 20th Century Hebrew Literature* (Boston: Academic Studies Press, 2010); David C. Jacobson, *Creator, Are You*

*Listening? Israeli Poets on God and Prayer* (Bloomington: Indiana University Press, 2007).

11. For similar discussions, cf. Haim Rechnitzer, "From Honolulu to Tel Aviv via Mt. Gilboa: The Rise and Fall of Shlonsky's Messianic *Halutz*," *Hebrew Studies* 55 (2014): 271–95; "To See God in His Beauty: Avraham Chalfi and the Mystical Quest for the Evasive God," *Journal of Modern Jewish Studies* 10, no. 3 (2011): 383–400.

12. For more on Goldberg, see, e.g., Amia Lieblich, *Learning about Lea* (London: Athena Press, 2003). Regarding the religiosity reflected in Goldberg's poetry, see Yehoyada Amir, "Prophecy and Halakhah: Towards Non-Orthodox Religious Praxis in (Eretz) Israel," *Tikvah Working Paper 06/12* (New York: NYU School of Law, 2012).

13. Amir, "Prophecy and Halakhah," 41.

14. Ibid., 39.

15. Ibid., 41.

16. The word *adam* can be also understood as the collective, humankind. But it seems to me that Goldberg speaks of asking forgiveness of an individual.

17. Leah Goldberg, *Taba'ot Ashan* (*Smoke Rings*), 1935; reprinted in *Poems I* (Tel Aviv: Hakibbutz Hame'uchad, 2003), 24 (my translation, DM).

18. Lieblich, *Learning about Lea.*

19. Leah Goldberg, "The Poems of the End of the Journey," in *Poems II* (Tel Aviv: Hakibbutz Hame'uchad, 1986), 154.

20. It was printed, for example, in *Ha'avodah Shebalev*, the Israeli Reform siddur (1982) and in *Mishkan T'fillah*, the American Reform siddur (2007). For more references, see Amir, "Prophecy and Halakhah," 46–47, n. 84.

21. Rachel and Arie Aharoni, eds., *Leah Goldberg: Diaries* (Tel Aviv: Hakibbutz Hame'uchad, 2005), 135; translation in Amir, "Prophecy and Halakhah," 41.

22. *T'fillat Haderekh* (literally, "the Road Prayer") is the title of the traditional prayer for beginning a journey.

23. Leah Goldberg, *Milim Achronot* (*Last Words*) (Tel Aviv, 1957), reprinted in *Poems II*, 221 (my translation, DM).

24. Talmud, Berakhot 29b.

25. For another exception, see Amir, "Prophecy and Halakhah," 52–53.

26. Lieblich, *Learning about Lea*, 237.

27. Bar-Yosef, *Mysticism*, 101.

28. Pinsker, "Never Will I Hear the Sweet Voice of God," 130.

29. From the documentary film *The Seven Tapes* by Yair Qedar (2012) on Yona Wallach's life and legacy (my translation, DM).

30. Yona Wallach, *Tat Hahakarah Nifreset K'mo M'nifah* (*Selected Poems 1963–1985*) (Tel Aviv: Hakibbutz Hame'uchad, 1992), 113; translation: Linda Zisquit, *Wild Light: Selected Poems of Yona Wallach* (New York: Riverdale-on-Hudson, 1997), 17.

31. For the collected group, see Yona Wallach, *Shirah Acharonim* (*The Last Poems*), ed. Dror Green (Safed Sfarim, 2007), 50–61.

32. Yona Wallach, *Selected Poems*, 165; translation in Zisquit, *Wild Light*, 9.
33. Marcela Sulak, *Twenty Girls to Envy Me: Selected Poems of Orit Gidali* (Austin: University of Texas Press, forthcoming 2016).
34. Orit Gidali, *Smikhut* (*Closing In*) (Tel Aviv: Hakibbutz Hame'uchad, 2009). I thank the poet Tania Hershman for translating the poem especially for this essay.
35. Avot Yeshurun, *Kol Shirav* (*All His Poems*), vol. 1 (Tel Aviv: Hakibbutz Hame'uchad, 2001), 279.

## Facing God's Face and God's Back: Hebrew Poetry as Prayer, by Dr. Wendy Zierler

1. Avi Sagi, *P'tsu'ei Tefilah: T'filah L'achar Mot Ha'el* (Ramat Gan: Bar Ilan University Press, 2011), 26.
2. Yehuda Amichai, *Patu'ach Sagur Patu'ach* (Jerusalem: Schocken, 1998), 29.
3. Rivka Miriam, *Kutonti Hatz'hubah* (Tel Aviv: Ekked, 1966), 30 (my translation, WZ).
4. Ibid. (my translation, WZ).
5. Admiel Kosman, *Higanu L'Elohim* (Tel Aviv: Hakibbutz Hame'uchad, 1998), 5 (my translation, WZ).
6. Abraham Joshua Heschel, *God in Search of Man* (New York: Farrar Strauss and Giroux, 1955), 29.
7. *Avot D'rabbi Natan* 17, "Rabbi Shimon" (my translation, WZ).

# Glossary

***Adonai*** (pronounced ah-doh-NA'I): The pronunciation for the tetra-grammaton (the four-letter name of God—see **Tetragrammaton**). Also, the beginning word (repeated) in the Thirteen Attributes (*Adonai, Adonai, el rachum v'chanum*, "Adonai, Adonai, merciful and gracious God"), the prayer at the center of this book.

***Chanukiyot*** (pronounced khah-noo-kee-YOHT); sing. *Chanukiyah* (pronounced khah-noo-kee YAH): The eight-branch candelabra used for lighting candles on Hanukkah.

***Chazel*** (or CHaZal, pronounced chah-ZAHL): An acronym for *CHakhameinu Zikhronam Livrakhah* (pronounced khah-khah-MAY noo zikh-roh-NAHM lihv-rah-KHAH), literally, "Our Sages, may their memories be a blessing"; hence, a short form for referring to the Rabbis of the first six centuries or so of the Common Era, the authorities who produced the Mishnah and the Talmud.

***Chesed*** (pronounced KHEH-sehd): "Loving-kindness," a Hebrew term implying God's mercy, compassion, or grace.

***Chutzpah*** (pronounced KHUTS-pah): Yiddish for "audacity" or "nerve."

***Erklären*** (pronounced ehr-KLEH-r'n): German for "explain," and hence, philosophically, a word used to describe the act of knowing an object by virtue of explaining it scientifically; in contrast to *verstehen* (pronounced fehr-SHTAY-'n), "understand," a word used philosophically for a deeper sort of knowing, the way we know history or another person, for example, by the utilization of human empathy.

***Etrog*** (pronounced eht-ROHG or, commonly, EHT-rohg): A citron, one of the "four species" of the autumn harvest (see Leviticus 23:40) used as a liturgical symbol of thanksgiving on the festival of Sukkot. The other three species are palm, willow, and myrtle branches tied together into a *lulav*. See ***lulav***.

**Grogger** (pronounced *GROH-g'r*): A noisemaker, used to drown out the sound of the name "Haman," the archenemy of the Jewish People, during the liturgical reading of the biblical book of Esther, on the holiday of Purim (pronounced poo-REEM, or, commonly, POO-rihm). As the story is read, people wield their *groggers* whenever the name "Haman" occurs.

**Hanukkah** (pronounced KHAH-noo-kah): The eight-day festival of light celebrating Jewish independence in the Hasmonean (called also Maccabean) revolt against the Seleucids in 167 BCE; the birth, therefore, of the Second Jewish Commonwealth.

**Kasher** (pronounced kah-SHEHR): From the same root as *kosher*, "fit," used primarily to mean "fit to eat," as opposed to *treyf* (pronounced TRAYF), meaning "unfit to eat"—referring to biblical and Rabbinic laws of food consumption. Used also as a verb, "to *kasher* our homes," denoting the necessary ritual preparation of stove and kitchen utensils—changing dishes for Passover, for example, as opposed to the dishes used the rest of the year.

**Lulav** (pronounced loo-LAHV or, commonly, LOO-lahv): A handheld bundle of three branches (palm, willow, and myrtle) tied together and waved ritually (along with the *etrog*, a citron) on Sukkot (see Leviticus 23:40) to symbolize gratitude for the autumnal harvest and the universal goodness of God, who provides us with our needs and ultimately promises deliverance beyond death itself.

**Megillah** (pronounced m'-gee-LAH or, commonly, m'-GIH-lah): Literally, "scroll"; hence, the name given to five biblical books (Ecclesiastes, Esther, Song of Songs, Ruth, Lamentations) read liturgically, from actual scrolls, on the five holidays of Sukkot, Purim, Passover, Shavuot, and Tisha B'Av, respectively.

**Minhag ta'ut** (pronounced mihn-HAHG tah-OOT): Literally, a "mistaken custom," with the implication of being an error in practice, a breach of Jewish tradition that should be avoided.

**Purim** (pronounced poo-REEM or, commonly, POO-rihm): Literally, "lots" in the sense of "drawing lots," a reference to the drawing of lots in the biblical book of Esther—the process by which Haman, the enemy who plots the destruction of the Jews, draws lots to determine the fateful day. Hence, the name for the late winter holiday of Purim, to celebrate the miraculous deliverance from destruction.

**Shavuot** (pronounced shah-voo-OHT): Literally "weeks," hence the name of the spring harvest festival marked by the ripening of wheat, seven weeks after Passover, traditionally accompanied by eating dairy products.

**Shivah** (pronounced shee-VAH, but commonly, SHIH-vah): Literally, "seven," and, hence, the shorthand name for the seven days of mourning following burial. The home in which the mourners gather is a shivah house.

*S'lichot* (pronounced slee-KHOHT; sing, *s'lichah*, pronounced slee-KHAH): Literally, "forgivenesses," from the singular "forgiveness," used also in conversational Hebrew as *s'lichah* = "Excuse me," "Forgive me," "I'm sorry." The plural, however, is also the name of a service and of the poems that compose the bulk of that service. The *S'lichot* service leads up to and introduces the High Holy Days. Communities differ on how long before the High Holy Days to begin saying it, but the climactic example is held late Saturday night (originally early Sunday morning) immediately prior to Rosh Hashanah (or if Rosh Hashanah falls in the first half of the week, two weekends prior to its arrival). *S'lichot* (as a type of poetry) also constitute much of the liturgy for Yom Kippur itself. *S'lichah* (in the singular) designates any particular such poem but is also the name for the fifth benediction (on the theme of forgiveness) in the daily weekday *Amidah*.

*Spiel* (pronounced SHPEEL): Yiddish for "skit" or "play," denoting the humorous skits performed on Purim.

**Sukkot** (pronounced soo-KOHT): Literally, "booths," denoting the temporary booths erected by biblical farmers for gathering the autumnal harvest; hence, the name of the autumn harvest festival, but also a reminder of living in booths upon being saved from Egyptian servitude (see Leviticus 23:42–43). Sukkot came rabbinically to symbolize, as well, the tenuousness of life itself and was accompanied, therefore, by the reading of Ecclesiastes, the biblical book on the fragility of life.

*Tashlich* (pronounced TAHSH-leekh): Literally, "you will cast," from Micah 7:19, "You [God] will cast all their sins into the depths of the sea"; hence, the name of a ritual practice of gathering at a running stream on Rosh Hashanah day, reciting the Micah passage, and casting our sins into the water.

**Tetragrammaton:** The technical term for the four-letter name of God that appears in the Bible (*YHVH*). Treating it as sacred, Jews stopped pronouncing it centuries ago, so that the actual pronunciation has been lost; instead of reading it according to its letters, it is replaced in speech by the alternative name of God, *Adonai* (pronounced ah-doh-NA'I). See *Adonai*.

**Thirteen Attributes:** Attributes of God mentioned in Exodus 34:6–7, taken to be God's thirteen attributes of mercy; hence, a way of designating the prayer at the center of this book, a prayer that is recited liturgically, as a reminder that God approaches sin and sinners with divine compassion and that God (according to the Talmud) has even made a covenant with Israel, with the thirteen attributes at the center.

*T'shuvah* (pronounced t'shoo-VAH or, commonly, t'SHOO-vah): From the Hebrew root *sh.u.v.*, "to return"; hence, "repentance." Also used technically as the title of the fifth blessing in the daily *Amidah*, a petition by worshipers that they successfully turn to God in heartfelt repentance.

*Un-taneh Tokef* (pronounced oo-n'TAH-neh TOH-kehf): A *piyyut* (liturgical poem) for the High Holy Days emphasizing the awesome nature of these days when we stand before God for judgment; but originally, the ninth part (called a *siluk*, pronounced see-LOOK) of a longer poem for the *Amidah* called *K'dushta* (pronounced k'-DOOSH-tah). Although widely connected with a legend of Jewish martyrdom in medieval Germany, the poem is actually the work of a Byzantine poet, circa sixth century. It is known for its climactic insistence that "penitence, prayer, and charity help the hardship of the decree pass."

*Verstehen* (pronounced fehr-SHTAY-'n): See *Erklären*.

*Yamim Nora'im* (pronounced yah-MEEM noh-rah-EEM): Literally, "awesome days"; hence, the Hebrew for "Days of Awe," the High Holy Days of Rosh Hashanah and Yom Kippur.

**Z'mirot** (pronounced z'-mee-ROHT): Literally, "songs," but generally used liturgically for songs that are sung around the table on Shabbat and holy days.

**Zohar** (pronounced ZOH-hahr): Literally, "splendor," hence the name of the most important mystical book in kabbalistic tradition, the *Zohar* ("The Book of Splendor"), written mostly by Moses de Leon in late thirteenth-century Spain.